Adobe® Illustrator® CS2 @work

PROJECTS YOU CAN USE ON THE JOB

Pariah S. Burke

 **SAMS** 800 East 96th Street, Indianapolis, Indiana 46240 USA

Adobe Illustrator CS2 @work: Projects You Can Use on the Job

Copyright © 2006 by Pariah S. Burke

International Standard Book Number: 0-672-32801-1

Library of Congress Catalog Card Number: 2005901041

Printed in the United States of America

First Printing: September 2005

08   07   06   05   4   3   2   1

Trademarks

Warning and Disclaimer

Bulk Sales

Sams Publishing offers excellent discounts on this book when ordered in quantity for bulk purchases or special sales. For more information, please contact

U.S. Corporate and Government Sales
1-800-382-3419
corpsales@pearsontechgroup.com

For sales outside of the United States, please contact

International Sales
international@pearsoned.com

Senior Acquisitions Editor
Linda Bump Harrison

Development Editor
Jonathan A. Steever

Managing Editor
Charlotte Clapp

Senior Project Editor
Matthew Purcell

Copy Editor
Margaret Berson

Indexer
Erika Millen

Proofreader
Tracy Donhardt

Technical Editor
Samuel John Klein

Publishing Coordinator
Vanessa Evans

Multimedia Developer
Dan Scherf

Designer
Gary Adair

Page Layout
TnT Design

Contents at a Glance

Table of Contents

About the Author

A 20-year graphic communications industry veteran and former Technical Lead to Adobe's Technical Support team, **Pariah S. Burke** is in high demand as a desktop publishing and graphic design workflow consultant and instructor. He travels all around North America training and consulting for advertising and design agencies, print and prepress production houses, and government and military agencies in Illustrator, InDesign, QuarkXPress, Photoshop, InCopy, PageMaker, Acrobat, Adobe Creative Suite, Variable Data Publishing, and more.

As a creative professional, Pariah has enjoyed success in nearly every field of print and web design, prepress, magazine publishing, and advertising. As the former co-owner of a prepress service bureau and principal for seven years of his own design and advertising agency, Pariah understands not only the designer's role in the market, but the concerns and processes of press and prepress production and creative direction.

He is the editor-in-chief of **Quark VS InDesign.com**, the founder of **Designorati.com**, and creator of the *Design Weblog*, the *Magazine Weblog*, and the *(Unofficial) Photoshop Weblog* for Weblogs, Inc. Additionally, Pariah is a contributing author to the book *Special Edition: Using Adobe Creative Suite 2* (Que, 2005), and his articles and tutorials have appeared in numerous other publications and periodicals.

Among Pariah's print and web design credits are work for Time-Warner, Black Crow Broadcasting, *UPSCALE Magazine*, whose look he helped redefine and whose print magazine he brought online in 1998. He helped the venerable monthly magazine integrate an Internet-based revenue stream into its publishing kingdom. He is most proud of his work for Playboy Enterprises, for whom he created and designed the Playboy Sun skin- and sun-care product line national launch campaign; including designing the line's brand identity as well as all product packaging, promotional materials, and photography.

In 2001, Pariah sold his design business, Imaginations Unlimited, and moved from Daytona Beach, Florida to Portland, Oregon to support and train Adobe Systems, Inc.'s North American Technical Support team. As Technical Lead for Illustrator, InDesign, InCopy, PageMaker, and Acrobat to that division, and as primary how-to guru and MVP for Photoshop, ImageReady, typography, color management, prepress, the Web, and QuarkXPress, Pariah taught Adobe's Technical Support team to use Adobe products and related technologies in real-world creative and production workflows.

After three wonderful years with Adobe, he returned full-time to explore exciting new projects in his life-long passions of graphic design and illustration, writing about the design industries and tools, and teaching on-the-job creatives.

Pariah lives in the crisp air and majestic beauty of the suburbs of Portland, Oregon with his beautiful fiancée, two lovely stepdaughters, a cowardly dog, five uppity cats, and two rowdy hamsters.

Dedication

For my partner in all things, Christy, without whose unwavering support and encouragement not a word of this book would have been written. For my mother, Sarah, who gave birth and nourishment to my imagination and my passion for creation, which led me through crayons, watercolors, and Rubylithe to computers, fonts, and Illustrator. And, for my grandfather, Dad, who taught me by his example to work hard, to do the best I possibly can in everything I do, and to live and work with honor, integrity, respect, and humility.

Acknowledgments

When I was 18 and packing to move from my parents' house to live on my own in a far-away city, my mother gave me a book by Dr. Seuss, *Oh, the Places You'll Go!* Many years later it remains among my most prized possessions—and an accurate record of my career and life.

The ups and downs and twists and turns and turnarounds that have led me here even I hardly believe, and I was there. An acutely shy person, I could never have dreamed I would one day spend much of my time standing in front of rooms full of strangers, teaching them to use the creative tools that impassion me as a creative pro. But I do, first to Adobe's Technical Support, now to agencies, designers, and illustrators all over the country. Working as a production artist on bar association directories in the early nineties, I would have scoffed at the idea that I'd ever see my name on a bookshelf. Yet here we are. I could never have predicted where the twisting roads of life and career would take me, though it has been an amazing trip.

Thank you to the people who have been there with me on every road, cheering me on as I climbed each hill, urging me up from every valley, Christy Siebler, Joanna Siebler, Stevie Siebler, Chris Dreyer, Jr., and Anna Gauthier.

Thank you to those who walked with me along this particular road, the wonderfully supportive staff of Sams Publishing: the patient and supportive Linda Bump Harrison; Jon Steever, the man who not only helped this book's clarity, but who is also directly responsible for the absence of the lamest of my jokes; the Queen of Grammar, Margaret Berson, who rescued many a dangling preposition; and Matt Purcell, who kept it all organized. Thanks also to the Sams production staff, who did such a wonderful job laying out the book.

Thank you, my friends and creative sounding boards, Samuel John Klein, who tech edited this book, every step by step, in each project, and the Graphic Designers Resource Group.

Thank you, Mary Bassham and Karen DeMichael, my arts high school teachers who sagaciously advised me that "graphic design is *not* a profession, and you will *never* go anywhere or amount to anything" in the creative fields. For you, an extra special and heartfelt: Nyah, nyah! *Pbbltht!*

To my granddad, George A. Taylor: Thank you for being my example, for showing me that I can do anything I set my mind to. Thanks for watching over me, Dad. I miss you. I hope I've made you proud.

And, most of all, thank you to my mother, Sarah Taylor, who opened the first door, the door to all roads, and all other doors. Oh, just look at the places I've gone, Mom!

We Want to Hear from You!

As the reader of this book, *you* are our most important critic and commentator. We value your opinion and want to know what we're doing right, what we could do better, what areas you'd like to see us publish in, and any other words of wisdom you're willing to pass our way.

You can email or write me directly to let me know what you did or didn't like about this book—as well as what we can do to make our books stronger.

Please note that I cannot help you with technical problems related to the topic of this book, and that due to the high volume of mail I receive, I might not be able to reply to every message.

When you write, please be sure to include this book's title and author as well as your name and phone or email address. I will carefully review your comments and share them with the author and editors who worked on the book.

Email: graphics@samspublishing.com

Mail: Mark Taber
            Associate Publisher
            Sams Publishing
            800 East 96th Street
            Indianapolis, IN 46240 USA

Reader Services

For more information about this book or another Sams title, visit our website at www.samspublishing.com. Type the ISBN (excluding hyphens) or the title of a book in the Search field to find the page you're looking for.

Introduction

Stop! If you're looking for the definitive desk reference on every nuance of each Illustrator tool and menu item, *don't buy this book*!

This book is *not* about teaching you software. This book is about showing you practical, efficient, and fun ways to use a tool, Adobe Illustrator CS2, to complete real-world, on-the-job projects and get your job done with as little wasted effort and as few headaches as possible.

Most people don't learn effectively when shown disconnected tasks utilizing generic subject matter.

Learning how to type text in one chapter, draw a flower with the Pen tool in another, and create envelope warps on a triangle in a third chapter, with hundreds of pages in between, will *not* teach you how to design a logo. Such books are wonderful for augmenting an existing workflow and finding new techniques. They don't, however, help you get the job done quickly if you have to spend most of your time flipping through the book, trying to decide if this section is more applicable than this other section to the project your client needs by 5 o'clock.

When I walk into a classroom I ask my students one simple question: *Tell me about your job.* Then I build a curriculum on the fly to answer the specific needs of my students.

I can't do that in a book; therefore, I looked back through my career in design and illustration, at my current and former client work, and at the myriad projects created every day in Illustrator by the people I've trained throughout the world. From hundreds of designs I culled the 11 most common types of projects, projects that nearly every creative pro has to complete every day at work.

Illustrator @work is *not* a list of tasks or features turned into projects. It was planned first as the 11 projects most often faced by professional users in today's marketplace, and then each project was broken down into its constituent tasks.

Neither is this book organized by tool or by the complexity of techniques or by your skill level. In any given Illustrator project one uses numerous tools taught in educational curricula and task-based books for novice, intermediate, and advanced users. Those labels have no application outside a classroom; when you're using a tool like Illustrator, you will never think to yourself, *Wow! I've just used an intermediate-level function!*

In any given chapter you will learn to productively use tools for work, without irrelevant skill-level labels. You will learn advanced mesh warp techniques in the step immediately following drawing your first rectangle, all in easy-to-follow steps that don't condescend.

Each chapter in this book contains a project or a group of closely related projects that will take you, start to finish, from a blank page to a polished drawing or design that's ready for output. Where possible I've provided tips and options for a variety of scenarios, though most projects include in the main flow of text the efficiency, productivity, and, of course, creativity techniques I've learned over the course of a 20-year career as a creative professional.

This book is tailored to the needs of nearly every Illustrator user—novice or old hand. I can't be there in person, spouting lame jokes and tailoring the instruction to your specific project, with your digital asset files, so I've done the next best thing by writing project-based instruction instantly adaptable on the fly to *your* project, with your assets, while you're doing it on the job.

What Will You Gain from This Book?

You will know how to complete at least the projects from this book that interest you, from start to finish. You will know where to find the tools, features, and options relevant to your project, and have an overall sense of Illustrator's organization and interface.

You will be able to identify logical starting points to projects you typically produce on the job, and complete them more efficiently and productively with professional results. You will have an efficient workflow more forgiving of changes to project goals and deliverables, and which will enable the inevitable changes to be made faster, more easily, and with less frustration.

You will also learn *about* projects as well as how to complete them. Learn to think about the considerations specific to each type of project you will face on the job. For example, for-print projects will help you consider and devise strategies for satisfying budgeting, paper and ink choices, bindery and special services.

This book will give you the confidence to say *yes* to new, untried projects because you know a comprehensive how-to is at your fingertips, waiting to walk you through the project from start to finish.

At the end of any given chapter you will have a sense of accomplishment—*I made this! I can do this now!* That sense of accomplishment will be multiplied when the tutorial completed was on the job, with a genuine, measurable achievement—*I just got my work done in a new, easier, more efficient way! And I can do it again on the next project!*

Organization of This Book

This book is divided into three parts:

▶ Part I, "Getting Started," takes you on a tour of Illustrator CS2, the newest version from Adobe. It was important not to make assumptions about what you do and do not know about Illustrator, so we've made sure that all the tools, palettes, and basic conventions of Illustrator are covered, as well as how it integrates with other Adobe products.

▶ Part II, "Projects," contains a variety of projects you'll likely be asked to complete on the job. The projects start with the common, but far from simple, development of logos and move through progressively more complex projects like development of corporate identity material, drawing near photo-realistic portraits, packaging, brochures, advertisements, DVD packaging, and even designing a website. This portion of the book will prepare you for almost any marketing-related requirement you may be asked to fulfill.

If you have your own resource files, fonts, logos, and images, feel free to use them as you work through each project.

But if you don't have those assets readily available, we've provided them for you on the publisher's website.

▶ In Part III, "Appendixes," you'll find Appendix A, "Glossary," which lists and defines the key terms used throughout the book. Appendix B, "Resources," provides additional tools and resources you may find useful when creating your own projects based on the teachings of this book, and links where you can find user groups and associations, training information, web and print publications, and help for many of Illustrator's known technical issues you may encounter. Appendix C, "Project: Identify and Recreate Logo Type" is a new project building on the logo creation and re-creation techniques from Part II, Chapter 2, "Designing a Logo (From Scratch or From a Scan)." In this new project you'll learn how to identify typefaces used in a logo utilizing various resources, and to re-create type with Illustrator CS2's Glyphs palette.

Downloading the Book's Project Files

The chapter-by-chapter project and media files are available at the publisher's website as Zip files.

To download the book's project files, go to http://www.samspublishing.com. Enter this book's ISBN (0672328011) in the Search box and click Search. When the book's title is displayed, click the title to go to a page where you can download the project Zip files.

CAUTION

Be sure you extract all the files from each Zip file with the option (for PC users) Use Folder Names selected so that you can get the same folders on your computer as included in each Zip file. Mac users can simply double-click the downloaded Zip file and the folder structure should appear intact, as named.

 TIP

Tips provide shortcuts to make your job easier or better ways to accomplish certain tasks.

 NOTE

Notes provide additional information related to the surrounding topics.

 CAUTION

Cautions alert you to potential problems and help you steer clear of disaster.

Conventions Used in This Book

This book uses the following conventions:

- *Italic* type is used to denote key terms when they first appear in the book, and occasionally for emphasis.

- A **special** font is used to show settings you will make, material you type, file-names you will enter, layer names, and URLs.

- A monospace font is used to show file-names and pathnames.

- Menu choices are shown separated by the ">" character, for example: choose Edit > Preferences > General.

- Keyboard shortcuts are shown with the Macintosh shortcut first and the Windows shortcut second: "press (Cmd-A) [Ctrl+A] to select the entire file."

The end result is a book that will be a hand—to hold for guidance the first time through a project, and to rest on your shoulder in reassurance the fifth time through. It contains the most common projects executed by the majority of Illustrator users at work. I hope it's useful to you—it's the result of hundreds of your peers answering the question: *Tell me about your job.*

@work resources

- **This indicates specific files that are available for download on the Sams website.**

PART I: Getting Started

Illustrator's Role in the Modern Creative Workflow

Let's get it out of the way right up front: Illustrator scares some people.

Facing the Fear of Illustrator

Now you. Admit to yourself that Illustrator scares you. Go on, you're safe here. No one will judge you. Admit to yourself that Illustrator scares you. Say it out loud. Good! Now again with conviction—"Illustrator scares me!"

Excellent! Owning up to your fear, recognizing its existence, is the first step toward overcoming that fear. If you also have a fear of heights, read this book while dangling your feet from the ledge of a very tall building, killing two birds with one stone...

But if you're not ready to tackle *that* particular fear yet, that's OK. We'll take it one step at a time (see Chapter 27, "Conquering Your Fear of Heights").

Illustrator Versus Photoshop

Illustrator is scary; it isn't as intuitive in even its basic reason for existence as Photoshop. *Everyone* understands the concept of a photograph, and even the flimsiest of imaginations can envision touching up and otherwise altering a flat image. *Raster*—pixel-based pictures like digital photographs—makes instant sense to us. Raster images have a correlation in the real, non-digital world—we've been snapping pictures for two hundred years.

For three thousand years humankind has stamped images onto paper, papyrus, bark, and other materials. We've been painting with implements including brushes, hollowed-bone airbrushes, and our fingers for 40,000 years. Making pictures is something human beings understand on a primal level; it's an understanding born of instinct only slightly more advanced than how to walk upright. In the real world, swiping a brush or finger across paper applies color to the picture; it happens, it's instant, it's *real*.

In the digital world, raster images are the natural progression of millennia of painting. Photoshop is the world's most advanced raster image tool.

So powerful and effective is Photoshop, so intuitive are its core painting and editing functions, that every creative professional in a hundred different industries uses or has used it, as do most serious hobbyists, or *prosumers.* Photoshop has no professional competition. It is, arguably, the world's single most pervasive software application. In recent years, Photoshop has even risen above the stature of a proper noun and moved so deeply into the public consciousness that it is frequently used as a verb—for example, "go Photoshop out those blemishes," or "I'm Photoshopping your head onto Oprah's body."

Photoshop performs its many and myriad tasks better than any application ever created for image editing, color correction, Web graphics creation, frame-by-frame video touchup, and many other tasks and work-flows. It is the world's most advanced raster painting and editing tool, but raster is itself limited and limiting.

Vector, the domain of Illustrator, is not the legacy of 40,000 years of human instinct—it is the product of 40,000 years of human *inge-nuity.* It is the culmination of millennia of innovation, utilizing the strengths of the analytical left brain to support and enable the unfettered indulgence of the imagination and creative right brain.

Vector is, underneath everything (try not to shudder), geometry—math. The very defini-tion of vector artwork is off-putting to right-brained creatives: two or more points connected by lines or curves to define a shape. Or, even more intimidating is the defi-nition given by sources such as the United States National Oceanic and Atmospheric Administration (see U.S. NOAA http://lcoris.noaa.gov/glossary/): "An abstraction of the real world where positional data is represented in the form of coordinates. In vector data, the basic units of spatial information are points, lines, and polygons. Each of these units is composed simply as a series of one or more coordinate points. For example, a line is a collection of related points, and a polygon is a collection of related lines."

To most right-brain creatives, not only is that definition nowhere near as sexy as Photoshop—it's downright chilling.

But vector *shouldn't* be scary. It's still math, points, curves, and shapes, but none of that matters with Illustrator. *You* don't have to do the math; *you* draw and create, leaving the math to the computer to perform in the background, invisibly if you like.

Pixel-based raster images have their own and very important roles, but they're limited for many types of creative work by the fact that, after they've been created, any change is destructive and cannot be reversed. Of course, in Photoshop, you have various func-tions to limit the destruction—things like layers, layer comps, snapshots, versions (with the help of Creative Suite's Version Cue), the History palette, and, until the document is closed, a limited number of multiple undos. However, compared to the ultimate and never-ending malleability of vector artwork, these devices are cumbersome and stop-gap measures. And they don't account for every-thing.

Consider adjusting an image's levels in Photoshop. The histogram, or chart of tonal or gray levels in the image, is permanently altered by adjustments such as Levels, Curves, Hue & Saturation, and, of course, the novice favorite, Brightness & Contrast. When gray tones are destroyed, they're gone forever; there's no way to get back the depth of tone in a raster image without repainting it by hand. In Illustrator, however, no color data is ever destroyed; colors can be adjusted in Illustrator infinitely, without ever losing one of the 256 levels of tone.

In Figure 1.1 is the histogram, the tonal range, of a typical photograph before and after a simple Levels correction. The black point of the image is to the left of the histogram, white to the right. Between are the intervening shades of all colors in the image. White gaps in the after image denote the tonal values of all colors that have been destroyed as a result of the Levels correction; those shades cannot be recovered.

Paint a shape in Photoshop or Corel Painter, then distort that shape with a filter, brush stroke, or other transformation—and, when you close the file or go beyond the allowed number of undo steps, the shape is altered forever. Even Photoshop masters can rarely distort the shape back to its original form without unsightly evidence of the initial transmogrification. In Illustrator, however, distortion and reformation is a simple matter of moving a point here, adjusting a curve there; the shape can be restored to its original form with much less effort and no lasting scars.

Embracing the Freedom of Illustrator

Raster images are *resolution-dependent*; they are created in a fixed *resolution* and a fixed size, and neither may be changed without detriment to the quality of the image. Vector drawings are *resolution-independent*; they print or save to the highest resolution of the device rendering them. Scale is irrelevant—vector artwork drawn inside a 1×1 inch square can be scaled up to 100×100 *feet* and retain the sharpest edges and smoothest color transitions. Vector artwork can actually be scaled up or down to infinity without loss of quality—portraits have been drawn on the head of a pin, then blown up to fill a poster.

Consider painting a photo-realistic portrait in Photoshop. For a raster image, the size and especially resolution of the portrait must be decided upon in advance, before the first stroke is painted. To determine resolution, at least the major uses for the portrait must be known—will it appear in a 1200 *dpi* magazine advertisement at scale? Will it need to be blown up to poster size? What about as the subject of a billboard? Will it need to shrink down for application to a coffee cup or business card? Every use is dependent on resolution, thus resolution must depend on the intended uses.

FIGURE 1.1   Original image histogram (left), and the same photo's histogram after applying Levels (right).

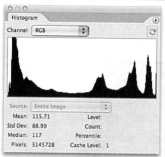 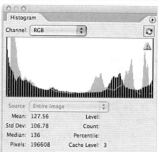

Now consider the same photo-realistic portrait painted in Illustrator. Oh, you think Illustrator can't create photo-realism? Not only can *it*, but *you* will create photo-realism in Chapter 5, "Illustrating an (Almost) Photo-Realistic Portrait." The portrait we will create is resolution-independent, with the ability to scale up or down infinitely. As proof, look at Figure 1.2. The image on the left is a screen capture of the portrait from Chapter 5 scaled down to roughly 1 × 1.17 inches; on the right is the same drawing scaled up to 12 × 14 feet—12,000% without a single telltale sign.

In vector artwork—in Illustrator—there is infinite *freedom*. Freedom to experiment and modify. Freedom to create without foreknowledge of where and how the artwork might or can be used, at what sizes, and in what resolutions. Every creative whim is yours to indulge with absolute impunity. The math is equally irrelevant—you *create*, and the computer will worry about the math. *You*, not a computer, control the quality and detail of your artwork.

Freedom is the root of every reason professional illustrators, digital artists, graphic designers, and production personnel choose to draw original artwork in Illustrator over Photoshop. Under the hood, vector drawing is about math; in Illustrator, vector drawing is about freedom.

If you opened this book because you didn't understand or were intimidated by Illustrator, know that your confusion and fear will dissipate like morning fog as you work through the projects in this book. You will learn not only the freedom and unadulterated creative power of Illustrator, but the pure joy inherent in creation without consequence.

Working Together

Although many projects begin and end with Illustrator, others often start in Illustrator and move out to other applications. For example, illustrations created in Illustrator are often placed into an ad or magazine layout created in InDesign or QuarkXPress. At the same time, projects like a poster may begin with a digital photograph color-corrected and touched up in Photoshop, then placed into Illustrator for tracing or to receive context from native vector objects. Vector drawings may even begin in another program and then move into Illustrator.

Photoshop and InDesign both have basic vector drawing tools, but those tools are there to eliminate the necessity of launching Illustrator for the simplest of tasks. They are not a replacement for Illustrator, nor are Illustrator's basic raster-editing tools a replacement for Photoshop or the multi-page

FIGURE 1.2 **The photo-realistic portrait from Chapter 5 in two sizes (both zoomed for screenshot): 1 × 1.17 inches (left), and 12 × 14 feet (right).**

CHAPTER 1: Getting to Know Illustrator Without Fear

technique taught in Chapter 8 a replacement for InDesign's native multi-page capabilities. When only a simple object is needed—an ellipse with a drop shadow, for example in InDesign—draw it in InDesign with its native tools. When that ellipse needs multiple fills, more than a single drop shadow, or other effects, however, it's time to take a trip to Illustrator.

Fortunately, even that much is incredibly easy. If an object begins in InDesign (or in most cases in Photoshop or GoLive), copy it, paste into Illustrator, make the changes, copy the new object, and paste back into InDesign (or Photoshop or GoLive). Each of the Creative Suite point products is aware of its CS and CS2 siblings, and can interact, to varying degrees, with copy and paste. The downside to copy and paste is that the pasted object(s) becomes embedded in the destination document; it does not exist as a free-standing document. Changes have to be made via the same copy-and-paste methodology, but more ominous is the fact that, should the destination document become corrupted, all objects embedded within it die too.

Will Illustrator and Photoshop Ever Merge?

Although I'm far too wise to ever use the word never (except when it comes to choosing for-press colors from a computer monitor), it is extremely unlikely that Illustrator and Photoshop will ever merge into a single product à la Macromedia's Fireworks. It's a common question, though, as many users see the areas in which the two applications overlap—Photoshop has Illustrator's basic Shape and Line tools and Illustrator has most of Photoshop's filters as well as slicing and other borrowed tools.

However, their unique roles divide them more than their similarities unite them.

Illustrator is Queen of Vectorland to the East, where resolution-independence rules supreme in the most enlightened of the world's vector societies. In Illustrator's Vectorland, of course, Photoshop maintains a small embassy of raster functions. Photoshop is King of the Realm of Raster to the West, a land populated by pixels and photographs, with a small pavilion of Illustrator representatives performing vector functions to the benefit of King Photoshop and their alliance. Together with Prince InDesign in the South and Duke GoLive's small, star-filled lands to the North, Queen Illustrator and King Photoshop rule benevolently over the world of professional graphic communications, cooperating along their respective borders to provide overlapping buffer zones; beyond those zones, however, each is its own land with unique topographies and laws.

Queen Illustrator, the first of them all, is naturally the most established. She is a veteran of the *Desktop Publishing Revolution*, and the direct descendant of the venerable PostScript bloodline. The other three rulers look to her for leadership and counsel, and her influence is undeniable among them all. Each has more in common, in function and role, with Illustrator than with one another. And, if it were necessary to pick a glue that holds the allied lands of the continent of Creative Suite together, it would surely be Queen Illustrator. Still, though relations are close and amiable with neighbors Photoshop, InDesign, and GoLive, she has her own unique and important role in the creative workflows that could never be occupied by, or joined with, any other—as do they all. Moreover, combining any of the two lands under a single rule would make them far too vast in area, complexity, and number of palettes to rule over effectively.

Adobe currently has no plans or even mead-induced fantasies about merging the queendom and kingdom into a single application.

Illustrator's User Interface

Let's just go over a few notable points about the Illustrator CS2 user interface.

The Adobe Common User Interface

Adobe, the originator of Illustrator, recognized many years ago that nearly 90% of the creative pros using one Adobe product also use a second. Almost 80% of those also use a third. When Adobe talked to those users, asking about their experience using these tools, Adobe learned an important lesson. The number one pain point cited by users of multiple Adobe products was that the applications looked and worked differently; switching between any two or more of Illustrator, Photoshop, PageMaker, and other Adobe applications required a period of adjustment—not just during initial learning, but whenever the user left one application momentarily to work in another. Similar commands were on different menus, keyboard shortcuts were inconsistent, and even identical tools—the Pen tool, for example, which appears in all of the above applications—functioned differently.

Disparity in the way Adobe's creative applications functioned was slowing down users' workflows and breaking their concentration. The Adobe Common User Interface (Adobe UI) was created to address the needs of Adobe's customers.

The Adobe UI was built in stages, first unifying the function of identical and similar tools across the applications, then by moving many commands and functions onto tabbed palettes that behave identically between the creative applications. As each new version of Adobe's products released, more was coordinated—and, in some cases, amalgamated—between them. In Creative Suite 2 and the CS2-designated products, even the chore of color management has consolidated into a single user interface on the Adobe Bridge.

After learning to use one Adobe creative application, the learning curve for each subsequent application is much shallower than before the Adobe UI. Working regularly in multiple applications entails learning fewer keyboard shortcuts and menus because they are mirrored when possible, and at least organized according to the same philosophies when it isn't. And, if a tool exists in multiple programs, it operates identically in all of them.

The functional result of the Adobe UI is threefold: increased productivity, reduced learning curve, and increased creativity because the tools are less important than the work.

Arranging Palettes

Every Adobe product built for the creative pro has tabbed palettes. For the most part, they all act and interact the same. Regrettably, Illustrator's 32 palettes enjoy neither Photoshop's palette well nor InDesign's side-docking ability. Still, there are plenty of ways to arrange your palettes.

To separate a palette from a group of palettes, click on the palette's tab—not on the title bar of the group—and drag it out and away from other palettes. The dragged tab will become free-floating (see Figure 1.3).

CHAPTER 1: Getting to Know Illustrator Without Fear

FIGURE 1.3 (Left) A palette grouped in a tabbed interface with other palettes. The bold outline appears all the way around a palette when dragging to group (center). When stacking, the bold line appears only at the top or bottom (right).

To join a palette with another in a group, drag the palette (either free-floating or in another group or stack) over the palette(s) with which you would like to group it. When a bold outline appears around the entire destination palette, drop. The new palette will now be tabbed in a group. Tabbed palettes occupy the same space, and therefore cannot appear onscreen concurrently.

To stack palettes so that two (or more) palettes do appear onscreen concurrently but still move as one unit, drag one palette's tab to directly below the bottom of, or above the top of, another palette. When the alignment is correct, a bold line will appear only on the bottom (or top) of the destination palette. After the palettes have been stacked, they will move as one and can even be rolled up or down together with the minimize button in the group's title bar.

Stacking palettes can be a tremendous aid when screen real estate is at a premium, such as in single-monitor systems or laptops.

Palette Menus

Many palettes, like the Gradient palette for example, include a menu with additional commands and options. Officially called the Gradient (or Symbols, Swatches, and so on) palette menu, these are often referred to as simply the Gradient (or Symbols, Swatches, and so on) menu or even just the flyout menu, for its manner of flying out from the palette.

Many useful commands and options are squirreled away on these palette flyout menus. In the case of list palettes like Swatches, Graphic Styles, and Symbols, their respective palette menus include display options, such as whether to present their various contents as swatches or lists in different sizes and styles. Many, like the Stroke palette (see Figure 1.4), include a Show Options command—that changes to Hide Options if options are already shown—providing access to vastly expanded controls.

FIGURE 1.4 The Stroke palette in default mode (left), and after selecting Show Options from the Stroke palette flyout menu.

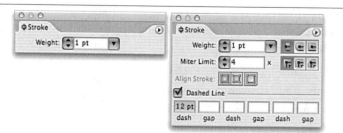

Still other palette menu commands, like the Paragraph palette's Adobe Single-Line Composer and Adobe Every-Line Composer, are commands that may *only* be accessed from a palette menu—they aren't accessible any other way.

Workspaces

New in Illustrator CS2 are workspaces: savable, shareable arrangements of palettes. All told, Illustrator includes 32 palettes. Even if you have dual monitors, that's still a heck of a lot of screen real estate taken away from a document window—even with all palettes in their default, options-hidden states. Unless you're taking screenshots for a book about Illustrator, you don't need all palettes onscreen at any given time. Depending on your screen resolution, you may not even be able to fit them all. Some palettes you may never use. If you aren't going to create data-driven graphics, for example, you'll have no need of the Variables palette.

Most often, however, you'll need a core set of palettes you will always use—probably Layers, Appearance, Navigator, and Info—as well as ones you use for specific types of projects. Setting type, for example, you will probably also want the Character, Paragraph, OpenType, Paragraph Styles, Character Styles, and probably Color and Swatches palettes on hand. While drawing a photo-realistic portrait you'll have no need of the type-related palettes, but you will need Color, Swatches, Stroke, and Gradient.

Workspaces enable you to create different arrangements—indeed, even different states and sizes of palettes—for every type of task you perform in Illustrator. Just open the palettes you need, arrange them as you need them, and close the palettes that don't apply to the task at hand. When everything is set, choose Window > Workspace > Save Workspace. Give it a meaningful name (I like task-based names such as **Typesetting**). Now reconfigure your palettes for the next type of task, and save a new workspace the same way. To switch between them, just select the desired workspace from the top of the Window > Workspace menu. To reset all palettes to their original, out-of-the-box configuration, choose [Default] from that menu.

Best of all, workspaces are shareable—create the workspace on your work desktop computer, and then copy it to your laptop or home computer. Copy workspaces from and to the following locations:

- ▶ On Windows: `C:\Documents and Settings\[UserName]\Application Data\Adobe\Adobe Illustrator CS2 Settings\Workspaces`

- ▶ On Macintosh: `[UserName]/Library/Preferences/Adobe Illustrator CS2 Settings/Workspaces`

The Tools Palette

The Tools palette or Toolbox is without a doubt the single most used palette in Illustrator. All your tools are there, thus the name (yeah, I know: here's my sign). The reason I so obviously obviated this point is that, because you will use these tools so often, it behooves us to take a moment to examine a few important features of the Toolbox.

First would have to be their amazingly convenient, single-key keyboard shortcuts (for most tools; see Figure 1.5).

Next it's important to note that not all the tools are showing on the Toolbox. The black arrow in the lower-right corner of tools like the Pen denote that other tools are hidden behind them (see Figure 1.6). Click and hold on such tools to reveal what's behind. At the far right of any of these tool flyouts is a tear-off arrow; clicking it will launch a free-floating toolbar containing those tools.

Finally, at the bottom of the Toolbox, below the tools, are some very useful feedback and function devices (see Figure 1.7).

- **Swap Fill and Stroke**—Exchange the stroke color for the fill color and the reverse.
- **Default Fill and Stroke**—Set fill to white and stroke to black.
- **Fill Swatch**—The currently active fill color, gradient, or pattern swatch.
- **Stroke Swatch**—The currently active stroke color or pattern swatch.
- **Color**—Set the foremost swatch to the solid color currently active in the Color

palette.

- **Gradient**—Set the fill swatch to the gradient currently active on the Gradient palette.
- **None**—Clear the foremost swatch of any color, gradient, or pattern.
- **Standard Screen Mode**—View the document along with menu bar, toolbars, and palettes.
- **Full Screen Mode with Menu Bar**—View the document and the menu bar only, hiding any palettes or toolbars.
- **Full Screen Mode**—View the document as the full screen, hiding the menu bar and any palettes or toolbars.

The Welcome Screen

When you first launch Illustrator CS2 you are greeted by the Welcome Screen, festooned with orange flowers. In this nifty screen you can

- Learn about new features, either by visiting the Illustrator CS2 page on **adobe.com** with the "Tell Me What's New" link, or via live, interactive demonstrators with the "Show Me What's New" link.
- Browse Cool Extras via the Adobe Bridge, including sample art, templates, fonts, and scripts.
- Begin a new document.
- Begin a new document from one of Illustrator CS2's dozens of predesigned templates.
- Open an existing Illustrator document.

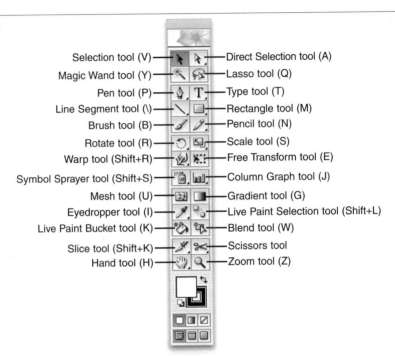

FIGURE 1.5 The Toolbox (shown in default state).

Selection tool (V) —— Direct Selection tool (A)
Magic Wand tool (Y) —— Lasso tool (Q)
Pen tool (P) —— Type tool (T)
Line Segment tool (\) —— Rectangle tool (M)
Brush tool (B) —— Pencil tool (N)
Rotate tool (R) —— Scale tool (S)
Warp tool (Shift+R) —— Free Transform tool (E)
Symbol Sprayer tool (Shift+S) —— Column Graph tool (J)
Mesh tool (U) —— Gradient tool (G)
Eyedropper tool (I) —— Live Paint Selection tool (Shift+L)
Live Paint Bucket tool (K) —— Blend tool (W)
Slice tool (Shift+K) —— Scissors tool
Hand tool (H) —— Zoom tool (Z)

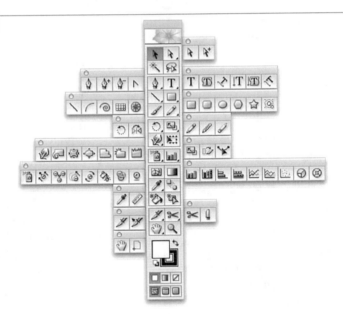

FIGURE 1.6 The Toolbox, with all hidden tools expanded into floating toolbars.

FIGURE 1.7   Bottom of the Toolbox.

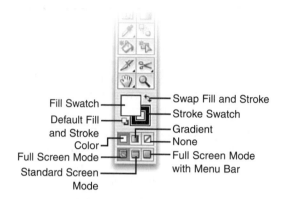

Though the Welcome Screen is cool at first, its novelty may quickly wear off. Tell it to stop bugging you simply by unchecking the Show This Dialog at Startup box in the lower-left corner. If, after clearing that checkbox, you want to get back to the Welcome Screen, just choose Welcome Screen from the Help menu.

New in Illustrator CS2

Illustrator CS (the previous version) was a major update of this now almost 20-year-old application. Released in October 2003 as part of the first edition of Creative Suite, Illustrator CS incorporated the greatest typographic controls this application (which was the first program created by Adobe) has ever had. It brought in the OpenType and Glyphs palettes, much more advanced character- and paragraph-level text control, as well as paragraph and character styles. That version also brought support for layered PDF files, improved color management, greater printing control and printer's marks, vastly tighter integration with Photoshop and InDesign, unified XMP metadata handling, improved linking of area and path type objects, programmable actions, and live 3D effects.

After all that—and a lot more I didn't list—Illustrator CS2, released in May 2005, simply couldn't follow up with as long a list of new features. That is not to say that Illustrator CS2 is not packed with new features; it just doesn't have as many core changes as were introduced with CS.

New Features

In Illustrator CS2 are several new features, including the following:

▶ **Live Trace**—Automatically trace raster images into vector paths instantly, and with supreme control over the final result. Live Trace replaces the Auto Trace tool (which wasn't very automated).

▶ **Live Paint**—Intuitively paint and color areas of multiple objects and paths as if they were a raster image or coloring book (it's a lot cooler to use than it is to try to describe).

▶ **Workspaces**—Included with all the first Creative Suite applications except Illustrator was the ability to save palette and screen arrangements in one or more workspaces. Illustrator now includes this feature, plus the ability to share workspaces between multiple computers and users.

▶ **Control Palette**—Similar to InDesign's Control palette or Photoshop and ImageReady's Options bar, Illustrator CS2 now sports a nifty, dockable Control palette that dynamically changes to feature options and commands relevant to the task being performed.

▶ **Support for Layer Comps in Photoshop Documents**—Layer comps in Photoshop documents can now be selected upon import into Illustrator.

- **Adobe Bridge**—Included with Illustrator CS2 (either standalone or as part of Creative Suite 2) is the Adobe Bridge application. A basic digital asset manager, Bridge is a hub for managing and modifying files, locating and licensing stock photography, and automating scriptable actions.

New Refinements

In addition to the new full features, there are numerous refinements of existing features, including the following:

- **Text Underline and Strikethrough**—After only 19 years and 12 versions, Illustrator can now underline text (without that dodgy underline-in-Photoshop-and-paste-into-Illustrator hack). There are even click-on, click-off buttons on the Character palette!

- **Stroke Alignment Options**—The addition of three little buttons to the Strokes palette enables changing the alignment of strokes from the default of straddling the path (half inside, half outside the path) to fully inside or fully outside. (If this is your first version of Illustrator, count yourself lucky that you will never know the fist-clenching, forehead-vein-bulging joy of working with strokes that are stuck on straddle alignment.)

- **Unified Color Management**—If you purchased Illustrator CS2 as part of Creative Suite 2, color management is simplified and unified across all the applications via the Adobe Bridge application—no more trying to manually mirror color management settings between Illustrator, Photoshop, InDesign, and Acrobat!

- **Sharable PDF Presets**—Create and share PDF presets across multiple computers or other Creative Suite 2 applications.

- **Swatches for Exchange**—A new universal swatches format can be exported from Illustrator and shared across the entire Creative Suite 2, not only Illustrator.

- **Improved Macromedia Flash (SWF) Export**—More control and an easier export process make creating static or animated Flash SWF files faster.

- **Increased PDF Formats**—Save as Acrobat PDF files that are compatible with Acrobat versions 4 through 7, including support for layered or multipage PDF files and press-standard PDF/X-1a and PDF/X-3 formats.

New Bugs in Illustrator CS2

As with any release of software, there are bugs—or what Adobe prefers to call "known issues." I have been intimately involved with Adobe Technical Support, discovering known issues alongside customers and Technical Support reps, and working with Adobe engineers to identify, troubleshoot, and resolve known issues. And, of course, being a dyed-in-the-wool creative pro user of Adobe software for just shy of 20 years, I understand better than most not only the impact of known issues and how they're resolved, but also how Adobe views them. The products Adobe publishes are cherished creations. Everyone at Adobe who works on or with Illustrator and other applications is emotionally vested in the success of the applications. When a known issue is discovered, the people who poured their passions into creating and improving the application zealously pursue a solution.

As a beta tester of Creative Suite 2 and Illustrator CS2—my first version tested from outside Adobe in several years—I found a number of known issues. Some have been resolved in the shipping release, some not yet. Odds are you will encounter some of these known issues—some arise directly while working through the projects in this book. In fact, I had to change some aspects of the projects from what I had planned because of what we call "show-stopper bugs," or technical issues that stop a workflow dead in its tracks and can't be overcome without changing the workflow.

In this book's Appendix B, "Resources," I've provided information about a downloadable list of known issues you will or may encounter as you work through the projects in this book. Also included in the list are techniques to work around those issues. The list is provided as a downloadable PDF rather than printed in the pages of this book to enable it to be kept up to date as Adobe resolves known issues.

Final Thoughts

If you're a die-hard Photoshop user, rest assured that after completing only a few of the projects in this book on the job, you will find yourself reaching for Illustrator for some projects on which you would have previously employed Photoshop. How can I be so confident? Because I see it happen every time I teach an Illustrator class, among thousands of my peers and students who hurdle their fear of Illustrator and allow the program the chance to carry their creativity aloft.

When you need the most powerful, elegant raster editor in the world, don't hesitate—grab Photoshop. But, when you're talking about genuine freedom of expression, unshackled sketching, and, most of all, professional-grade illustration… well, silly rabbit, pixels are for kids.

PART II: Projects

CHAPTER 2: Designing a Logo (From Scratch or From a Scan)

About the Projects

In this chapter you will learn how to draw while creating logos starting from scratch and from scans of rough sketches or rasterized versions of a logo—two methodologies typical of today's logo development process. You will also learn to incorporate transparency and special effects, and how to prepare and output your logos for all their myriad uses, known and unknown.

Prerequisites

It would be helpful if you had a basic operational knowledge of a scanner and scanning software (if you plan to scan your own artwork) and the ability to apply fills and strokes.

@work resources

Please visit the publisher's website to access the following Chapter 2 project files:

- ▶ **Chap02** (complete projects to use as a reference while you work: **Logo - Final.ai, Logo - Grayscale.ai, Logo - B&W.ai**)
- ▶ **Chap02\Assets (Scan-Hand Trace.tif)**
- ▶ **Chap02\Finished Project** (where you place your finished projects)
- ▶ **Chap02\Extras (HowTo – Identify and Recreate Logo Type.pdf, Logo-From-Website.gif)**

Planning the Projects

In planning to design a logo, there are many crucial questions and considerations.

The path you choose depends on your starting point. Do you have a sketch of reasonable quality on paper? If so, hand-tracing a scan of your sketch is a viable option. Depending on the complexity of your sketch, it might even be faster to forego the scan and start drawing. Is your starting point a rough pencil sketch or no sketch at all? In that case, beginning with type or just grabbing the Pen tool and drawing would be the way to go. Is your task not to design but to simply vectorize a raster image of a logo? There Live Trace could be extremely helpful, though trying to identify typefaces and fonts might be a faster kickoff depending on the logo itself.

In this project and special appendix we will work from all three types of starting points. By the end of this chapter, you will not only be able to trace over or redraw any of these, but you will also have the skill to design a logo from scratch onto a blank page.

> ## ◎ TIP
>
> When conceptualizing a logo, make separate lists of adjectives, adverbs, and verbs describing the product, service, or company identified by the logo. Consider what the brand *does*, what its products or services are, and how consumers perceive it. Make your lists as long as possible, and then whittle them down to the three most important words each. An effective logo should communicate all nine words.

Those are the mechanical considerations. Contrary to the amateur designer's (and, regrettably, many clients') expectations, mechanics are the *least* important concern in creating logos. Various planning whys and whats far outweigh the hows.

First and foremost is the recognition that designing a logo is *not* a half-hour job. Working through this project with the sample files provided will be relatively fast, but that is only because you will be following the mechanical steps to build a logo into which I have already put the legwork. When designing a new logo or redefining an existing one, plan on several revisions, extensive market and trademark research, and the involvement of an intellectual property attorney.

Don't let the "we'll design any logo for $50" online shysters set your expectations of the cost of a professionally designed logo. Those are cookie-cutter, clip-art–driven logos where one business's logo will likely be virtually identical to his competitor's—negating the whole purpose of a logo as the unique identifier of a particular business and brand. Professional logo designers always do their research, investigating not only the brand and its market(s), but also existing trademarks; often, an intellectual property attorney is hired to perform a thorough trademark search. It is because of the research required to do the job right that a professional typically charges upwards of $2,000 for logo design.

Ahead of its inventory, its trade secrets, and its patents, the most valuable asset of any commercial endeavor is its *brand*. The logo is the harbinger of a brand. It must be protected at all costs—thus the need for state and federal trademarks. It may seem as if the designer's concern ends when the logo is delivered, but in reality it is the designer's responsibility to design a logo that is reasonably free of both copyright and trademark infringement. You are, after all, not creating a piece of art; you are building a mark whose uniqueness is legally protectable, and that is legally *required* to be unique.

Consider colors—signature colors that will create an instant identification with your client's brand. Quick: What is UPS's signature color? Right! Brown. In fact, color is so important to the UPS brand that the tagline was changed a few years ago to "What can Brown do for you?®" The UPS brand survived a logo overhaul, and no one needs to see the logo to recognize a brown van or brown uniform as UPS. When you run a delivery company, the most important aspect of your marketing strategy is being seen while delivering.

What color(s) you choose for your client's logo is critical to the logo's perception. Colors have meanings to the human psyche. For example, red inspires passion and anger. To most people, yellow signifies cheer and vibrancy, but to a significant portion of the world's population a subdued or pastel yellow means the opposite—in fact, it prompts feelings of depression and dissatisfaction. Put red and yellow together, however, and they inspire hunger—one of the big secrets behind the success of McDonald's restaurants and its competitors, Burger King, Checkers, Pizza Hut, Taco Bell, and Wendy's, all of whom employ brands made up of variations on the red-and-yellow combination.

And these are only *some* of the considerations to keep in mind as you embark upon logo design. Numerous books are devoted to this subject alone!

Effective logo design is all about the choices you make *at the start*. Wise choices at the inception of the project will lead to strong brands and logos; poor choices... well, garbage in, garbage out, as the old saying goes.

Project: Logo Sketch

We'll scribble a rough sketch for our logo in three easy steps:

1. Fast sketching with the Pencil tool
2. Simplifying and smoothing the Pencil tool sketch
3. Positioning points

Sketching a Logo Concept

Quick! You've got an idea! Uh, no; not about a way to impress the hottie in Accounts Receivable. No, this idea was about a logo design. For days you've been wracking your brain as to how to build the logo for this brand, pouring through market data and cell-phone-captured digital pictures of competitors' brands. Nothing you tried seemed to work.

Now, as you were playing Zuma, the perfect design flashed across your mind. Get the idea sketched out fast—before it's gone! You can either reach for the trusty mechanical pencil with the broken pocket clip, or you can jot down the design in Illustrator, where it will end up anyway.

STEP 1 ▼
Fast Sketching with the Pencil Tool

Get that idea down fast!

1. Begin a new Letter-sized Illustrator document entitled **Logo – Sketch**. Because this document will only hold the logo, and because we will define a crop area, the size is as irrelevant as a PICT file. Still, we must work with something. So go ahead and set the *Artboard* size to Letter and Units to Inches. Make the Orientation *portrait* (the left button), and set the Color Mode to *RGB* to allow us the widest possible range of colors with which to work. Click OK.

2. Grab the Pencil tool from the Toolbox and draw. That's it. Just click and drag to draw. Get those rough shapes onto paper (so to speak).

   With the Pencil tool, as long as the left mouse button remains depressed, you're drawing. Release it, and drawing stops. Move over to the next shape, click and drag again, and you're drawing a whole new path. While you quickly scratch out your idea, I'll sketch mine (see Figure 2.1).

FIGURE 2.1   A quick Pencil tool sketch of the REV logo drawn with stylus and tablet.

3. Got your idea down? If you had colors in mind, you can fill them in now. Don't worry that the sketch is as rough as the morning after a bachelor's party in Vegas. We'll clean it up in a moment. Save your document (and close down Zuma—Illustrator might need the RAM).

◎ TIP

Need to change the shape of a path? Click somewhere on the path with the Pencil tool and draw your revision; it will automatically be added to, removed from, or incorporated into the existing path. Hold the Shift key as you begin drawing to initiate a new path atop the first, without interacting with the first.

STEP 2 ▼
Simplifying and Smoothing the Pencil Tool Sketch

Now that we've got the rough idea down— rough indeed!—we need to clean it up into something a little more workable.

1. Because I'm careful and always want a bread-crumb trail leading the way back until I'm finished with a design, I'll duplicate my working layer. I recommend you do so as well. On the Layers palette, drag **Layer 1** and drop it

on the Create New Layer button at the bottom of the palette. That will create **Layer 1 Copy**. Hide **Layer 1**.

2. With the original messy sketch preserved on its own layer, let's grab the Selection tool and remove some of the clutter around the main subject of the sketch by clicking on each extraneous path and pressing Delete (see Figure 2.2).

FIGURE 2.2   Now that the sketch is reduced to the most important elements, I can begin the cleanup.

3. Choose Outline from the top of the View menu so that we can see and work with what's really important.

⊚ **TIP**

Illustrator has two primary working modes: Preview, which shows the finished artwork, including fills, strokes, patterns, and effects, and Outline, which enables more precise path work by hiding everything but the paths themselves. There are other preview modes, but we won't need them in this project.

4. Select any path in your drawing and you will see all of its *anchor points*. When drawing with the Pencil tool, you *will* get too many points. We have to clean them up.

    We need to work with closed paths, so if there are any gaps in your paths (see Figure 2.3), use the Pencil tool to close them. Just click on the anchor point at one end of the gap, and draw until you reach the anchor point on the other end of the gap.

FIGURE 2.3   Gaps render a path unusable for many effects and transformations, so they need to be closed.

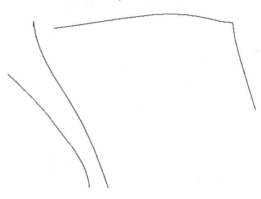

5. Click and hold on the Pencil tool button in the Toolbox to access the Smooth tool behind it. Drag the Smooth tool along any line segment with too many bends and anchor points. It will reduce the number of both (see Figure 2.4).

FIGURE 2.4   Before the Smooth tool (left), and after (right).

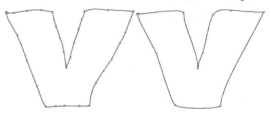

⊚ **TIP**

Any icon in the Toolbox that bears a black arrow in its lower-right corner (like the Pen tool) has additional tools behind the first. Clicking and holding on the tool will reveal the others in a flyout.

6. The Smooth tool simplified my path quite a bit, but it still has too many anchor points. If your path is the same way, let's select Object > Path > Simplify.

In the Simplify dialog, turn on Preview and play with the various options until you get as close as possible to your desired drawing. In my case, because I'm drawing a V, I've checked Straight Lines (which eliminates curves and disables the Curve Precision slider), and set the Angle Threshold, the maximum allowable corner angle, to **40°**. This cleans up my V path tremendously (see Figure 2.5).

FIGURE 2.5   After I've simplified my path, it looks very close to its intended form—a heavyweight capital V.

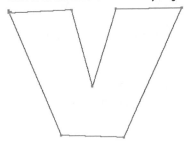

STEP 3 ▼
Positioning Points

With a simpler path that's almost ready for prime time, let's finish it off by positioning our anchor points where they belong.

1. Click on, and drag from, the vertical ruler to create a vertical guide. Line it up with the left-most edge of the path. Now drag another vertical guide to where the right edge *should* be. Do the same thing for the horizontal guides, dragging from the ruler at the top of the window. The goal is to create a box defining the area for our path.

2.   With the Direct Selection tool, either click directly on a point or click and drag a selection rectangle such that only the desired point falls within it. Now that point is selected and ready to be manipulated independent of the other path points.

3. Click on the point and drag it where you want it. Working with my V, I want the top-left point to align with the intersection of the top and left guides; the top-right point will go to the intersection of those guides. The other points along the top parts of the V will need to be aligned to the horizontal guide defining the top of the box.

4. Do the same thing for all the anchor points in your path. If you can't get the precise placement you need with the mouse, nudge with your keyboard arrow. As you get close, the point should snap to the guides.

> ◎ **TIP**
>
> If the arrow keys on your keyboard move objects or points too much (or too little), adjust the distances they nudge with each press. Go to Edit > Preferences > General and adjust the Keyboard Increment setting. Experiment with different values to get what works for you.

5. Save your document. If smoothing, simplifying, and manually positioning points doesn't completely fix your path as it did mine (see Figure 2.6), don't despair. Keep working through this chapter; by the end, you will be able to fix any path, any way, any time.

FIGURE 2.6   V for Victory. My quick, hand-drawn Pencil sketch is now a recognizable object.

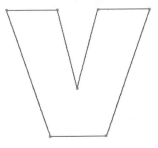

Project: Trace a Scan

We'll trace a scan of a drawing of the logo in four steps.

1. Preparing the tracing template
2. Drawing with the Pen tool
3. Adjusting curves with the Direct Selection tool
4. Knocking one shape out of another

Tracing a Scanned Sketch

Cleaning up after a Pencil tool sketch is sometimes more work than redrawing with the Pen tool. And, if you're starting with a scanned pencil, marker, or pen drawing, the Pen tool is usually the way to begin.

In cases like this, we need to trace over the scans (or Pencil tool scribbling) by hand.

In this section we'll draw and modify paths with the Pen tool and its brothers. Although everything in this project is important to drawing by hand as well as tracing, we'll work with a scan of an original pencil sketch. Like all the world's great art, the sketch began life on the back of a cocktail napkin.

STEP 1 ▼
Preparing the Tracing Template

Let's set up for drawing. If you would like to continue working with your Pencil tool sketch, ignore the references in this step to the placed scan and continue working in the same document.

1. Start a new document with the same settings as the last one (letter size, portrait orientation, RGB, and Units set to Inches), and title it **Logo-Hand Trace**.

2. Go to File > Place, which will pop up a Place dialog very similar to the Open dialog. Navigate to the location of this chapter's resource files, and choose `Chap02\Assets\Scan-Hand Trace.tif`. Make sure you check the Link option in the Place dialog so that a copy of the image does not embed in the Illustrator document. The scan should wind up in the middle of your artboard; position it if necessary.

> ### 🚫 CAUTION
> If you don't see the scan, check the View menu. Are you in Outline or Preview mode? By default, images will not appear in Outline mode.

3. Open the Layers palette from the Window menu. The scanned pencil sketch is on **Layer 1**, so double-click **Layer 1** in the palette (be careful to double-click on either the icon or the name, **Layer 1**, not on anything else). When the Layer Options dialog comes up, title the layer **Scan** and check the Template option, which should automatically trigger Lock and Dim Images. Click OK.

   If you're working from a Pencil tool drawing, make the original sketch the template layer.

   Notice how the **Scan** layer is now locked and italicized, and the image itself is dimmed? This is a template layer, which makes it easy to trace without inadvertently moving the scan itself. Double-clicking again on the entry in the Layers palette will enable converting it back to a regular layer just as easily (don't do that now).

4. At the bottom of the Layers palette, click the New Layer button. Double-click the resulting layer and rename it to **Tracing**, but do not make this a template. We'll draw on this layer.

5. Before going any further, we need to define the space in which the R must reside. If your rulers are not already showing across the top and down the left side of the document window, turn them on by pressing (Cmd-R) [Ctrl+R].

6. Click on, and drag from, the vertical ruler to create a vertical guide. Line it up with the left-most edge of the R. Repeat to align vertical rulers to the right edge of the stalk (the thick vertical stroke of the R) and the right-most edge of the letterform.

7. Now do the same thing for the horizontal guides, dragging from the ruler at the top of the window. Position guides across the top and bottom of the R, as well as even with the top and bottom of the hole (the "counter" in typography terms), and even with the join of the outer rounded part (the "bowl") and the diagonal bar (see Figure 2.7).

If you can't quite tell in your scan where everything will be, take a guess; it's not set in stone. Save your document.

STEP 2 ▼
Drawing with the Pen Tool

The Pen tool is the true power of vector illustration. It was perfected with the release of Illustrator 1 in 1986, and it has remained almost unchanged since.

1. Select the Pen tool, set the fill color to none and the stroke color to lime green, red, magenta, or something else equally conspicuous (you can use the Swatch palette for the easiest method). Zoom in on the R until it fills the document window without cutting off.

2. Click once with the Pen tool where the top-left corner of the R should be (where the guides intersect). Now click where the bottom-left corner should be (another intersection of guides). See the line? Refer to the diagram in Figure 2.8 for numbered points we'll use throughout this section.

FIGURE 2.7   My R with guides positioned.

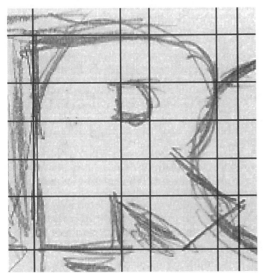

FIGURE 2.8   As you work, refer to this diagram of the nine points (and five additional in the counter) that define all the path direction and/or curvature changes in the R.

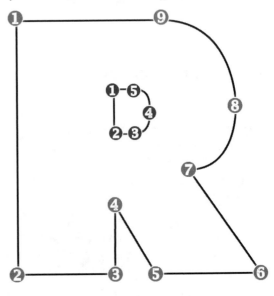

Every time you click with the Pen tool, you create a new anchor point. After the first point, each subsequent point automatically connects to the prior one with a straight line—more accurately, it connects to the prior point with a path segment of the same *angle* and type. Thus a series of rapid clicks would beget a series of points connected by straight lines.

Anchor points should only be where a path changes direction—when the line follows a different angle or curve from the point before it, or if the point leads into an angle while the previous point leads into a curve (or the other way around).

3. Keep going counterclockwise, creating the points (and line segments) to define the straight surfaces of the R. Stop after you connect point #6 to #7.

TIP

If you make a mistake while drawing with the Pen tool, pressing (Cmd-Z) [Ctrl+Z] will undo the creation of the last point, not the entire Pen tool usage as it would with the Pencil tool. If you press (Cmd-Z) [Ctrl+Z] multiple times, you can step backward through the creation of all points (or any actions). To *redo* press (Cmd-Shift-Z) [Ctrl+Shift+Z].

4. Now that you have drawing straight lines down, it's time to draw the curves of the R's bowl. Your path should still be selected, with the #7 point filled and all others hollow, which indicates that any new points will connect off from #7. Click *and hold* on the new point (#8) at the midpoint of the bowl. Don't let go. Now count to 10,000 like this: *One Mississippi, two Mississippi,...*

Just kidding! Don't count. [The publisher of this book accepts no responsibility for carpal tunnel syndrome or other injuries incurred by readers as a result of the activities in this chapter. All reader participation is "at own risk" and strictly voluntary. –Ed.] Just hold the mouse button down and move the cursor around a bit. Now you're creating curvature as indicated by the appearance of Martian antennae sprouting from the point (these are *curve handles*).

Try to create a curve segment that properly defines the lower half of the bowl. In a few moments we'll work with making curves; for now, just do your best.

5. Create point #9 by clicking and dragging to create the curve at the top of the bowl.

TIP

The first time you click and release, you make an anchor point that inherits the curvature of the point before it (the second time reverts to a corner point and straight segment). When you click and drag, however, you create a smooth point and begin changing the curvature of the new line segment. When curve inheritance is undesired, Opt-click (Alt-click) on the source point before creating the new point.

6. Click and release on point #1 to close the path. Notice that you already have another curved path segment instead of a straight one? There's that sometimes convenient, sometimes inconvenient inheritance.

Unless you are already pretty good with the Pen tool, you should be staring down an R that looks as if it lost a brawl with Mr. T.

STEP 3 ▼
Adjusting Curves with the Direct Selection Tool

Points and curves are all about geometry, but *please* don't let that scare you if you hated junior high school geometry. Manipulating points and curves gives instant feedback; though it makes things more intuitive, it is *not* necessary to understand their underlying science to learn how to work with them. (I had a crush on my sixth-grade geometry teacher, so, with some deftly orchestrated after-school tutoring from Miss Rovin, I got the subject down. Calculus is another story entirely.)

Any time you select an anchor point that has a curve on either (or both) end, curve handles appear. Each handle corresponds to its path segment, meaning that the handle on the left of a point controls the path segment on the left. The length of the handle is in direct proportion to the depth of the curve. A short handle creates a shallow curve, a long handle a deep curve. Click on the handle point and you can drag it around anywhere, with instant feedback from the curve.

1. In the Toolbox, click and hold on the Pen tool. While cleaning up the R and building the E, we're going to make extensive use of these four tools, so let's tear them off into their own free-floating toolbar by clicking the tiny arrow to the far right. Position it somewhere convenient on your screen.

2. After careful consideration we've realized we want a flat top on the R, so select point #9, at the top of the R's bowl, with the Direct Selection tool. Both curve handles should appear (see Figure 2.9).

FIGURE 2.9   Selecting a curved anchor point displays its curve handles.

3. Point #9 is a smooth point, but to get a flat roof on the R we need to convert it to an angled or corner point. What to do, what to do... Ah, yes! From the floating Pen toolbar, select the Convert Anchor Point tool and click on #9. Because we've converted the point type, the path segment between #1 and #9 is now straight, with no curve handle. Of course, the segment between #9 and #8 is looking a little worse for wear.

4. Any time you select a point, the curve handles on either end of the curve—belonging to the next anchor points to either side along the path—also become active because they control how the adjoining curve comes off *them* (see Figure 2.10). So, with #9 still selected, take the handle coming off point #8 and drag it with the Direct Selection tool to get the best possible curvature for the upper bowl.

If you drag the handle around you will eventually stumble onto this. But I've got to get on with writing the rest of this book, so I'm just going to tell you: Drag the handle to the intersection of the planes on which points #9 and #8 reside—which should be the convergence of the guides running along the top and right edges of the R. Perfect upper bowl curve!

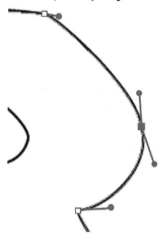

⊗ NOTE

Working with handles can sometimes be an exercise in hand-eye coordination. Because handles are ethereal devices and not real objects, zooming has no effect on their size on screen. Even worse, when they're close to an anchor point it can sometimes be difficult to discern which is a point and which is the end of a handle. Take deep breaths and remember that practice *does* make perfect.

5. Select #8 directly now, and try adjusting the bottom curve. Did it alter #8's upper curve? Of course it did. Before you get frustrated and run out to buy *Adobe Photoshop CS2 @work* in hopes of learning how to do logos in *that* program, allow me to show you the trick.

   Grab the Convert Anchor Point tool again. If you click on the #8 anchor point, you'll convert it from a curved point to an angled point, ruining the R. However, if you click on one of the curve handles *themselves*, you will make the two path segments coupled by #8 independent from one another.

(Incidentally, although Photoshop also has vector path tools, they operate just like Illustrator's—and they're just as frustrating until you get the hang of them.)

6. *Now* try changing the curvature of the segment between #8 and #7. Better, right? Work with the curve handles of both anchor points until you have a smooth, slightly elliptical bowl with no discernible bumps around #8.

   Check your drawing against Figure 2.11. Do they look the same? If not, examine points #7 through #9 to see if you inadvertently converted an anchor point that shouldn't have been converted, or a point you forgot to convert that should have been converted.

FIGURE 2.11 Note the smooth bowl of the R and its counter.

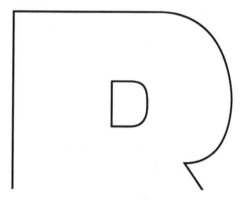

7. Select the R path with the Selection tool, and fill it with a solid color like black. With the R still selected, lock it by pressing (Cmd-2) [Ctrl+2].

8. Press D to reset the swatches to their defaults. Now draw the five-point counter in the R using the same techniques as drawing and massaging the outer path.

Knocking One Shape Out of Another

Because Illustrator treats every path as a separate object, the hole in the R is not really a hole; it's a white-filled path sitting atop a wholly whole and hole-less R.

It's time to make the donuts.

1. Choose Object > Unlock All to unlock and select the outer R path.

2. With the R still selected, Shift-click on the hole to select it without deselecting the R.

3. Open the Pathfinder palette from the Window menu, and click the Subtract From Shape Area button. Then click the Expand button. *Now* we have a dyslexic French cruller.

Project: Shape Drawing and Modification

We'll build and modify part of our logo from scratch in two simple steps.

1. **Drawing the basic shapes**

2. **Adding and subtracting anchor points, and joining path segments**

Combining Simple Shapes to Make Complex Paths

The lowercase e is, in its most canonical form, an ellipse, so the fastest way to draw it is not with either the Pencil or the Pen tool. Rather than build a common shape from scratch, *start* with the shape and then modify it your needs.

Drawing the Basic Shapes

Define the shape of things to come.

1. Find the center point of the *e*—do it by eye because the joy of vector is that everything is always malleable. Now draw horizontal and vertical guides to intersect at that center point.

2. Click and hold on the Rectangle tool to get to the Ellipse tool behind.

3. With the Ellipse tool, click and hold on that center point. While pressing the (Opt) [Alt] key, drag away from the center point at an angle. Press (Opt) [Alt] to draw the ellipse from the center outward. Make an ellipse that is slightly wider than tall. Extend the height just beyond the guides that define the top and bottom of the R and V.

4. Because we estimated the center point, odds are the ellipse will not line up perfectly or be the exact size desired. Switch to the Selection tool by pressing V on your keyboard, and click on the ellipse. Around it will appear the bounding box, whose control handles resize or distort when dragged (see Figure 2.12). Use the boxes on the *sides* (not the corners) and hold (Opt) [Alt] while resizing to force the opposite side to follow suit without distorting the perpendicular dimension. When you click and drag the path, the Selection tool will reposition the ellipse without changing its dimensions.

5. When the ellipse is in the desired position, double-click the Scale tool in the Toolbox. This will bring up the Scale dialog.

FIGURE 2.12 The bounding box controls scaling and rotation of an object.

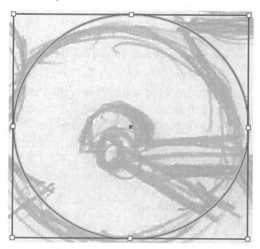

6. By clicking Preview on and off, estimate the best scaling percentage to draw the counter to knock out of the E. Because this is an ellipse, you will probably want non-uniform scaling. When you have the scaling in the range you need, click the Copy button to create a copy of the original ellipse at the percentages specified, leaving the original unaltered.

7. The scaled copy is aligned to the center of the original, so hold (Opt) [Alt] as you manually scale one axis and/or the other to tweak the size of the inner ellipse via its bounding box. If you can't see the copy, change its fill to a different color than the original.

⊚ **TIP**

To ensure perfect sizing between objects, a tried-and-true trick is to draw a rectangle the exact size of the first object—in this case the width of the R's stalk with a small height. Then drag the rectangle onto the second object—the E—and line it up with the outer edge of that object. Adjust the size, shape, or spacing of the second and subsequent object(s) to accommodate the rectangle's volume.

Before subtracting the smaller ellipse from the larger one with the options on the Pathfinder palette, subtract the crossbar from the inner counter.

8. Although I *could* ask you to reinforce your Pen tool skills by drawing custom shapes to knock out of the ellipses—and you would do it, too, because I'm a nice guy and I don't ask much of you—I want you to do things the easiest and fastest way possible. So, let's do it the faster way by grabbing the Rectangle tool (behind the Ellipse tool, as you may recall).

9. Decide where the crossbar of the E will be and draw a rectangle to represent it. Make sure the rectangle completely bisects the smaller ellipse, that it is wider than the smaller ellipse, and that it's the height you want (see Figure 2.13).

FIGURE 2.13 Stop me if you've heard this one: Two ellipses walk into a bar...

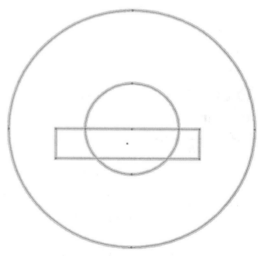

10. Select both the rectangle and the inner ellipse.

11. On the Pathfinder palette, click the Subtract From Shape Area button and Expand. You now have the eye and the curve of the aperture. Subtract these from the outer ellipse the same way (see Figure 2.14).

FIGURE 2.14 **Starting with three simple shapes, we created a more complicated path with a few button clicks.**

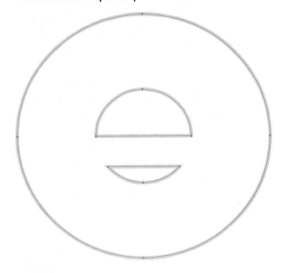

STEP 2 ▼
Adding and Subtracting Anchor Points, and Joining Path Segments

It's time to learn path modification skills by opening the lower hole into a true aperture.

1. Switch into outline mode and zoom in on the E.

2. With the E selected, all the anchor points in the path should be visible. Choose the Pen tool and move your cursor over one of those anchor points. Notice anything different about your cursor?

Click on one of the anchor points—go on, I double dog dare ya. Did the anchor point disappear? If not, you didn't click directly on the point. Try clicking on a path segment, away from an anchor point. You got a new point, right?

With amazing convenience, the Pen tool changes itself into *eight different tools* depending on what type of construct you're clicking on (see Table 2.1 for the various Pen tool cursors and functions).

TABLE 2.1 Pen Tool Cursors

	Begin a new path.
	Add anchor point to this path.
	Delete this anchor point.
	Convert this anchor point.
	Continue path from this anchor point.
	Join path segments.
	Close path.
	Adjust curve of this point.

3. Referring to Figure 2.15, click the Pen tool onto the path segments in these five places, adding five new anchor points.

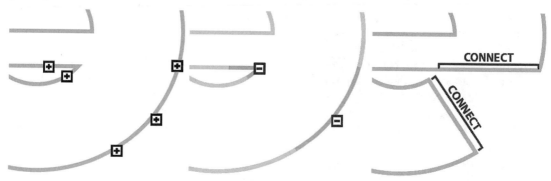

4. Then delete the indicated pair of points by clicking directly on them with the Pen tool.

5. Finally, to close the path again, join the open segments by clicking first on a point at one side of the gap, then the point at the next. Move on to close the second gap. Your E is now complete.

Project: Logo Refinement

In six easy steps we'll refine and polish the logo:

1. **Loading and using spot colors**
2. **Drawing the star effect**
3. **Defining opacity masks and clipping masks**
4. **Creating motion with warp effects and pathfinder jitters**
5. **Drawing the speedometer**
6. **Implying motion through feathering**

Refining the Logo

Armed with the means to draw or trace anything quickly and efficiently (and, of course, the skills to create logo forms from scratch), we're now ready to pick the colors and apply the styling that will make this logo distinctive of its brand.

STEP 1 ▼
Loading and Using Spot Colors

Color, of course, is critical to branding and logo design. Equally important is the mechanics of choosing colors, for, if done incorrectly in Illustrator, the results on press will be unpredictable, at best, and expensively unusable, at worst.

1. Using whichever technique you prefer, complete a logo drawing of the REV letters, and go to File > Save As and save a new copy as **Logo-FINAL.ai**. Delete the layer(s) containing your scan, pencil rough, or other temporary construction materials. Now that we have the finished letterforms, we don't need the sketch.

2. The REV energy drink is a vibrant green brew, so I chose bright greens, which contrast beautifully with black, an appropriate secondary color. Of course, I chose the colors from my PMS swatch books. Specifically, I chose colors from the Pantone Process Coated library, which are swatches that print in standard CMYK rather than as additional premixed inks called *spot colors*.

Illustrator includes the Pantone Process Coated library and many other libraries, under Window > Swatch Libraries. Open the Pantone Process Coated library, which will load as a new palette. You can load any (or all) the Swatch Libraries listed—as well as more if you choose.

3. From the flyout menu at the top of the PANTONE Process Coated palette, choose List View for an easier way to work with the swatches.

4. One at a time, find each of the following colors and drag their swatches to Illustrator's normal Swatches palette: **DS 298-4, DS 294-3, DS 286-2, DS282-1**. Close the PANTONE Process Coated palette.

5. Select the R. Open the Gradient palette (Window > Gradient) and activate a Linear gradient from the Type drop-down (you may need to Show Options from the palette menu). It will probably start out as a horizontal white-to-black gradient (see Figure 2.16).

FIGURE 2.16 Default options for a new gradient. Note the gradient stop color indicators beneath the gradient preview—white on the left, black on the right.

6. Drag the **Pantone DS 286-2 C** swatch from the Swatches palette and drop it directly onto the white color gradient stop in the Gradient palette. The preview and your R should instantly change from a black to a green gradient. If you wind up with a tri-tone gradient, you missed the target when you dropped the green swatch. Undo with (Cmd-Z) [Ctrl+Z] and try it again.

   Make a swatch from this gradient by clicking the New Swatch button at the bottom of the Swatches palette.

7. Fill the V and the E with the same gradient swatch, but change the angle on the V gradient to **180°** and the E gradient to -**90°**.

STEP 2 ▼
Drawing the Star Effect

One of several ways in which the REV logo implies motion and activity is the star pattern radiating through the R and V.

1. Create a new layer and title it **Star and Mask**. Lock the layer containing the REV letterforms.

2. Select the Star tool, which hides behind the Rectangle tool, and click once in the artboard to bring up the Star dialog. There, choose a high number of points (I used 25) and set Radius 1 (the peaks) to **2 in.** and Radius 2 (the valleys) to **1 in.** You should wind up with a nice star like mine (see Figure 2.17).

FIGURE 2.17 The result of using the Star tool.

3. Position the star dead center over the E, press (Opt) [Alt] to resize its height downward, and then press (Opt) [Alt] to resize its width outward until you get good spread across the R and V (see Figure 2.18).

4. On this first star, clear the fill and give it a **6 pt** stroke of **DS 282-1 C**.

5. Go to Effect > Blur > Radial Blur, and set a Zoom blur with Good quality and an Amount of **47**.

FIGURE 2.18 Resized and repositioned, the star radiates across all three letters.

6. Duplicate the star with Copy and Paste In Front, and then set its stroke as none and the fill to **DS 294-3 C**.

7. Duplicate one more time, setting the third star's fill as **DS 298-4 C**, and scale the star down until it's just barely visible (see Figure 2.19).

FIGURE 2.19 All three stars styled and in place.

STEP 3 ▼
Defining Opacity Masks and Clipping Masks

To make the stars appear as desired and only within the letterforms, we must turn to opacity and clipping masks.

1. Select all three stars and group them.

2. Draw a rectangle that completely encompasses the letterforms but doesn't over-reach them too far on either side.

3. Clear any stroke that may be on, and set the fill to be a radial black-to-white gradient. Black should be on the left with its location (on the Gradient palette) set to somewhere around 77%. The goal is to have the black obscure roughly the

inner one-third of both the R and V while almost completely obliterating the E.

4. Select both the gradient box and the three-star group.

5. Open the Transparency palette and, from its palette menu, choose Make Opacity Mask. If you set up the gradient-filled rectangle correctly, you should see something like Figure 2.20.

FIGURE 2.20 **The Transparency palette with opacity mask applied.**

Now for the clipping mask.

6. For a moment, unlock the **REV** layer. Copy the REV letterforms and Paste In Front on the **Star and Mask** layer.

7. Select all three letters and choose Object > Compound Path > Make. Lock the bottom layer again, and then Select All on the **Star and Mask** layer, which should get the compound letterforms as well as the opacity-masked stars.

8. From the Object menu choose Clipping Mask > Make. The stars are now clipped to appear only within the area of the letterforms (see Figure 2.21). Lock the layer and save the document.

FIGURE 2.21 **With opacity and clipping masks applied, the star now radiates only within the letterforms.**

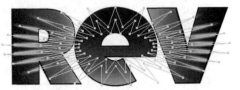

Creating Motion with Warp Effects and Pathfinder Jitters

The next motion trick is the jitter effect on the end characters. Don't *you* get the jitters. This will be fun.

1. Start a new layer and title it **Jitters**. Hide all other layers.

2. You should still have the (individual) REV letterforms on the clipboard, so Paste In Front. Now delete the E.

3. We need five copies of the V in addition to the actual black-to-green–filled front V. To make things easier, we're going to work in reverse order, pasting each successive one in front. So, copy the V, but don't paste.

4. Set the fill as **black** and the stroke to **none**.

5. From the Effect menu choose Warp > Squeeze, and input the following settings: **Vertical**, **11%**, and Distortion of **33%** and **-2%**.

6. Paste in Front again and fill this V red (or another obviously out-of-place color) with no stroke. Rotate it **-10** degrees.

7. Make your third V also red with no stroke, and Warp Squeeze it with **Vertical**, **7%** Bend, and **14%** and **10%** Distortion.

8. On the fourth V, make a new gradient that goes from **DS 286-2 C** at **50%** tint—with the Gradient palette color indicator selected, go to the Color palette and drag the tint slider down to **50%**—to **100% black**. No stroke. And, again, choose Effect > Wrap > Squeeze with **Vertical**, **4%**, **7%**, and **-9%**.

9. The fifth V is going to be like the second—filled with **red**, no stroke, no Warp—but this one will be rotated **-8** degrees.

---

10. Paste in Front one final time to get our normal, green-to-black V. This one we will use solely as a reference to monitor how our effects look.

11. The trick to pulling this off is to move and (slightly) resize or rotate the Vs until you get exactly the right look. The three red Vs will become negative space, knocking out of Vs #1 and #4. Figure 2.22 shows how I set up my Vs.

FIGURE 2.22   All five Vs in place, ready to begin path subtractions.

⊙ TIP

There are several ways to select stacked objects without changing their order. In a case like this, the best way is by looking to the Layers palette. Beside the layer name is an arrow. Clicking that arrow to rotate it downward opens up the content of the layer, with each object (group, path, guide, sublayer, and more) having its entry. On each entry is a Target circle. Click once on the Target circle to select the object, as indicated by an outer ring; and by a square beside it. The square is the color of the layer, which changes with every new top-level layer.

You can select multiple object layers by Shift-clicking their Target circles.

12. When you have your Vs arranged as you like them, begin subtracting the red ones from the others via the Pathfinder palette. In the case of the black V (#1), subtract both #4 and #3 from it.

If you don't get exactly the look you are after, undo, move things around (or size and rotate them), and hit the Pathfinder palette again.

13. When the V is done, delete the front-most V and group the rest. Because we used Paste in Front the whole time, the jitters should already be lined up with the real V on the REV layer.

14. Repeat steps 3–13 with the R, but when it comes to warping, rotating, and moving the Rs, reverse the horizontal numbers. The V jitters to the right, but the R should jitter out to the left. For example: For V #1 squeeze Horizontal Distortion was **33%**. To reverse the direction of the squeeze on R #1, the Horizontal distortion should be **–33%**.

Some settings will need to be changed to accommodate the fact that the R and V are different shapes. For example: With V#1, we used a Vertical Distortion of **-2%**, but on R #1 I liked the result of dropping that to **-9%**. The goal is get a balance—in both form and color—between the R and V jitters.

STEP 5 ▼
Drawing the Speedometer

Letterforms? Formed. Star effect? Stellar. Jitters? Ch-ch-check. Great! Then all that's left is the speedometer in the E.

1. Make a new layer called **speedometer** and lock the rest.

2. With the Line tool, draw a **0.25 in.** long line with a weight of **4 pts** and **DS 286-2 C** stroke color.

On the Stroke palette set a round cap. Line up the stroke (approximately) to the top of the E's crossbar and close to—but not touching—the outer edge of the E.

3. Make a second copy of the line and drag it to the opposite side of the E.

◉ **TIP**

Hold (Opt) [Alt] while dragging an object to make a duplicate. Hold Shift while dragging to constrain the motion to a multiple of 45 degrees—for example, 0, 45, 90, 135, 180 and so on. Both may be held simultaneously to make a copy with its angle constrained.

4. Make a third copy, rotate it **90°**, and drag it to the top center of the E.

5. Rotate the last two copies **45°** and **-45°**, positioning them at the midpoints between the horizontal and vertical marks. (Creating and rotating guides relative to the center of the semicircle created by the lines might help.) These are your tick marks.

6. Grab the Type tool and, inside the left, top, and right tick marks, type the numbers **0**, **70**, and **140** in the same color as the tick marks. Choose a typeface that will be legible at extremely small sizes—I chose Impact, but any clean, narrow, and beefy type-face would work equally well.

7. Select the type and tick marks, and group (Object > Group) and lock.

8. Draw a small black circle in the center of the E's crossbar; this will be the base of the needle (see Figure 2.23).

9. The needle itself is a very simple object—everything in a logo needs to be simple. Just use the Pen tool to create the full needle, angled from the

base to around the 140 mark, with pointed ends. Fill it with **DS 294-3 C** and a thin stroke of black.

10. As a separate object draw the shadow face of the needle and fill it with **DS 282-1 C**.

11. Draw two to four little slivers of the needle and position them around the dial above the needle to imply such rapid motion that it leaves afterimages. We'll call these the afterimages.

12. Draw a triangle the width of the needle whose point meets the needle's inner end, and whose lower edge meets the needle's body. This will be the needle sweep.

FIGURE 2.23   The E speedometer, up to this point.

STEP 6 ▼
Implying Motion Through Feathering

The final touches are just a matter of feathering and applying a little transparency.

1. Needle: Choose Effect > Stylize > Drop Shadow. Settings: **Multiply, 50, 0 in., 0.05 in., 0.02 in.**, Color (**Black**).

2. Needle Shadow edge: Choose Effect > Stylize > Feather. Settings: **0.05 in.**

3. Afterimages: Fill them the same color as the needle itself, but make them

successively lighter as they move away from the needle. On the Transparency palette set the blending mode to Hard Light, and the Opacity 50% for the first afterimage, dropping sharply for each subsequent afterimage. Give them all a **0.03 in.** Feather.

4. Needle sweep: Fill it with a **DS 294-3 C** to **DS 282-1 C** gradient angled to roughly **168°**. Adjust the color sliders until you get the gradient you want. Then feather the whole thing **0.19 in.** and set the Transparency to **Lighten** at **65%** (see Figure 2.24 for the final result).

FIGURE 2.24   The finished REV logo.

Project: **Saving for Print, Web, and Microsoft Office**

We'll prepare the finished logo for virtually any possible use in six easy steps:

1. Exporting to legacy EPS format for print
2. Saving as a TIFF file
3. Saving for the web
4. Saving for use in Microsoft Office
5. Converting your four-color logo to grayscale
6. Converting your grayscale logo to 1-bit black and white

Saving the Logo for Print, Web, and Microsoft Office

Our logo is polished and ready for delivery to the client—almost. We have no idea what software the client or her clients and vendors may use the logo in, so we can't be certain that they can read Illustrator CS2 format. To be responsible designers, we need to provide the artwork in formats suitable for typical uses—and capable of being used in workflows we can't anticipate.

STEP 1 ▼
Exporting to Legacy EPS Format for Print

EPS is the most widely accepted vector file format. It can go anywhere professional graphic, layout, and RIP software may be found—even the ancient *PostScript* Level 2 systems still used in some smaller print shops. However, most of the effects we used— the opacity mask, feathering, drop shadows, and other transparency effects—are usually not supported by applications outside of Creative Suite 2. We need to take care of that—no, not by forming a posse and muscling everyone else into getting CS2 (I'll pass that idea along to Adobe for you, though).

1. Draw a rectangle around the logo, covering the entire logo but extending only to the four edges. Go to Object > Crop Area > Make. This will define the limits of your logo file, regardless of the page size. Save your **Logo-FINAL.ai** file.

2. The very next thing to do is Save As a new Illustrator file. We're going to eliminate our ability to edit major portions of the logo in this process, and there's no reason to risk an accidental save of our working document. It is *much* less frustrating to delete a temporary working copy of a file than to re-create the whole thing—trust me on this.

3. Unlock all layers.

4. From File > Document Color Mode, select CMYK color.

5. You have real text in the logo—the speedometer numbers, remember?—and that won't do. Too much likelihood of embedding or RIP issues there. So do a Select All on the whole document.

   If we were only concerned with the type, we would do the old-fashioned Create Outlines maneuver from the golden years on the varsity fontball team. But this is the new millennium, man! This is the age of transparency and a mature, refined, post-graduate Illustrator. We can go for a touchdown on the transparency *and the type* all in one play.

6. From the Object menu select Flatten Transparency and configure it thusly: Pick the [High Resolution] preset, and then turn on Convert All Text to Outlines. Leave everything else as set.

7. Go to File > Save A Copy. In the dialog choose Illustrator EPS (*.EPS) from the Save as Type drop-down. Give it a name like **Logo.eps**.

8. In the EPS Options dialog our goal is to maximize compatibility, so set the Version to be Illustrator 8 EPS. There's no reason to go all the way down to Illustrator 3 EPS; you'll lose a lot in terms of coloring and design. You are working with Illustrator version 12 right now. If your client's vendor cannot handle the 1998 technology of version 8 files, they need to upgrade.

9. Set the Preview to TIFF (8-bit Color) and Transparent.

10. Turn off Embed Fonts and leave the rest of the options as they are. Click OK, say Yes to the redundant warning, and we're done.

STEP 2 ▼
Saving as a TIFF File

In situations where EPS files are not feasible, TIFF (or TIF) is the next most ubiquitous format. Because TIFFs are resolution-dependent raster images, when you deliver to the client, recommend that his first choice be EPS, and recommend TIFF only when an EPS will not do.

1. First, undo the Flatten Transparency step, which will be at the top of the Edit menu. Illustrator flattens everything to raster as it saves to TIFF, and flattening twice can degrade quality.

2. Choose File > Export, and the Save as Type should be TIFF (*.TIF). Give it the **Logo.tif** filename.

3. In the TIFF Options dialog, Color Model should already be CMYK, but set the Resolution to High, and turn on Anti-Alias and LZW Compression. Because we have no idea how the client might use the file, Byte Order should be IBM PC for maximum compatibility on both Windows and Mac machines (some lower-grade applications like Microsoft Publisher have had issues reading TIFFs with Macintosh byte ordering). Check the Embed ICC Profile; applications that don't understand color management will simply ignore it.

STEP 3 ▼
Saving for the Web

Odds are, someone is going to want to use the logo for a website. If possible, find out the actual size of the logo needed. When you save it for the web, you will fix both the resolution and dimensions; if the logo is sized up or down after that, it's going to look poor (and that will reflect on you).

1. Go to File > Revert to take the document back to before we did anything with the EPS. That should back the document out to RGB color mode (as indicated by the title bar).

2. Size the logo as needed via the Transform palette, and then reset your crop area by going to Object > Crop Area > Release, which will give you back the box you made. Size and position it, and then make it a crop area again.

3. Now, choose File > Save for Web (I love how logical Adobe has made all this).

4. In the Save for Web dialog box, you have many options that are too intricate and subjective to go through fully here. So, here are the highlights:

   Along the top are four tabs, Original, Optimized, 2-Up, and 4-Up. Original is your original image; Optimized is what the image would look like with the current Save for Web settings; 2-Up is a side-by-side comparison of both; and 4-Up is your original plus three different optimization settings.

   Up on the right is where all the brainpower gets consumed. You have presets (of course) that determine the settings below the Preset drop-down, though you can manually edit the settings boxes as well. The file format drop-down is where you pick the, uh, file format (I need a better thesaurus). Subsequent options vary with the file format chosen. In Chapter 11, "Designing a Website," we go through the Save for Web dialog in more depth. For now, work with the settings here and watch how they affect the image displayed on the Optimized tab.

5. The settings you use here depend entirely upon the client's needs for the logo—where it will be used, the dimensions desired, file size limitations, and so on. Every situation is different, so I'm afraid I can't tell you the options to check here. Use your best judgment.

STEP 4 ▼
Saving for Use in Microsoft Office

Microsoft Word is the world's leading word processor on both Windows and Macintosh. Word, Excel, and PowerPoint are as much standards of the business world as Photoshop, Illustrator, and Acrobat are of the creative world. Businesses need to get their logos and other graphics into Office applications—especially PowerPoint—but, in Microsoft's infinite wisdom, Office applications have never handled EPS files well (seriously yucky EPS display), and they flat out don't do Illustrator .AI files. Recognizing that businesses employ designers' work in Office, Adobe sagely built into Illustrator a means of exporting artwork in a special PNG format flavored just for Office—it's like digital bonbons; Office can't get enough.

1. If you skipped Step 3, "Saving for the Web," turn back to that and do the first two steps before proceeding.

2. Done? Good. Choose File > Save for Microsoft Office. Click Save. No options. As Peggy Bundy would tell you: You can't improve on bonbons.

STEP 5 ▼
Converting Your Four-Color Logo to Grayscale

To make your client ready for any situation—or, if you prefer, to make sure your work looks good under all circumstances—it would behoove you to create grayscale and black-and-white versions of the logo and provide those in EPS and TIFF formats. Why? Well, look at it this way: Logos are often used in grayscale and one-color environments like newspapers, Yellow Pages, fax cover sheets, screen-printed apparel and products, and even used for non-ink procedures like embossing onto books, binders, cases, and other paper, plastic, and metal products.

If you don't do the work now, someone else might down the road. How much do you trust the client to get a professional to do the conversion—which will involve color changes and possibly even removal of certain design elements? How much do you trust the average production artist at the local newspaper or packaging plant?

1. Save As `Logo - Grayscale.ai`.

2. Unlock all layers and Select All.

3. From the Filters menu choose Colors > Convert to Grayscale. As the warning reveals, gradients (which we have) and patterns (which we don't) won't be converted. The rest of the colors, the solid areas like the star and speedometer, should desaturate to their grayscale equivalents.

4. One at a time, select the remaining colored objects and convert their gradients to percentages of black. For the main green-to-black gradient in the letterforms, for example, you might try 25% black to 100% black.

STEP 6 ▼
Converting Your Grayscale Logo to Black and White

And now the straight 1-bit black and white...

1. Remove the stars, needle sweep, needle shadow, and afterimages; fill the speedometer numbers and needle with white; change the tick marks' strokes to white and thicken them another point or so for added contrast at small sizes; outline the needle's base circle with white; delete the inner set of R and V jitters, and; finally, fill the letterforms themselves with black while giving them a **2-pt** white outline as clear separation from the jitters.

2. Remember to save the black-and-white version as a separate Illustrator .AI file that you retain.

3. Export both the grayscale and black-and-white versions to new EPS and TIFF format (if not also Microsoft Office-flavored PNGs) deliverables for the client.

   See Figure 2.25 for the final REV logos.

Final Thoughts

Whether you sketch, draw, or trace your logo depends on how and what you begin with. You have the skills to start from any point and end at whatever destination your imagination conjures.

One common method of logo redrawing that we didn't cover in this chapter is how to re-create a logo by identifying typefaces. Well, you're in luck. I slipped it in as Appendix C, "How To—Identify and Recreate Logo Type." In that quick project we'll learn how to use Internet- and Illustrator-based tools to identify fonts used in a rasterized logo. Then we'll set and modify the shape of type to redraw the logo.

Why didn't we use Live Trace, you may ask. Live Trace is a wonderful addition to Illustrator with CS2, but it's all but useless with rough scans like our pencil sketch. Its real strength is in vectorizing photographic quality images or at least rasterized drawings with clean lines. Check out Chapter 5, "Illustrating an (Almost) Photo-realistic Poster," to see what Live Trace can *really* do.

FIGURE 2.25 Final REV logos in full-color (trust me) and black and white.

Where will the client use her new logo? Anywhere. Everywhere. Thanks to you. It's all about careful attention to detail—choosing colors that translate without additional cost into any typical use, making text readable and legible when the logo is used at small sizes, and using vector to ensure that elements always print with the highest quality even when used at large sizes. Logos show up everywhere, on all sorts of things, in all sorts of places. Rarely do designers know ahead of time every ultimate use for a logo.

With the color, grayscale, and black-and-white EPS, TIFF, web, and Microsoft Office PNG files, your client will be prepared for any situation, ready to use your professional-quality logo anywhere, any time, any way.

CHAPTER 3: Adding Logos and Artwork to Non-Flat Objects

About the Projects

Adding logos to objects such as mugs, jars, and banners for mockup is a common task. In fact, it's the only reason some users own Illustrator. In this project we will use Illustrator's Envelope Distort and mesh tools to brand common promotional items, including a travel mug, angled snack jar, and a lanyard, whose shape and slogan we will wave, twist, and shade into near photo-realism.

Prerequisites

It would be helpful if you had a basic understanding of raster and vector image formats, selecting and moving objects and anchor points with the Selection and Direct Selection tools, drawing basic shapes with the Pen and Rectangle tools, and setting and changing fills, strokes, type, and type-styling options.

@work resources

Please visit the publisher's website to access the following Chapter 3 project files:

- ▶ Chap03 (Decal-Cup.ai, Decal-Jar.ai, and Lanyard.ai)
- ▶ Chap03\Assets (Logo.ai, Logo - B&W.ai, Jar of Treats.psd, and Steel Mug.psd)
- ▶ Chap03\Extras (Project-How to Draw the Clasp.pdf)
- ▶ Chap03\Finished Project

Planning the Projects

Is Illustrator CS2 the right tool for the job? Photoshop CS2 includes perspective painting and cloning tools as well as the Liquefy command (the last since version CS). If your goal is to simply distort artwork, and keeping it at a fixed resolution is not an obstacle for your project, Photoshop might be the better tool for the task. If, however, you need nondestructive distortion with a high degree of control—or the ability to adjust the distortion later—Illustrator is your best bet. Illustrator is also the right tool for the job of decaling logos or other artwork to photographs (or drawings) of non-flat objects like a coffee mug.

Prepare the Artwork

Do you have the logo or other artwork ready for application onto an object? If it's an Illustrator drawing you want to apply to a non-flat object, complete the drawing first and save it as its own file. If you have a photograph to map, is it prepared in Photoshop? If the image is not rectangular, make sure it has either a transparent background or a clipping path. This *can* be accomplished in Illustrator CS2, but it's easier to set transparency or clipping on raster images in Photoshop ahead of time.

 TIP

In Photoshop (versions 7–CS2), often the fastest way to save an image with a transparent background or a clipping path is by using the Export Transparent Image wizard. Open the image and then, from the unlikely location of Photoshop's Help menu, choose Export Transparent Image, and follow the wizard's prompts.

Prepare your logo or artwork (we'll call it the decal from here on out) *flat*—don't distort it or create any dimensionality in the original image. We'll do all that in this chapter's projects, with much more flexibility and forgiveness of mistakes than you could get from distorting an original image.

The next obvious question is: Do you have the photograph or drawing of the non-flat object itself—the target surface—ready? Do you have the image? Have you done all the correction and touch-up needed? Is the image in the color space and resolution required for its ultimate use?

If you are working with the Chapter 3 resource files, you're all set.

Promotional Items

When you're planning promotional items (swag or tchotchkes in the parlance of those who live for freebies) like t-shirts, jars of goodies, mugs and cups, stress balls, or lanyards, do your market research. The primary purpose of emblazoning logos, slogans, or other information onto promo items is to keep the brand in front of the recipient as long and as often as possible. The secondary purpose is the important goal of causing the recipient to act as a walking billboard, spreading brand awareness wherever she might take a tchotchke. The only way to meet either goal—and, of course, ideally both—is to provide branded items the recipient will actually *use*.

Look closely at the product's or brand's target market. What are the needs of this market that could be filled inexpensively with promotional items? What types of items does the market typically buy or use that don't necessarily answer a need? Make a list of the market's needs and a separate list of its wants (toys and edibles are often excellent choices). Then list ways to answer those needs and supply those wants.

 TIP

Though promotional items sometimes carry direct sales potential (a coupon, for example), they are rarely about calls to action or sales. Primarily their purpose is branding—getting the name out there.

First, remove from the list any items that may reflect negatively on the brand; unless the brand is directly related to alcohol, tobacco, or medicine/pharmaceuticals, avoid these categories of tchotchkes like the plague. Although private label wines or decaled lighters are useful to many people, vocal minority segments of any broad market will infer negative associations between the brand and the promo item—an ardent nonsmoker, for instance, will typically see the lighter as endorsing cigarette smoking rather than considering how useful it would be for lighting candles or campfires.

Whittle the "safe list" down based on the feasibility and costs of production. Present the top 3–10 items (depending on the budget and campaign size) to the client as mockups, like those we will create in this chapter.

Promote Responsibly

Be wary of political and social convictions and of common health issues. If your promotional items are cosmetic or hygiene products, verify that the manufacturer does not test on animals—and advertise that on the ingredients label. Animal-based foodstuffs like meat and cheese—and the brand that hands them out—will not be auspiciously received by vegetarians and vegans.

A large percentage of the population is allergic to compounds found in products containing dairy, shellfish, peanuts, or peanut oil. For many, an allergic reaction to one of these substances could be fatal—in particular peanut oil, which is an ingredient in a surprising number of unlikely products. Scrutinize the ingredients list meticulously. (Although it is generally true that no publicity is bad publicity, killing one's customers proves an exception to that rule—most of the time.)

Project:
Logo Decaled onto a Rotated and Angled Jar

We'll apply a logo as a transparent decal to a rotated and angled jar in four easy steps:

1. Placing and locking the surface image
2. Defining the target surface area
3. Applying the distorted decal
4. Making the decal transparent

Mapping a Vector Logo to a Rotated and Angled Jar

REV has decided to debut its energy drink at a big graphic design conference this year. In addition to complimentary bottles of its drink, the company would also like to give away branded promotional items. Because pens, mouse pads, and private label hot sauce have become cliché, REV asked us to come up with some alternate ideas for tchotchke. After examining REV's target market (20-, 30- and 40-something professional creatives), making our lists, and consulting with several manufacturers of branded promotional items, we've come up with a few ideas to present to REV, which we want to do in context.

> **TIP**
>
> Where can you find promotional items to brand and vendors to do the job? With a search engine, of course! Search for "promotional gifts" (with the quotes).

The first item is a jar of snacks. Working from a photo the manufacturer provided, we'll add the full-color REV logo to the jar so that the client can see what the finished silk-screened or label-affixed item might look like.

STEP 1 ▼
Placing and Locking the Surface Image

First, let's get the jar in place.

1. Begin a new document 11×8.5 inches in RGB color mode. Title it **Decal-Jar**.

2. Choose File > Place and select the Jar of Treats.psd file; make sure Link is checked.

3. When you have the jar positioned to roughly the center of the artboard, lock its position with (Cmd-2) [Ctrl+2].

STEP 2 ▼
Defining the Target Surface Area

Notice how the jar is both rotated and angled? It's a good photo for getting a sense of the size and depth of the jar, but it means we can't use a straight-on decal. Not to worry, though; it's just a simple matter of moving the decal into the third dimension.

1. Look closely at the jar and try to identify the four corners of the flat surface on the dominant face. Starting with one corner, use the Pen tool to draw a shape that defines the target face (see Figure 3.1).

FIGURE 3.1   The target surface shape, representing the area into which the logo must be decaled.

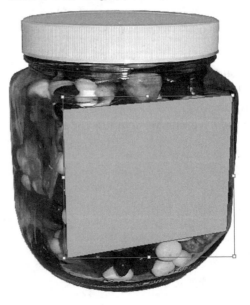

2. Fill the shape with a solid, contrasting color to assist in drawing. The colors you use are irrelevant to the final work; this shape will disappear momentarily.

3. Use the Direct Selection tool to refine the position of the corner points if needed.

STEP 3 ▼
Applying the Distorted Decal

Now to apply the logo as the decal.

1. After deselecting the shape we created in step 2 (just click away from it with the Selection tool, place the REV logo from the `Logo.ai` file.

2. Position the logo roughly centered on the target surface shape. The logo should be larger than the target surface shape.

3. Open the Links palette (Window > Links), and look for the `Logo.ai` entry. Select the entry, and, from the Links palette's flyout menu, choose Embed Image.

4. Now send the REV logo behind the target surface shape but still in front of the jar photo. The easiest way to accomplish this is by selecting the logo with the Selection tool and either choosing Object > Arrange > Send Backward or simply using the Cmd-[(Ctrl+[) keyboard shortcut.

5. With the Selection tool still active, Shift-click on the target surface shape to select both it and the logo.

6. From the Object menu, select Envelope Distort > Make with Top Object. Your drawing should now look like mine (see Figure 3.2), with the logo distorted and scaled such that it looks as if we've merely photographed a jar with the logo already imprinted on it.

FIGURE 3.2 Envelope distortion matches the decal to the shape and perspective of the target surface.

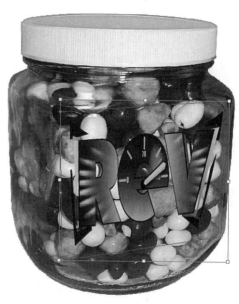

STEP 4 ▼
Making the Decal Transparent

If we wanted an opaque label such as what we'd get from silk-screening directly onto the jar, we'd stop there. For this particular tchotchke, however, I think we want a transparent vinyl decal.

1. Open the Transparency palette from Window > Transparency. The logo envelope should still be selected.

2. From the Blending Mode drop-down (it probably says Normal), choose Hard Light. Voilà! Instant translucent decal (see Figure 3.3).

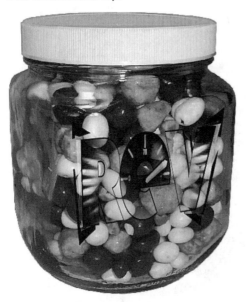

Project: Logo Decaled onto a Cylindrical Mug

We'll apply a logo as a transparent decal to a rotated and angled jar in three easy steps:

1. Building a shaped grid
2. Applying the cylindrical decal
3. Blending the decal into the object's lighting

Mapping a Vector Logo to a Cylindrical Mug

Coffee fiends (like yours truly) and tea drinkers far outweigh fans of any other beverage, so coffee mugs are a safe bet for promotional items. Even more universal, though, is a travel mug, which can be used for hot and cold beverages. Of course, you can also employ the following technique to apply any artwork to thermoses, paper cups, glasses, balls, bald heads, and any other

rounded surface. (I recently used it to apply a tattoo onto a bare arm for an article I wrote on tattoos and copyright.)

STEP 1 ▼
Building a Shaped Grid

With a ballpoint pen, plastic spork, and six inches of twine—no, wait, that was McGyver. And it was a hydro-electric generator, not a shaped grid.

You *could* use the same technique for decaling cylindrical objects as we did on the jar. The only drawback to the jar method is that the decal will fill the area of the target surface shape—it's a full-surface application. What if you only want your decal to cover a portion of the surface? Right, you make a smaller target shape. But creating an accurate target shape by eye on a cylindrical or round object is easier said than done. Fortunately, we can build a shaped grid to make it a much simpler process.

1. Start a new 11×8.5-inch RGB document and name it **Decal-Cup**.

2. Place the Steel Mug.psd image and lock its layer. Create a new layer called **Shape Grid**.

3. With the Pen tool, draw a curve along the top edge of the steel body, where it meets the plastic top. Your curve doesn't have to be precise, but will work better if it contains three points (one on either end, then one in the middle). Ensure that the curve runs edge-to-edge (see Figure 3.4).

4. Draw another curve along the mid-body curve, where the cup begins to narrow. Again, go edge-to-edge and use at least three points in the curve. Somewhere between these two curves is

where we'll place the logo. While you work, think about where in that area it should appear.

FIGURE 3.4 **My curves, lining the top and bottom of the possible target surface.**

5.   Grab the Blend tool and click once on the left point of the upper curve, then on the left point of the lower curve. A number of lines should appear between them. Note how the curvature of the lines blends between the two original curves? This is *a blend*.

6.   With the blend still selected, select Object > Blend > Blend Options. Set the Spacing to Specified Steps and enter whatever number of blend steps is necessary to align steps to the top and bottom of the area you've chosen for the placement of the logo.

7.   Lock the blend like any other object—(Cmd-2) [Ctrl+2], remember?.

8.   Again using the Pen tool, draw vertical lines that appear to (but don't actually)

connect the top and bottom of the first blend on either side. Follow the contour of the cup. Blend these two lines together, adjusting the blend options as needed (see Figure 3.5). Lock the **Shape Grid** layer.

FIGURE 3.5 **With the grid in place, we can now easily identify where we should apply the label.**

STEP 2 ▼
Applying the Cylindrical Decal

The shaped grid lines will act as guides, enabling us to define an accurate target surface shape.

1.   On a new layer, draw a target surface shape to define the size and position of your logo, using the grid to define the shape. Use at least three points in your curves for best results. When the target surface shape is finished, hide the **Shape Grid** layer.

2.   Place the Logo - B&W.ai artwork.

3. Send it behind the target surface shape, then create an envelope distort via Object > Envelope Distort > Make with Top Object (see Figure 3.6). If the envelope needs to be edited, use the Direct Selection tool. However, if you need to modify the logo itself, select Object > Envelope Distort > Edit Contents, at which point the original logo paths become accessible.

FIGURE 3.6 The logo is now in place, matching the contour of the travel mug.

STEP 3 ▼
Blending the Decal into the Object's Lighting

Although the logo decal has the correct *shape*, it's still just floating above the travel mug. The white bits in particular look out of place. To accomplish the illusion of being part of the mug, the logo needs to be just black and, more importantly, adopt the lighting and shadow of the original photograph. Do we need to go back to the Logo - B&W.ai file for this or even undo the envelope? No, sirree.

1. With the logo still selected, open the Transparency palette from the Window menu.

2. Set the blending mode to Multiply. Instantly the white disappears.

3. Now for the seemingly impossible task of sharing all those streaks of light with the black logo. Set the Opacity to something less than 100%—whatever looks good to you. I used 65% (see Figure 3.7). Let your light shine through.

FIGURE 3.7 The finished travel mug. The blending mode and opacity settings allow the highlights to shine through, creating realism.

Project: (Almost) Photo-Realistic Waving Lanyard

We'll create and map textual artwork onto a near photo-realistic waving lanyard in six easy steps:

1. Drawing the basic shape and importing swatches
2. Scribbling the basic shape
3. Distorting with a mesh
4. Releasing, reusing, and editing meshes
5. Painting with a gradient mesh
6. Finishing the lanyard

Drawing a Near Photo-Realistic Lanyard and Mapping Text to It in 3D

Envelope distortions created with two-dimensional target shapes are actually very simple in their depth, shape, and the amount of perceived distortion they create. When you need absolute command over any aspect of depth, shape, distortion, or color transitions, turn to meshes.

Because REV Creativity Drink will debut at a trade convention, and convention-goers are typically issued badges for entry into the show floor, panel discussions, parties, and various other functions, a lanyard would make a good promo item. After the convention, a fair number of attendees will continue to use it to hold their office security badges around their necks—thus spreading the REV name far and wide like walking, talking, iPod-jamming billboards.

Consider a lanyard printed with repetitions of the tagline and website address. How would you draw it in Illustrator? Just a long rectangle with type set atop it?

Well, you *could* do that, I suppose. But a drawing like that certainly won't give the client the sense of seeing the physical item. Let's go the extra mile for our client and give them something they can almost reach out and touch. It will pay off with the satisfaction of hearing the client's fingernails click on the monitor.

STEP 1 ▼
Drawing the Basic Shape and Importing Swatches

1. Begin a new 11×8.5-inch document in RGB. Name it **Lanyard**.

2. From the flyout menu on the Swatches palette, select Open Swatch Library > Other Library. When the dialog comes up, navigate to, and open, the `Logo.ai` file. A new palette entitled Logo will appear; in it will be the REV corporate color swatches (see Figure 3.8).

 TIP

To make swatches available to all CS2 applications independent of documents, choose Save Swatches for Exchange from the Swatches palette's flyout menu. Then load the ASE Swatch Exchange File into the applications' Swatches palettes from their flyout menus.

FIGURE 3.8 The imported swatches palette (in List View).

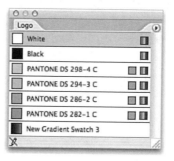

3. Draw a long, narrow rectangle approximately 10.5 inches wide by 0.375 inches tall. Fill it with DS 282-1 C. Give it a stroke of none.

4. Set your type over the box, in approximately the same shape and size. Enter REV's tagline and website address separated by bullets: **REV Up Your Creativity**™ ▶ **www.RevDrink.com**. Style and color them however you like—I used Myriad Pro Bold Condensed, 18 pt, with the tagline in white, the URL in black, and the bullet in DS 294-3 C.

5. Copy the text, and paste it repeatedly until it completely fills the text box.

STEP 2 ▼
Scribbling the Basic Shape

Because lanyards are typically knitted thread, let's simulate a knitted texture.

1. Select the green box (lock the text if needed).

2. On the Appearance palette (Window > Appearance), click the flyout menu and choose New Fill. Make this DS 282-1 C as well. You should now see two identical fill attribute entries in the

Appearance palette—only the upper one will be visible on the artboard, however.

3. With the upper fill attribute selected in the Appearance palette, go to Effect > Stylize > Scribble. Make a nice tight scribble. My settings are: Angle: **90°**; Path Overlap and Variation: **0**; Stroke Width: **0.03 in.**; Curviness: **10%**, and Spacing: **0.04 in**—the last two settings both got variations of **0**.

You should see bumpy upper and lower edges on your box, but no gaps between the Scribble strokes.

4. For texture, let's add a third fill via the Appearance palette, this time DS 286-2 C.

5. Let's scribble this new fill with the following settings: Angle: **90°**; Path Overlap and Variation: **0**; Stroke Width: **0.02 in.**; Curviness: **10%**, and Spacing: **0.07 in**. Once again, all variations are set to **0**.

Does your rectangle look more like woven fabric now (see Figure 3.9)? Feel free to play with the Scribble options. When you're satisfied, group the rectangle with the text—(Cmd-G) [Ctrl+G].

6. Duplicate the layer, and hide the duplicate.

FIGURE 3.9 **Though it has tremendous potential for abuse, Scribble also has practical applications—such as creating a knitted texture.**

CHAPTER 3: Adding Logos and Artwork to Non-Flat Objects

STEP 3 ▼
Distorting with a Mesh

This is where the fun *really* begins. A mesh under your control can actualize any kind of twisting, crunching, squishing, stretching, turning, and distorting you can imagine. So bring your twisted vision and let's do the Monster Mesh.

1. With the group selected, go to Object > Envelope Distort > Make with Mesh.

2. The Envelope Mesh dialog defines how the mesh is initially broken up. For such a long and narrow shape, let's try one row and ten columns. When you click OK, your artwork will display a grid with points at all intersections. You are no longer working directly with the group of text and scribbled box; now you're working with the distortion mesh.

   The points of a mesh behave like anchor points in a path. Solid points are selected, hollow unselected. Mesh points also have curve handles that affect the curvature of *mesh patches* on either side of the point—just like path anchor points.

◎ TIP

Drag multiple mesh points to distort multiple patches and larger segments of the drawing. Drag the points defining one plane of a mesh patch toward other points to squish the patch's content; drag them away to stretch. Shift-drag a mesh point to constrain its motion to the mesh line, either horizontally or vertically.

3. Using the Direct Selection tool, move the mesh points around and distort your box until it resembles one length of a loosely arranged lanyard, with bends and curves and maybe even folds (see Figure 3.10). Adjust the distance between the mesh points at the top and bottom to create depth, such as a bend pushing the lanyard toward or away from the viewer.

◎ TIP

Because lanyards are fabric, they rarely form sharp angles. Keep your distortions graceful by adjusting curve handles.

4. When you're happy with the first side of the lanyard, show the second layer and do it again to create the other length of the lanyard. A lanyard is a continuous length of fabric, so remember to match up the ends of the two pieces (see Figure 3.11).

FIGURE 3.10 My lanyard, with the mesh showing.

STEP 4 ▼
Releasing, Reusing, and Editing Meshes

So you've done all of this neat twisting and distorting with your mesh. What if you want to make a second object with the same distortion effects (which we do)? Must you try to re-create each and every push and pull? Nope.

1. Duplicate one of your current layers (either the front or back strips of the lanyard), locking the original and the other original.

2. With the Selection tool, click on your new object, copy, and choose Object > Envelope Distort > Release. You should have your original, uninteresting scribbled box and text group, as well as the mesh, now a distinctly separate object.

3. To mirror the distortion of the lanyard ribbon with another object, you would select the target object and the now

independent mesh, and use the Object > Envelope Distort > Make with Top Object method we learned with the jar and travel mug—which we are not going to do now.

4. Instead, delete the undistorted scribble group, leaving the mesh itself.

5. Zoom in on the left edge of the mesh and grab the Mesh tool. Until your mouse is over the mesh (or an object that can be converted to a mesh) it will display a no-mesh cursor. Position the cursor roughly at the midpoint of the left edge of the mesh, however, and you will see the Add Mesh Point tool. Click here. Notice that you have now split the entire length of the mesh into two rows where previously it was one.

   If you clicked on a different area of a vertical mesh patch border. you would add additional rows; click on a horizontal border to add columns, and click somewhere inside a mesh patch to add both a column *and* row simultaneously.

6. The more mesh patches (columns and rows) you create, the greater your command over distortion or (as you will see in the next step) color. The drawback, of course, is that you have more mesh patches and mesh points to wrangle when you want to make large changes— so don't go nuts with the Mesh tool.

STEP 5 ▼
Painting with a Gradient Mesh

Having fun? Well, try to contain yourself—it gets better. *Way* better.

The lanyard is distorted beautifully now (I have faith in you). But it still doesn't look real, does it? What's missing? C'mon. You know what it is. Take your time; I need to go to the little boys' room anyway.

Okay. I'm back. Did you figure out what's missing? Right! It's missing highlights and shadows to give it depth.

1. If you did go nuts with the mesh tool, undo with (Cmd-Z) [Ctrl+Z] until you get back to two rows and ten columns. We'll probably add more as we go along, but for now, let's keep things simple.

2. Position your mesh object directly over the distorted lanyard it matches. Be sure it lines up on all points (adjust mesh points if necessary). Open and arrange the Color, Swatches, Transparency, Layers, and Toolbox palettes on screen together. We won't need any others for this section.

 TIP

If this palette arrangement is one you will use again, for example if you find yourself painting meshes frequently, create a workspace for it by choosing Window > Workspace > Save Workspace.

3. Duplicate the current layer; then hide the duplicate.

4. Select the mesh with the Selection tool, and, on the Transparency palette, set the blending mode to Luminosity— which should make the distorted lanyard beneath visible.

5. Now look at your distorted lanyard. Make two decisions: First, where is the light source in relation to your lanyard? And, with that in mind, where should the lanyard be shaded? Got that?

6. Drag the black swatch from the Swatches palette and drop it into any mesh patch to be shaded. It's okay to gasp. Do it with another mesh patch— try an area that should be highlighted.

7. Now click on a point that touches one of the mesh patches you just filled. With the point selected, choose a contrasting color swatch on the Swatches palette (or mix a color on the Colors palette). See how smoothly they blend? This is called a *gradient mesh*. Each colored path or point will blend smoothly in all directions into the next colored path or point.

8. Set all your highlight and shadow areas by either method. Use different shades of gray for more realism than simple black and white. Add or remove mesh points as needed. And don't forget to leave some points and patches unshaded; we want the REV colors to show through.

Adjust the opacity of the entire mesh object with the Transparency palette if needed—I used Luminosity at 40%. In the end, your "light mesh" should look similar to mine (see Figure 3.12).

FIGURE 3.12 With a gradient mesh, colors flow smoothly in whatever direction needed—in this case, creating smooth lighting and shadow transitions.

STEP 6 ▼
Finishing the Lanyard

By now, half your lanyard should be looking close to real. There's just one more mesh to create before repeating the light and shadow work on the other half.

1. Lock your light and shadow layer but keep it visible.

2. Turn on the duplicate you made earlier in the project, and move that layer *beneath* the actual lanyard in the Layers palette. This will be our cast shadow layer—feel free to rename the layer to **Cast Shadow**.

3. Its shape should loosely follow but not mirror the shape of the lanyard—that would be unrealistic. So distort *and* color it (with shades of gray) to create credible shadows cast by turns, twists, and puckers of the lanyard relative to the light source direction you chose.

4. Set the blending mode for this mesh to Multiply—so only darker colors will appear, thus making the shadows believable atop any color, object, or image. Keep the opacity at 100% to enable deep shadow.

5. Either after distortion and color or during, soften the edges of your cast shadow with Gaussian Blur (Effect > Blur > Gaussian Blur). I used **7.4 px** as my Gaussian blur setting, but select what looks best to you, with your object. The lower the Gaussian Blur setting, the sharper your shadows, which implies that the object is closer to its shadow as well as fewer and closer light sources.

6. When this half of the lanyard is exactly the way you want it, give the other half highlights and shading and a cast shadow as well (see Figure 3.13).

 TIP

When shading with black (or gray), set the Color palette to display a Grayscale slider from the Color palette flyout menu for faster access to all shades.

FIGURE 3.13 My finished lanyard, with highlights and shading and a cast shadow provided by gradient meshes, and all parts distorted with distortion meshes.

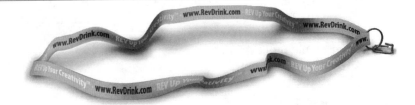

Final Thoughts

From a distance (or zoomed out), the lanyard should look very close to photo-realistic. Enlarged, however, the illusion of a photograph might not hold up. We built a quick sketch to present an idea; if your illustration is destined for high-resolution work or print, spend a little more time on the shading. I would also strongly recommend working more with the scribbled pattern, varying its colors and texture to look more realistic—perhaps through multiple meshes with their own blending modes. Giving your lanyard volume by thickening the edges shown to the viewer by folds or rotations would also go a *long* way toward creating realism. That too can be accomplished easily by layering multiple mesh objects with slight fluctuations in their shapes.

Now that you know how to do the Monster Mesh, look back on your jar and mug projects. Could a mesh have helped you with those? What about some of your recent Photoshop projects—could they have been created with Illustrator's meshes, with the freedom of live effects, easy changes, and the resolution independence of vectors?

Curious how I created the ring and clasp at the end of the lanyard (see Figure 3.14)? Check out the `Project-How to Draw the Clasp.pdf` in the **Extras** folder in this chapter's resource files!

FIGURE 3.14 Don't forget the details! What good is a lanyard without a clip?

CHAPTER 4: Designing Corporate Identity Material

About the Projects

In this chapter we will create essential corporate identity material, including business cards, letterhead, and an exploded envelope. In fact, we will build business cards for multiple employees in a single file. The files will then be prepared for delivery to a print provider as press-ready PDFs.

Prerequisites

It would be helpful if you had an understanding of spot and CMYK process colors. You should have a basic operational knowledge of, and access to, Acrobat Standard or Professional 6 or 7, or at least Adobe Reader 6 or 7 (see Appendix B, "Resources," for the URL of the latest version of the free Adobe Reader).

@work resources

Please visit the publisher's website to access the following Chapter 4 project files:

- ▶ Chap04 (Business Cards.ai, Letterhead.ai, Envelope.ai)
- ▶ Chap04\Assets (Logo.pdf, bg_bc.psd, bg_env1.tif, bg_env2.tif, bg_lttrhd.tif)
- ▶ Chap04\Extras (bg_bc-back.pdf, bg_lttrhd Back.tif)
- ▶ Chap04\Finished Project

Planning the Projects

Designing corporate identity material is one of the most common reasons a creative calls upon Illustrator. Regardless of whether you have designed this kind of project a hundred times or this is your first time through, the success of the project depends on planning.

The Logo

Start with a logo. Never begin designing identity material until you have already established the identity. A company's logo is the single most important visual element in a brand identity; business cards and letterhead only serve as vehicles to communicate that brand.

Chapter 2, "Designing a Logo (From Scratch or From a Scan)," will help you draw a new logo. The finished logo from Chapter 2 is included in this chapter's resource files, if you want a head start. If you have your own logo ready in *.EPS*, *.PDF*, or Adobe Illustrator *.AI* format, feel free to use that throughout this project.

Business Cards

Business cards are typically the piece that's the most expressive—and most difficult to—design of any identity package. In a scant 3.5 × 2 inches (7 square inches) you must establish the brand identity, communicate the marketing story, create a memorable impression of both the brand and the person handing over the business card, provide clear contact information, and identify an individual representative of the brand. Laying out all this information to be clear and uncluttered is challenging. It takes planning and careful attention to the details of the design.

Open your wallet for excellent examples of poorly designed business cards. Grab any card you received from someone else and try to remember what the company does. Do you remember the face of the person who handed you the card or what you and she discussed? What are the company's chief products or services? Can you figure out the company's attitude—are they fun and welcoming, serious and reserved, or risk-takers?

Now look at *your own* business card and ask the same questions.

If your business card meets each of the objectives, the answers to these questions should be obvious. Design an effective business card by constantly asking yourself—and your client—these same questions.

Copy Proofs

Making copy (text) changes in identity material takes time, but clients who don't understand the design and production processes rarely realize the amount of work involved. To them, a task like adding the "WWW" to the company's URL on a dozen business card designs, letterhead, two sizes of envelope, fax cover sheet, and Rolodex cards is just a matter of quickly typing three letters. To the creative, such changes often entail adjustments of type alignment, positioning, and size—all of which might necessitate alterations to other elements.

Without adequate preplanning, many designers get stuck making the changes for free. And, when something is free, it's easy to ask for more: "Take the 'WWW' out again, I liked it better without." "Can we try a different font, just to see what it looks like?" "Didn't so-and-so tell you? I wanted all 12 departments listed on the Rolodex card, not just the main number and address." It can go on indefinitely, monopolizing your time, taking billable hours away from other clients.

Before you put Pen tool to artboard, place the responsibility for copy accuracy and completeness on the client. Get a *copy proof.*

Send your client a fax (or a dated PDF) containing all (and *only*) the text that will appear anywhere in the material you are to design. Include the company name, tag line, any personnel names that will be used in your work, phone and fax numbers, email addresses, URLs, mailing address(es), and so on. Have the client make any changes directly on the copy proof, and then sign and return it to you. In your contract it should also be stipulated that changes made subsequent to client proof approvals may incur additional charges at your normal hourly rate above the estimated (or quoted) amount.

With a signed copy proof and a clause communicating your right to charge for changes requested after proof approvals, you are free to fix the client's typo in her fax number at no charge. But you also have the choice and right to charge for the hour it takes to add the "WWW" across all the pieces.

Even if your contract doesn't contain such a clause, have the client sign a copy proof. It will make the client look more critically at the copy, and it will indemnify you against being saddled with the printing costs if the client's typo makes it all the way through to press—the odds against that happening are not as long you think. It happens.

Project: Business Cards

We'll create business cards for several employees in four easy steps:

1. **Getting started and setting the bleed area**
2. **Setting the crop area**
3. **Placing the design's common elements**
4. **Using layers to create multiple layouts in one**

Designing Business Cards for Multiple Employees

Most creatives will build cards for five employees by designing the basic layout first, using one employee, and then making four copies of the file to hold the revised name, phone number, email address, and other non-recurring information. Although that workflow works, it is a lot more complicated than it needs to be with current technologies. What happens when the client wants to make changes? You wind up making the same changes five times, that's what.

Making the same change in five different versions of the project not only increases the odds of a mistake sneaking through to press five times over; it is repetitive, and it wastes your time. As you will learn throughout this book, there are three things I hate (other than ketchup on my eggs): wasting time, unnecessary repetition, and using *Comic Sans* in anything but a comic book or greeting card. Although I can't do anything about the crimes against *typography* that have been perpetrated in the name of Comic Sans (other people are trying to right this terrible injustice with the Ban Comic Sans grassroots campaign: http://www.bancomicsans.com), I *can* help you dramatically reduce wasted time and repetition in working with closely related designs.

In this project we are going to plan for changes in our designs (because there will *always* be changes) and build a workflow that will reduce the time and work involved in making them.

STEP 1 ▼
Getting Started and Setting the Bleed Area

Before getting to the fun stuff, we need to know where we can and cannot place elements.

1. Begin a new document by pressing (Cmd-N) [Ctrl+N] and title it **Business Cards**.

2. Set the document width at **2 in.** by **3.5 in.** in height. Our business cards are going to be formatted vertically for a little extra attention; to create standard wider-than-tall business cards, swap the width and height measurements.

3. Set the measurement Units to inches, *Pica*, or any other system with which you feel comfortable—anything except Pixels because this is a for-print project. Choose *CMYK* Color for the Color Mode, and click OK.

 TIP

Almost every measurement box in Illustrator will take any measurement system, regardless of the units chosen in the New Document dialog or even those displayed in the measurement box; Illustrator will do the conversion for you. For example, if the New Document Units are set to inches, replacing the entire contents of the Width field (including the "in" notation) with 21p will make Illustrator convert from pica to inches, resulting in a width of 3.5 inches.

4. If the rulers are not already showing, choose Show Rulers from the View menu, or press (Cmd-R) [Ctrl+R]. Click inside the top ruler and drag downward to create a horizontal guide. Position it **0.125 in.** *inside* the artboard. It is important to set the guide at exactly the correct position—not an easy thing to do by hand.

 TIP

Keep the Info Palette in view and watch its X and Y coordinates change as you drag guides and other objects to help with precise placement.

5. If you cannot get the guide to the exact placement, don't fret. Drop the guide as close as possible, then go to View > Guides > Lock Guides. Unlike many other items on the View menu and its submenus, Lock Guides will not change to Unlock Guides. Instead, when guides are locked, a checkmark appears next to the menu item; the checkmark is absent when guides are unlocked.

When Lock Guides is turned off, click on the guide you just placed to select it (it should change color), and we will use the Transform palette (or Control palette docked beneath Illustrator's menu bar, if you prefer) to align it precisely (see Figure 4.1).

FIGURE 4.1 Positioning the final guide via the Transform palette.

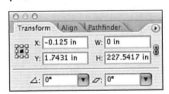

Illustrator starts the vertical ruler, the 0 point, at the *bottom* of the artboard, so our top guide needs its Y coordinate positioned **0.125 in.** below the **3.5 in.** top of the artboard. What is that coordinate, you may ask. I have no idea.

If you are not entirely right-brained, you can do the subtraction in your head, or just grab the pencil and notepad that should be standard equipment on your desk. Or, check out the killer tip that follows for the fastest, tree-saving way of doing basic math in Illustrator.

> ## ◎ TIP
>
> Illustrator's measurement boxes can all do math. Instead of breaking your concentration hunting for a pencil and paper or reaching for the calculator, try this: In any measurement box type the numbers and symbols. Illustrator understands addition (x + y), subtraction (x - y), multiplication (x * y), and division (x / y). And it can work with disparate measurement systems! For example: To position an object precisely 1 pica inside the left edge of an 8.5 × 11 in. page, select the object, and, in the Transform palette's X coordinate measurement box, type 0 in + 1p. Tada! Illustrator does the math and the unit conversion simultaneously, positioning your object at 0.1667 in.

6. Repeat the previous step to place guides **0.125 in.** from the bottom, left, and right edges (drag vertical guides from the vertical ruler on the left).

7. Now repeat this process once more to set guides **0.125 in.** *outside* the artboard area—thus your top guide should be 3.5 + 0.125 in.

When you have all eight guides in place—four inside and four outside the artboard—lock them by toggling Lock Guides on from View > Guides (see Figure 4.2).

FIGURE 4.2 **All guides in place around the artboard.**

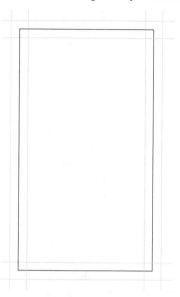

The guides surrounding the outside of your artboard are the four sides of your *bleed* edge. Nothing between the artboard and the bleed area should print in the final trimmed piece, but the design needs to extend out to the bleed edge to prevent ugly ink gaps if the paper shifts on-press. Paper shifts, or *misregistration*, are an unavoidable fact of printing.

> ## ⊘ CAUTION
>
> The size of the bleed area should be checked with your printer or service bureau before beginning the design. A bleed of 1/8 inches (0.125 in.) is the de facto standard in American printing, and should be used when in doubt.

Bleed and Live

In *offset lithography* (also called simply "offset print-ing"), by far the most common type of commercial printing, paper is imprinted and conveyed through the machine by a series of rollers. Inherent in this process is the probability that stacked paper will build up a slight shift throughout the course of a long run. In that case, the colors of ink line up, but the entire image is not in exactly the same place on the page from the top of the paper stack to the bottom. Shift happens.

Because offset lithography uses paper stock that is larger than the final trimmed piece, after printing and drying the paper must be trimmed in stacks of up to 5,000 pieces on a large mechanical guillotine. Full-page displacements, because they are so gradual and slight (typically only a few *points*), are all but undetectable before trimming. In non-bleeding designs, it is rarely noticeable even after trimming. However, when it happens to bleeding designs, where ink prints all the way to one or more edges of the paper, the cutting machine's blade can leave unsightly slivers of unprinted paper on one or two sides of the trimmed stock.

The compensating factor for the inevitability of paper shifts is the 1/8-inch bleed area. When you extend designs outward from the final trim size 1/8th in. (or 0.125 in. decimally) and push all critical design elements and copy 1/8-inch *in* from the trim edge, the guillotine still slices ink if it misses the trim edge. The white slivers are eliminated.

Always thoroughly inspect your print job at the print house before taking possession of it or signing the invoice. If you find pieces in your job where noticeable shifting has occurred (more than a few points), you have the right to ask the printer to reprint the job to provide usable replacements. If the printer refuses, do not take the printed work and do not pay the invoice. Wait a day. Nine times out of ten, the printer will call agreeing to fix the job—if she has not already done so. If the printer does not call, take your job to another shop.

 NOTE

When paper shifts on the printing press, image data from outside the trim on one or two sides prints onto the card, but that also means that image data inside the trim area on the opposing one or two sides is cut off. The inner set of guides is the *live area* of the design; everything important in the design—the logo, text, *everything*—must stay inside the live area to prevent unwanted cropping if the paper shifts on-press.

 TIP

The following table shows the fraction-to-decimal conversions of common measurements:

Fraction/Decimal Equivalent:

1/16 = .0625	1/8 = .1250	1/4 = .2500
1/2 = .5000	5/8 = .6250	3/4 = .7500
7/8 = .8750		

STEP 2 ▼
Setting the Crop Area

Next, we will set the crop area, which works differently in Illustrator than in InDesign or other programs with which you may be familiar.

1. Using the artboard as your guide, grab the Rectangle tool and draw a rectangle that completely covers the artboard, from edge to edge, side to side, and top to bottom. The fill and stroke color and the stroke width, if any, are irrelevant.

2. With the rectangle still selected, check its positioning using the Transform palette; if the reference point is set to the top left, the rectangle should be positioned at exactly **X: 0 in.** and **Y: 3.5 in.** Also in the Transform palette, check that the width and height equal **2 in** and **3.5**, respectively.

3. Keeping the new rectangle selected, go to Object > Crop Area > Make. Your rectangle should disappear, replaced by little lines—*crop marks*—floating around the corners of the artboard (see Figure 4.3).

 TIP

When you print (or Save for Web, in not-for-print projects), your document will crop where the implied lines of the marks meet, tossing out any artwork that appears outside the crop marks. When a commercial printer runs your job on-press, the crop marks themselves, as well as everything out to the bleed edge, will print. After the printing press, the crop marks will guide the guillotine operator when cutting down the paper to the *trim size*.

FIGURE 4.3   **Crop marks.**

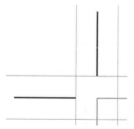

Now would be a good time to save your Business Cards.ai file.

STEP 3 ▼
Placing the Design's Common Elements

Now that the document is prepared for printing and we can see our bleed area, the trim size, and the live area, we know where we can design. So let's get to the fun part and begin designing our client's business cards!

1. Because REV is an energy drink marketed to creative types, the brand is bold and vivacious; the identity material must instantly communicate that.

   Place the bg_bc.tif background image from the Chapter 4 resource files into your layout. Use the Transform palette to set its size to be exactly **2.25 in.** × **3.75 in.**, and the top left corner to be at the coordinates **-0.125 in.** and **3.625 in.**

2. This will be the background of the business card, and we don't want to inadvertently move it around or modify it while we work on objects above it. So, with the background selected, go to Object > Lock > Selection—or simply press (Cmd-2) [Ctrl+2]. Now *nothing* can happen to that image until it is unlocked.

3. Bring in the REV company logo by choosing File > Place, and then navigating to where you saved the finished Logo · Final.ai file from Chapter 2, the Logo.pdf file from the Assets folder of the Chapter 4 resource files, or another Adobe Illustrator, EPS, or PDF logo you may have. Make sure the Link box is checked but Template is unchecked.

4. When the Place PDF box comes up (with .AI and PDF format logos), choose Crop To Art. The navigation buttons at the bottom should be grayed out as they only appear with multi-page PDFs to let you choose which page to place (see Figure 4.4). Click the Place button.

FIGURE 4.4 **The Place PDF dialog box.**

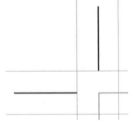

The first thing you should notice is that the logo is pretty darn big. The next thing is that it has an X through it. The X signifies that the drawing is linked rather than embedded—Illustrator treats it like a flat file; you cannot manipulate the constituent elements of the logo. We want it this way. If the logo needs to be modified, do so in the original file, not when in use as part of

a separate layout. That way, any changes made to the original logo affect all uses of the logo—less time, less work, narrower margin for error.

Because the logo came in so large, the first thing we want to do is scale it down to a manageable size. The beauty of vector drawings is that they can be resized up or down infinitely without losing quality.

5. Zoom out by pressing (Cmd--) [Ctrl+-] until the logo's edges are within view.

6. Click on one of the corner control points and, while holding both the Shift and Alt keys (Mac use Shift and Opt), drag the *bounding box* until the logo fits comfortably well inside the artboard. Press (Cmd-0) [Ctrl+0] to fit the artboard in the window once again.

With the Transform palette (Window > Transform) let's now precisely position and size the logo. On the Transform palette is an odd-looking grid of nine boxes connected by lines; one of those boxes is filled black. These are your *reference points*, corresponding to the corners, sides, and center of an object's bounding box. Changing the reference point determines to which part of an object transformations such as scaling, positioning, and rotating will be relative. When centering an object's position, always reference the object's center point, which enables precise positioning without the need to break your concentration to do the math.

7. Where is the horizontal center of a 2-inch card? Right: 1 inch. So, with the logo selected, click the center reference point on the Transform palette, and set the X coordinate to **1 in**. Set the Y coordinate to **2.2 in**. Now the logo is positioned, but it still needs to be sized.

8. ⛓ See the little chain link icon to the right of the width and height fields in the Transform palette? Click the chain to lock the width and height fields in proportion to one another—signified by the line that now runs between them; the width and height fields are now linked—precision resizing to scale is enabled (see Figure 4.5). Set the logo's width to **1.75 in**. Did the height change accordingly? Did you notice that the logo resized from the center point? Despite the scaling, the logo is still aligned to the 1-inch center of the business card. Cool, huh?

FIGURE 4.5   The Transform palette with linked width and height values.

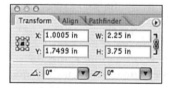

9. Ⓣ Click the Type tool on the Toolbox and, at the top of the live area, starting from the guide that defines the left side of the live area and going all the way across to the right side, click and drag out a rectangle about **0.75 in**. tall. When you let go of the mouse button the cursor will automatically appear inside the type area, ready to type out the address.

Because REV is a fictitious company, type in the following—if it doesn't all fit, type it anyway:

100 Creative Avenue

Anytown, US 98765

10. ▶ From the Toolbox grab the Selection tool, which should keep the text box selected. Now open the Character palette (Window > Type > Character) and choose an interesting—but *very* legible—typeface and type style for the address. Set its size to somewhere between **9** and **11** points.

The *font* you choose will be the signature typeface for all of REV's identity and future marketing materials, so choose wisely. Your choice should be a clean typeface that is easy to read at very small sizes—step back six feet from the computer and squint.

I chose Adobe's Myriad Pro Semibold, which came free with Illustrator.

◎ **TIP**

With Illustrator CS2 Adobe gave you 85 high-quality, OpenType fonts. If you own the full Creative Suite, you have over 140 free fonts. Check the Resources section of this book (Appendix B) for a full listing of the free fonts you own, and where to find them.

11. Keep the text box selected, and set the type color to black by choosing the black block in the color ramp at the bottom of the Colors palette.

12. On the Paragraph palette—this should be (by default) the next tab to the right of the Character palette—click the second button along the top row to align the paragraph to center. Does the address

look lined up? Check the positioning of the text box in the Transform palette and adjust as needed. Is the full address showing in the box, or is it cut off? Drag the bottom of the text box downward until it fits. If the text sits on more than two lines, make sure it is set to no less than **9 pt** and no more than **11 pt**, or choose a different typeface, or adjust the width of the type on the Character palette (you may need to Show Options from the little round palette menu flyout at the top of the palette).

13. Create another text box just above the logo and type the REV tagline: **REV Up Your Creativity™**. The tagline should be in a bolder version of the address typeface and white (I used Adobe Myriad Pro Black).

14. At the bottom of the design, typeset the REV website address—**www.RevDrink.com**—in the same style and using the same method as the tagline. Save your document.

STEP 4 ▼
Using Layers to Create Multiple Layouts In One

That's it for the common elements, the content that will be identical across all employees' business cards. It's now just a simple matter of laying down the employee-specific information.

1. Open the Layers palette (Window > Layers) and lock Layer 1 by clicking the blank area between the visibility eyeball and the layer expansion arrow. The padlock indicates that the common elements are now impervious to accidental repositioning or deletion.

2. At the bottom of the palette, click the Create New Layer button, which will create **Layer 2**. Double-click on Layer 2 to bring up the Layer options dialog, and rename the layer to **Robert Smith**. Click OK.

3. Create a new text box that spans the width of the live area between the logo and REV URL. Now type the following information, each line separated by a return:

   Robert Smith

   President & CEO

   rjsmith@revdrink.com

   503-555-1212 x200

   If everything doesn't fit, increase the height of the box by dragging its bottom edge.

4. Highlight all of the copy by clicking and dragging within the text box, and this time make the text black. Set the leading (next to the point size field) a bit higher than the default—something between **13** or **17 pts** should be good, but it depends on your layout and your font choice. Center the type via the Paragraph palette.

5. Select just the top line, with Robert Smith's name, and style it similar to the tagline and website line, but black instead of white.

Now let's give Bob some breathing room.

6. Switch back to the Paragraph palette with the **President & CEO** line selected. From the flyout menu choose Show Options. At the bottom of the Paragraph palette you should now see two measurement boxes: Space Before and Space After. Using the up and down buttons, increase the space after the paragraph until Bob's title has a comfortable separation from his email address without being disconnected. I went with **7 pts**, but feel free to choose what looks good to you.

Your business card should be pretty close to mine (see Figure 4.6).

7. Now that the boss's business card is done (that will please him if he happens to look over your shoulder), the other four business cards are a breeze. Making sure Bob's layer is highlighted in the palette, go to the Layers palette flyout menu, and choose Duplicate **Robert Smith**. A duplicate layer should appear.

8. Hide the lower **Robert Smith** layer by clicking the eyeball beside the layer name, and then double-click the upper layer and rename it to **Jane Doe**. Click OK.

FIGURE 4.6 My finished business card design.

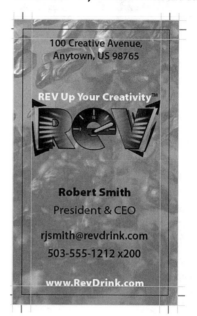

100 Creative Avenue,
Anytown, US 98765

REV Up Your Creativity™

Robert Smith
President & CEO

rjsmith@revdrink.com
503-555-1212 x200

www.RevDrink.com

 TIP

Save money by setting all the employee-specific information in black.

Black is the most opaque of the process inks (though not fully opaque, mind you), and is the last ink applied to *overprint* the three other process colors—cyan, magenta, and yellow. In a job like this, thin areas of black (like the type) will not *knock out* of the other colors; it will simply be printed right on top of continuous background colors. Thus, if you can set the employees' variable information in black only, just one set of cyan, magenta, and yellow film will be needed for all five sets of business cards. At an average cost of $15–$25 per piece of film, that's a direct savings of $180–$300!

Additionally, by eliminating any differences in the cyan, magenta, and yellow ink needed for each set, you will enable the print shop to run the entire five sets at once. Your printer will save the time and overhead expenses inherent in changing out plates and *running up* and *running down* each set for all but the black ink. If you ask nicely, she might pass that additional savings along to you.

9. By selecting each line of text one at a time and typing over it, make Jane's business card her own (be careful not to highlight past the last character in the line):

   Jane Doe

   CFO

   jdoe@revdrink.com

   503-555-1212 x300

10. Now repeat the previous three steps for each of the remaining business cards for Michael Johnson, Mary Jones, and William Black—make up their titles and other information.

Your result should be six layers in the Layers palette (see Figure 4.7)—one for each employee and Layer 1 (which a shrewdly organized designer like myself would rename

to "Common Elements"). If you build all five cards in one file, changes to the design become faster and more facile to accomplish. A typo in the REV address or URL is a single change that covers all five designs; the same with resizing the logo, touching up the background, or other typical changes that clients request. Even better, there's now only one file to manage, track, and send to the printer, not five.

 NOTE

To make the workflow genuinely efficient, we should have created *paragraph styles* when we set up Bob's card. Then, if Bob or anyone else wanted changes to the typography—typeface, color, paragraph spacing, alignment, and so on—we would only have to make the change once for it to apply to all five individual employees' cards. But we covered a lot in this portion of the project, and I don't want to overwhelm you.

FIGURE 4.7 With five different documents contained within one file, management and changes become easier, faster, and less susceptible to error.

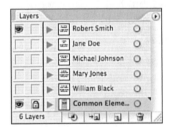

Save your Business Cards.ai file, but leave it open. We're going to need it again for the rest of the identity package.

Project: Creating Corporate Letterhead

Second only to business cards, letterhead is a mandatory part of any identity package. Every business writes letters, right? The identity of the business must carry through to its stationery. Using the business card design as a jumping-off point, design the letterhead on your own. You already have the skills.

 TIP

Placing files into a document with File > Place, as we did with the logo in the business card design, is one way to import external content. But when another document already has the placed files you need, there's a faster way.

Just arrange both the source and destination document windows on screen, select the content you want to copy in the source window, and drag it to the destination document—for example, the logo and address elements. Voilà! If the content consists of placed and linked files, the links are maintained in the destination document.

Keep the following points in mind, and if you get stuck, examine the `Letterhead.ai` file in the resource files (see Figure 4.8).

1. In the U.S., business standard letterhead is **8.5 × 11 in.**; in the U.K. the standard is **A4**.

2. Set the same bleed and live areas of **0.125 in.** each.

3. I've included a full-page background image, `bg_lttrhd.tif`, to match the business card and create a truly distinctive letterhead for REV.

FIGURE 4.8   The finished REV letterhead.

 NOTE

Rarely does a letterhead design call for a full-page background image—or any design elements more complicated than a rule here and there. Nevertheless, that rarity creates opportunity for those exceptional cases wherein a background or other decorative elements do have a place and function in the design. The vast majority of corporate letterhead is printed on white paper; creative letterhead design is construed as printing on gray-flecked, pale blue linen, or another subtle paper color. Pristine, high-contrast, and understated is the rule in letterhead design. And rules are made to be broken, right?

Wrong! Rules are made to be followed in all but the most extraordinary of circumstances, and only those who *fully* understand the rules, the trade-offs, and the hazards inherent in violating them should break the rules.

If this letterhead were for any other brand, it would almost certainly have a more reserved design on white or another light-colored stock. Fortunately, the REV brand is vivacious, energetic, creative, and even somewhat audacious. The brand *justifies* breaking certain rules typical of letterhead design.

Project:
Exploded Envelopes

In three easy steps we'll design a custom envelope:

1. Drawing the exploded envelope, and creating guides from paths

2. Manually building crop marks, fold lines, and labels

3. Applying background images with clipping masks

Designing Exploded Envelopes

Well-designed business cards and stationery needs equally well-designed and matching envelopes. If the letterhead were more standard (white linen or another common stationery stock), we could print just on the front of the same stock envelope, which would be a simple matter of creating a document the size of a #10 envelope's front panel (9.5 × 4.125 in.). However, the full-page, full-bleed image on the letterhead demands that the style carry through to full-bleed envelopes. Therefore, we are going to design an *exploded* envelope—a folded piece designed unfolded—which is how any folding project with two or more printed surfaces must be laid out.

STEP 1 ▼
Drawing the Exploded Envelope and Creating Guides from Paths

Because an exploded envelope is not a simple rectangle, setting up our bleed, trim, and live area guides is a little more involved than simply dragging from the rulers. It's a great chance to introduce a couple of tremendously cool and highly useful features, including creating guides from paths and the Pathfinder palette.

1. Begin a new document and set up the artboard as **17 × 13 in.** in landscape orientation, and in CMYK color mode. Name it Envelope.

2. Draw five rectangles with the following sizes and position them as in Figure 4.9 (I numbered my rectangles for your reference; don't number yours.)

   1. **9.5 × 4.125 in.**

   2. **9.5 × 2 in.**

   3. **9.5 × 3 in.**

   4. **0.75 × 4.125 in.**

   5. **0.75 × 4.125 in.**

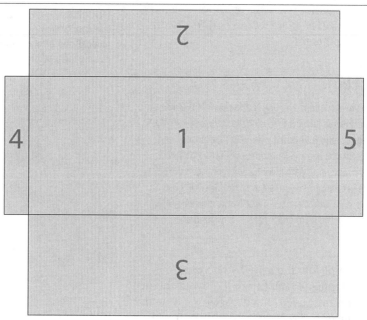

FIGURE 4.9 Each rectangle is a panel of our envelope. Note that panels 2 and 3 are rotated 90 degrees. When the envelope is folded and sealed, these panels will be upright on the back of the envelope, so they must be designed upside down.

3. Using the Transform palette, precisely align the boxes to each other. Begin with **box 1**. Select its top-left reference point in the Transform palette and note the X and Y coordinates (it helps to use a pencil and paper). Then select **box 2**, the back flap, and choose its bottom-left reference point; set the X and Y coordinates to equal the top-left coordinates of box 1. Do the same for the other three boxes, using the various reference points of **box 1** as the key. When finished, center the group of boxes to the artboard.

4. For safety's sake, let's duplicate Layer 1, rename it to **Trim Boxes**, and hide it.

5. Select all five boxes and copy them to the clipboard—don't paste yet. Now, with the boxes still selected, let's convert them to guides via View > Guides > Make Guides. Your boxes should disappear and be replaced by cyan guide lines.

6. Either by using the Edit menu's Paste In Front command or simply pressing (Cmd-F) [Ctrl+F], paste your boxes back in.

 TIP

The Paste In Front command differs from traditional Paste in two key ways: First, it will paste in front of the selected object(s), or, if nothing is selected, in front of all objects on the layer. Second—and more useful—it will insert objects at exactly the coordinates from which they were copied. Conversely, the inconsiderate Paste command arbitrarily inserts objects in the center of the document window with no regard whatsoever to what *we* want, how *we* feel, or what *we* need.

7. One at a time, for every box except **1**, select each and increase its dimensions by **0.125 in**. in all directions. The fastest way to do this is to ask Illustrator to do its math magic. Making sure to select

the center reference point for each box, add .25 in. (0.125 × 2) to both the width and height.

8. Duplicate the layer by choosing Duplicate **Layer 1** from the flyout menu on the Layers palette. Then rename the layer to **Bleed Boxes** and hide it. It will not be needed until the "Applying Background Images with Clipping Masks" part of the project.

9. Now select all five boxes once again. If everything is going correctly so far, the Transform palette should define the total area as **11.25 in.** wide and **9.375 in.** tall. Keeping the new set of boxes selected, open the Pathfinder palette (Window > Pathfinder). Click the Add To Shape Area Button. Your boxes should merge. Click the Expand button to expand the path to the new shape (see Figure 4.10). This merged path will become the bleed area.

10. Convert the merged shape to guides just as you did for the first set of boxes.

11. Repeat steps 6, 7, 9, and 10 to create your live area—this time *reducing* the size of the boxes (including **box 1**) by **.25 in.** You should wind up with three concentric sets of guides, each equidistant from its neighbors (see Figure 4.11).

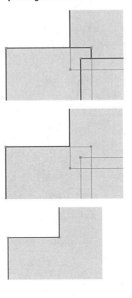

FIGURE 4.10 Separate paths (top) become merged paths with the Pathfinder palette's Add To Shape Area Button (middle) and, after expansion (bottom), a single path encompassing the total area.

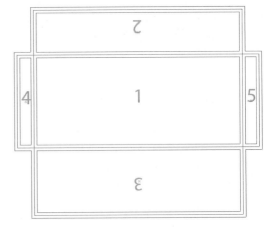

FIGURE 4.11 All guides in place—bleed on the outside, trim in the center, and live area on the inside.

STEP 2 ▼
Manually Building Crop Marks, Fold Lines, and Labels

Now let's create the crop and fold marks so that the print house finishers know where to trim and fold the envelope.

1. 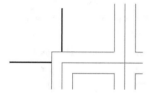 Using the Line tool, create a vertical (90-degree) line that is **0.5 in.** long and **1 pt** in weight (use the Stroke palette). Place this mark at the top left corner of **box 2**, even with the middle guide (the trim size) but *outside* the bleed area. (See Figure 4.12.)

FIGURE 4.12 Crop marks align to the trim borders but appear outside the bleed guides.

> ◎ **TIP**
>
> Hold the Shift key as you draw a line to ensure that it remains straight and constrained to an angle of 0, 90, or another multiple of 45 degrees.

2. 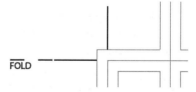 Set the stroke color to *registration*, not black. If you look at the Swatches palette, the first swatch on the top row is none, represented by a white square with a red slash through it. Just beside that is the registration crosshairs on the registration swatch. Registration may look black, but it isn't. Set your crop mark strokes (and, in step 4, fold marks and fold labels) in registration, but be careful not to set any other elements in registration.

3. Repeat this process until you have vertical and horizontal crop marks around all the outside corners of your live area. Position them precisely using the Transform palette—it may help to Paste In Front your original boxes again.

When all crop marks are in place, use the Selection tool to select them all by clicking and dragging a rectangle that touches all the crop marks. Now lock them to prevent accidental movement.

4. The last sequence in building the envelope template is to create fold marks, which we will accomplish by drawing dashed lines similar to the crop marks. So, draw a **.05 in. 1 pt** horizontal line and align it outside the bleed area to the place where **box 1** meets **box 2**, the upper back flap. It should look like an extension to the horizontal crop mark already there. Make sure these too are set to registration color.

5. On the Stroke palette check the Dashed Line checkbox; the default **2 pt** should be fine. Your line segment should break into a dashed line (see Figure 4.13.)

FIGURE 4.13 Dashed line fold marks should appear to be extensions of the crop marks, with the fold label set as shown.

---

6. With the Type tool, click once just below the dashed line and type in all caps **FOLD**. Set this as **8 pt** Arial or Helvetica and, like the marks themselves, registration color. For vertical fold lines, rotate the text boxes -90 degrees.

---

7. Repeat the last two steps for every fold point—everywhere the front of the envelope (**box 1**) adjoins another flap. It may help to open my `Envelope.ai` resource file and examine where I have placed the fold marks.

When finished, double-click the layer—which should be **layer 1 copy**—and rename it to **Template**. Lock the layer and save **Envelope.ai**.

STEP 3 ▼
Applying Background Images with Clipping Masks

With a completed and reusable envelope template, it's time for laying out the envelope's design elements.

1. Make a new layer and entitle it **Elements**. This is where we will do the creative work.

2. Like the business cards and letterhead, we would have already created background images in Photoshop, so place `bg_env2.tif` and then `bg_env1.tif`. If you lose track of which is which, open the Links palette. Its thumbnails will guide you.

3. Align both images so that they completely cover the bleed area and their coordinates match perfectly.

4. Remember creating the **Bleed Boxes** layer? Now we need it. Lock the **Elements** layer (and any other layers that may not be locked), and unlock and unhide **Bleed Boxes**. Select all objects and copy the boxes to the clipboard.

5. Hide **Bleed Boxes** once more; unlock and click on **Elements**. Paste In Front and the bleed boxes should line up perfectly with the guides beneath. If not, line them up.

Lick Your Lips

Envelopes must be glued to do their job. (For some reason beyond my comprehension, the post office is not keen on simply folding one piece of paper into another.) Three of the four back panels will be glued together during production. The top flap usually has a moisture-activated strip of glue, which was specially designed in the late 1700s by Vincennes prison guards watching over the prolific letter-writer, Marquis de Sade, to facilitate the infamously cruel tongue-of-a-thousand-paper-cuts torture technique.

Because the glue must be applied by special machinery, it is not available in all print shops—though most printers know where to sub out such work. Find out ahead of time if your chosen print provider can handle the envelope portion of the job, or if you need to take it elsewhere.

Then ask the provider whether they would prefer that you draw strips to indicate the placement of glue, or if they will take care of it. Most want to do it themselves.

Nowadays envelope flap glue comes in various forms. There's the self-adhesive type, covered in easy-peel strips of wax paper—by far the easier, but more expensive type. And, of course, there is the old-fashioned lick-and-stick kind, which is available in standard I-can't-feel-my-tongue-now flavor, as well as already-been-chewed-bubble gum, I-can't-believe-it's-not-berry, and my favorite, lint-covered-Tic Tac-mint.

Sufferers of the Celiac Sprue disease, and those allergic to wheat, should avoid licking envelopes as the glue is often made with wheat.

6. With the boxes still selected, go to the Pathfinder palette and merge them—don't forget to press Expand.

7. You should be able to see "bg_env1.tif" around the edges of the merged boxes. Shift-click to select the image without deselecting the boxes.

8. Go to Object > Clipping Mask > Make. The boxes amalgamation should disappear and the background image should take on its shape (see Figure 4.14). Clipping Mask is a non-destructive means of hiding all but the desired portion(s) of images and objects, and can be used on any type of object in Illustrator—placed images, paths, text, blends, and so on. Send the masked image to the back with Object > Arrange > Send To Back or by pressing (Cmd-Shift+) [Ctrl+Shift+]. It should be completely hidden behind bg_env2.tif.

9. Draw a rectangle to define the trim edges of the front panel—or copy **box 1** from the Trim Boxes layer—and use it to make a clipping mask on **bg_env2.tif**.

What you should now have is a fully painted envelope, with the front panel a lighter shade than the other panels. The content of the images should line up perfectly as they transition between the front and other panels.

Just as you did with the letterhead, drag in the REV logo, tagline, address, and website URL. Then style them to your tastes to fit the theme begun by the previous pieces of the identity package. You can see my final design in Figure 4.15.

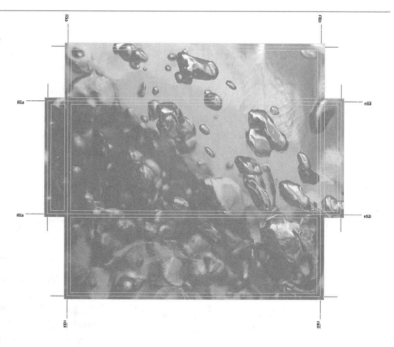

FIGURE 4.14 **With the Clipping Mask > Make command, the foreground objects mask-in the background image.**

FIGURE 4.15   The final REV
exploded envelope design.

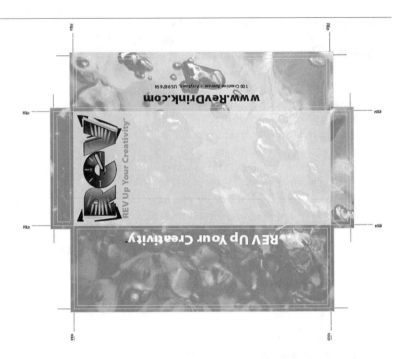

Project: **Press-Ready PDFs**

We'll get our corporate identity materials
ready to go to press in two simple steps:

1. Making press-ready PDFs
2. Making a layered PDF file

Making Press-Ready PDFs

For-press designs don't serve much purpose if
they can't make it to press. Because
Illustrator is the industry standard in vector
drawing, odds are overwhelmingly in favor
that your service bureau or printer will
accept native .AI files. But do you want to
send them? More specifically, does your print
provider(s) need the ability to change your
designs? The pros and cons on that subject
are worth discussing—at another time.

When native Adobe Illustrator files are not
preferred, PDF is the way to go.

For Just the Price of a Phone Call

Always try to consult the provider who will RIP your
digital files to film (or direct to press) before even
beginning to design a job. If that is not practicable—
sometimes providers can't be selected beforehand—at
the very least speak to the provider before generating
PDFs. Short of not paying invoices, the best way to earn
a bad reputation among press and prepress vendors is
to consistently send them improperly formatted files
that they must then fix. In addition, although some
providers will often be nice enough to make the repairs
(if they can) gratis the first time, they will charge for
repair time on subsequent occasions.

Dumb questions left unasked become stupid mistakes
that print providers must fix. Don't be afraid of asking a
dumb question. Every printer or prepressman in the
industry would rather spend 10 minutes answering
questions he has addressed a hundred times than spend
30 minutes fixing problems he has had to repair a thousand times. A simple phone call will go a *long* way
toward smoothing the production of your job, saving
you money, and building your reputation as a smart
creative willing to learn to do things the right way.

STEP 1 ▼
Making Press-Ready PDFs

Since the late nineties, PDF files have been a printing industry standard, so your printer or service bureau has the ability to take and *RIP* them—assuming you create them properly. Here's what you need to do:

1. Open your `Letterhead.ai` file and look it over to make sure everything is set to go. Check the Links palette for yellow caution signs and red circles, which indicate that a linked file has been updated or is missing, respectively.

2. From the Effects menu, select Document Raster Effects Settings. In the resulting dialog, ensure that Color Model is CMYK; Resolution is set to either High or Other (if you use Other, enter in the PPI field the exact resolution needed by your print provider); that Background is set to Transparent, and; that, in the Options section, only Preserve Spot Colors When Possible is checked. Click OK.

3. From the File menu, choose Save A Copy. Change the filename from `Letterhead copy.ai` to **Final Letterhead**, and choose Adobe PDF (*.PDF) from the Save as Type drop-down. The extension for your file will automatically change to reflect the new format. Click Save.

4. In the Save Adobe PDF dialog, choose from the Adobe PDF Preset drop-down [Press Quality], [PDF/X-1a:2001], or [PDF/X-3:2002]. Note: Do not use either PDF/X preset unless your print provider has specifically requested them. Similarly, do not set a PDF/X standard from the Standard drop-down. PDF/X files require particular systems in place at your provider's shop.

Check with your provider about the Compatibility desired—which version of Acrobat and which version of PDF. When in doubt, use Acrobat 5 (PDF 1.4).

5. If you have decided to prevent your provider from editing your files, uncheck Preserve Illustrator Editing Capabilities. Leaving it checked creates a file that is, in every respect that matters, identical to a standard .AI file.

6. Check View PDF after Saving because it is *always* a sound practice to review the final form of your file before sending for output. Check Optimize for Fast Web View. All other options should be grayed out. If they *are* accessible, check your Standard. It should be set to None.

◎ TIP

Optimize for Fast Web View is a misnomer; the word "Web" should be dropped and it should be called Optimize for Fast View. Though it was originally added to PDF's repertoire to make online PDFs faster to view, it is useful for PDFs in general. It orders the PDF file's code to group together all the bits and bytes necessary to draw each page, and it orders the grouped code according to the page order. The net result is that page 1 draws completely before page 2 begins loading, enabling the viewer to read the first page while the second is still downloading or rendering. This sequential rendering is of particular utility in any PDF with complicated vector drawings, robust raster images, or transparency, all of which take time to render in Acrobat or Reader.

7. Unless otherwise directed by your provider, the settings on the Compression tab should be left alone. They determine if and by how much your design's elements will be compressed and rendered. Any change here affects the ratio between quality

and file size. Don't make the mistake of lowering these to save on file size; files going to press are *supposed* to be big. Quality is the overriding concern here.

8. On the Marks and Bleeds tab, make sure Trim Marks is unchecked (because we created our own), and that Bleeds are set on all four sides at **0.125 in.** Whether to include the remaining marks—*Registration Marks, Color Bars,* and *Page Information*—should be determined by conversation with your output provider.

9. The Output tab is very important, but the most crucial part of it, the Destination profile, can only be provided by your print provider. Ask for the *ICC profile* of her output device—the imagesetter, platesetter, or digital printer. The provider will already have the .ICC file for her device, and will gladly provide it to you for installation on your system. You must choose that profile in the Destination drop-down.

TIP

Install ICC profile files under Macintosh OS X to the **Library/ColorSync/Profiles** folder, and on Windows into the **Windows/system32/spool/drivers/color/** folder. Illustrator (and all color-managed applications and technologies) will automatically detect and enable the use of the new profile.

Choose Convert to Destination (Preserve Numbers) as your Color Conversion option. Set the Profile Inclusion Policy to Include Destination Profiles to, as the sign says, minimize the risk of unexpected color changes. If using the Press Quality preset with Standard set to None, the PDF/X area will be grayed out. If your provider has asked for a PDF/X-based file, she will also supply what she wants here (see Figure 4.16).

FIGURE 4.16 The settings of the Output tab determine whether the colors that roll off the press look anything like they do on screen.

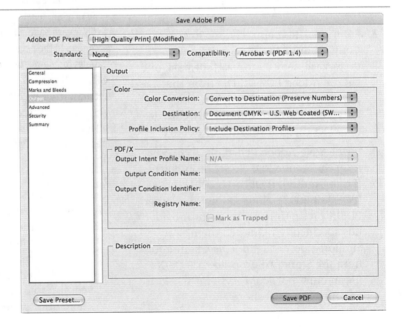

10. For what we are doing, Fonts should be the only section available on the Advanced tab. And we want it set at its default: 100%.

Fonts in PDFs: Embedding and Subsetting

PDF files can embed the fonts used to create their content. This enables the designer to rely on her work appearing as intended regardless of the viewer's computer platform and what fonts he may have installed. If your wedding invitation foolishly uses Comic Sans, you can be certain that viewers of your PDF will wince and bear witness to your tragic typographic faux pas.

However, if PDF files included the entire font for each typeface and style (bold, italic, bold-italic, and so on) you used, the PDFs would get huge rapidly—more importantly, someone would figure out how to extract the fonts from the PDF, making Adobe an unwitting accomplice to rampant software piracy. So one of the many ways in which Adobe keeps PDF files as small as possible—and legal—is by *subsetting* included fonts.

Instead of attaching the entire font file to the PDF, only the glyphs in use get embedded in the PDF, with all remaining glyphs and the data necessary to make them a standalone font left out. In simplest terms: If your document contains every letter from A through Y, Z will not be embedded.

11. Leave all options on the Security tab turned off because we don't want to make an instant enemy of your provider by hindering her from doing what she needs to do—opening, printing, and possibly changing the PDF (usually in non-design-related ways).

12. It's a good idea to review everything we've set to this point on the Summary tab. Critical, though, is that the Warnings section is empty. If it isn't, cancel and fix the problems before returning to save the PDF.

13. Now, one last step before saving the PDF is to determine whether you will ever use these settings again—and you will with the envelope. So click the Save Preset button, which will enable you to add a new entry to the Adobe PDF Preset drop-down that instantly restores all of the options you have just spent five minutes of your life configuring. Give the preset a descriptive name like `Margaret`, `Jorge`, `The Funky Chicken`, or even something vague and obscure like `Identity Package`.

14. Click the Save PDF button and sit back while Illustrator does the conversion.

15. In a moment, Acrobat (or Adobe Reader, if you don't have Acrobat) will open to display your newly created PDF file. Review it carefully; this is what is going to become your print job. Is everything *exactly* the way it was in Illustrator? Are the colors and typefaces the same? Are there any extraneous marks or substituted characters? Do your linked files—the logo and the background—appear in smooth color with sharp edges?

16. If everything is as expected, close Acrobat and return to Illustrator.

17. Now make a PDF of your `Envelope.ai` file. This time, when the Save Adobe PDF dialog appears, just select the `Jorge` preset you created. It should fill in all the options for you, requiring you to do nothing more than check the Summary tab for warnings.

STEP 2 ▼
Making A Layered PDF File

With the letterhead and envelope designs ready for shipment to your print shop, the last step is to create a PDF of the business cards. This will differ from the other PDFs in one important way.

Assuming you have already obtained agreement from your provider to accept a layered Acrobat 6 or 7 PDF, we are going to continue our streamlined business card workflow by making one PDF for all five cards stored in the one Illustrator document.

1. Open your Business Cards.ai file and give it a final review. Check the Links palette for yellow caution signs and red circles, and set the Document Raster Effects Settings as we did in the previous step sequence.

2. Begin the PDF process by saving a copy, again, as we did for the letterhead and envelope, and choosing your preset file from the Adobe PDF Preset list.

3. In the Compatibility drop-down, choose either Acrobat 6 (PDF 1.5) or Acrobat 7 (PDF 1.6), which will cause the Create Acrobat Layers from Top-Level Layers option to become available. Check that option. Everything else should remain the same.

4. When the new final Business Cards.pdf file opens in Acrobat or Adobe Reader, look it over for problems.

5. Although you probably only see Bob's name and information, everyone else's is in there as well. In Acrobat, go to View > Navigation Tabs > Layers to show the Layers tab, which will appear on the left. You should see six layers—the common elements and each employee's specific information (see Figure 4.17).

6. Click the eye beside the **Robert Smith** tab to turn him off, and do the same beside **Michael Johnson** to turn him on. See? All five business cards in one PDF file!

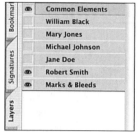

FIGURE 4.17 Acrobat's Layers (Left) tab mirrors Illustrator's palette (Right). Note that including printers marks during PDF creation adds the Marks & Bleeds layer to the PDF.

Final Thoughts

There are as many variations on the way corporate identity material may be designed as there are brands in the world. Each identity package will be—and *should* be—unique to the brand, putting different demands on your skills as an Illustrator user and as a graphic designer. Some designs will not even have a logo, and will be as simple as typing out contact information with the default text options (I will pray to the goddesses Creativia and Typographia that you never do anything so horrible as to deserve such a project).

Others will be far more interesting, involving not only full bleeds and exploded envelopes but also multiple types and sizes of envelopes, branded fax letterhead, folding business cards, die-cut letterhead, numerous spot colors, and non-standard sizes of everything. Follow the workflows you learned in this project and you will be able to build (and make changes to) any identity package, with a minimum of wasted time and effort.

Options

Many design decisions have an effect on the cost, time, and availability of printing. Talk to your print provider(s) as early as possible, and throughout the design process, about your choices for inks, paper, bleeds, and any special needs like folding or bindery.

Your palette is not limited to merely CMYK *process colors*. *Spot colors* and other special processes can enliven and inform a design. Consider adding a *varnish plate* on part of your business card for added impact. You could also entertain *embossing*, foil stamping, and even custom *die-cutting* to create non-rectangular shapes or make negative space truly negative by actually cutting holes into the card. Consider whether the design calls for something special, and then talk with your print service provider about the options available to you and their rates and limitations.

Layered PDFs

The technique of using layers to create multiple versions of a design in a single file is not limited to business cards. Many designers proof clients with several (usually no more than three) variations on a design. If you create the variations in a single, layered Illustrator file and save it as a layered PDF, clients can quickly compare versions without opening and closing different files. Even better for both you and the client, the client's comments and revisions on all designs stay in one file.

In my own creative work I have found that this proofing method has the added benefit of reducing confusion for everyone involved, and it often leads to more focused feedback and more productive collaboration between the client's personnel and myself.

Envelopes

As you design envelopes keep in mind these points:

- ▶ The grippers on mail machines require that a **0.5 in.** margin all around the edges of the envelope be clear of addressee and return address blocks and postage.

- ▶ If you include a Place Postage Here box, make sure it appears no more than **0.5 in.** from the top and extends (inclusive of its content) no more than **1.75 in.** inward from the right edge.

- ▶ The address block should begin no more than **4.5 in.** from the left edge and no more than **2 in.** from the top edge. Similarly it should not extend closer than **1 in.** to the right edge of the envelope.

- ▶ When setting the addressee block type, leave sufficient room for the addition of a delivery point barcode either above the addressee's top line, below its bottom line, or in the lower-right corner of the envelope.

- ▶ If the envelopes are addressed without integrated barcodes, the Post Office may affix a label during routing for that purpose to the bottom edge of the envelope. Such labels are typically on the right edge or centered horizontally and approximately **0.625 in.** tall. Be wary to avoid setting important design elements in this area.

With envelope design there are critical considerations beyond aesthetics. The postal services in most countries have strict regulations regarding dimensions of envelopes, placement of certain features, and even areas that must be blank (the light background we used on the front panel should be fine). In the United States the Post Office even produces a booklet, *Publication #95*, with all the specifications and diagrams for proper placement of elements. You can pick it up free from your local General Mail Facility (the really big post office).

About the Project

By drawing an (almost) photo-realistic portrait in this project we will explore the true beauty and versatility of Illustrator artwork.

Prerequisites

It would be helpful if you had a basic understanding of drawing with the Pen and Pencil tools, modifying paths with the Direct Selection tool and other tools, using the Pathfinder palette, applying fills and strokes, placing external graphic files, and working with layers.

@work resources

Please visit the publisher's website to access the following Chapter 5 project files:

- ▶ **Chap05** (complete projects to use as a reference while you work: **Portrait.ai**)
- ▶ **Chap05\Assets** (**Model.psd, Model's Hair.psd**)
- ▶ **Chap05\Extras** (**Monster Mesh.pdf**)
- ▶ **Chap05\Finished Project**

Planning the Project

Illustrating in Illustrator is done a thousand different ways, for a million purposes. That being the case, there isn't much I can impart in the way of planning considerations for an illustration. There are just too many possible scenarios in which you would choose to illustrate—realism or any other style. Yes, you *can* use the photo I've provided—that's why I've provided it. However, this is an intricate and deep project—think hours and days, not minutes. If you're going to put that much effort into a project, wouldn't you rather do it with a subject that has relevance to you—on the job or personally?

Because the conceptual planning steps for a project like this are sparse, it affords us a unique and excellent opportunity for a primer on copyright for the creative professional—which is exceedingly relevant to this project.

First, a legally mandated disclaimer: I am *not* an attorney, nor was I educated as one. My remarks about copyright consist of information and best practices I have accumulated as a result of 20 years creating and working with copyright- and trademark-protected creative work. I have spent many hours in consultation with various intellectual property and other attorneys retained by me or by firms and agencies for whom I have worked or which I owned, and I have sat on both sides of a courtroom during copyright and other intellectual property lawsuits. Though, again, that does not make me an authority on the topic. *Always* consult a bar-certified intellectual property attorney in your district prior to making decisions related to copyright, trademark, or patents. The information in this section is not legal advice, and neither the author nor publisher or any of their cats bear any responsibility for what you may or may not do with it.

Automatic Protection

You are a creative. Only creatives would be reading this (well, my girlfriend and the various editors at Sams will read it too, but you know what I mean). You are a creative, which means you *create something* (usually visual art) from raw materials or from nothing. What you make, either for a living or as a hobby, is born of your vision, talent, skill, and labor. Clearly, if you're reading a how-to book, you're investing your time and energy into fortifying your skills—skills that not everyone possesses. In the eyes of the law, your skills have value, and thus the fruit of your skilled labor has intrinsic value. The law protects items of value and the individuals who own them. Your creations are your valuable possessions, and copyright law protects both their value and your ability to possess them.

In the United States and in most of its trade partner countries, copyright protection is automatic—the instant a work is created, it and its creator are protected under federal copyright laws. Registering a copyright with the U.S. Registrar of Copyrights (or equivalent agency in another country) is not required for copyright protection; it merely makes the government aware of your existing protection. In the event of a copyright dispute, the certificate of registration issued by the Registrar establishes the date on which you possessed the work in a fixed form (the form submitted to the Registrar). In that way, the Registrar becomes a witness during any copyright infringement proceedings.

And, because all copyright dispute matters are handled in federal court, that's an important witness to have.

Multiple Rights

Copyrights are, as the plurality of the name implies, more than a single right. The phrase "all rights reserved," in addition to being antiquated and superfluous, states that the creator of a work retains and has not licensed any of her rights. She has the ability to license or assign any or all of her rights individually. Such rights include, but are not limited to: first publication rights, the right to publish a work for the first time; serial rights, the right to serialize or break a work (typically a written, film, or animated work, or a collection of works) into segments to be published over a period of time; and film rights, the right to make a film, DVD, Webcast, instructional video, or any type of broadcast based on the original work. These are but three of many rights afforded to the creator of an original work in this global, Internet-enabled economy. Any or all of them may be sold, temporarily licensed, given away, or otherwise assigned to other entities. Further, they may be regionalized. For example, American book publishers typically secure from authors the first North American publishing rights, thus enabling the publisher to publish and distribute an author's work throughout the United States, Canada, and Mexico. If the same or another publisher wishes to translate the book into a different language and publish the translation in another country, the publisher must secure from the author additional publishing rights specific to that country (or continent) as well as the right to translate the author's work into a derivative work.

Derivative Works

Derivative works are ones based upon or closely related to another copyright-protected work. In this project we're going to take a photograph that is owned by photographer Lacey Gadwill—she owns the copyright. She licensed to Sams Publishing and me several of her rights in the work—the right to publish, distribute, and create derivative works from—her photograph. Lacey still retains ownership of the photograph, and, presumably, the rest of her rights thereto. Our use of her photo does not impinge upon Lacey's ability to use it for other purposes, just as you allowing a magazine to publish your illustration in an ad would not threaten your other rights. Unless you specifically give away one or more of your rights somehow, you retain each and every one of them.

> **✖ NOTE**
>
> The preceding is a broad, generally true statement, but it can be contradicted by a number of factors. Always consult with an intellectual property attorney prior to transferring or assigning any rights in and to a copyright-protected work.

In drawing a photo-realistic portrait from Lacey's photograph, we're creating a derivative work. Though we're changing the form of the artwork from a photograph to an illustration, and though we're modifying or eliminating portions of the original photograph, the illustration still features the same model, in the same pose, with the same (lack of) background, with the same lighting. It was the photographer's vision that created the photograph. We're borrowing her vision and *adding* to it with our own. Therefore the outcome will be a collaboration between us rather than a completely original work. This makes it a derivative work.

Derivative works are a violation of the copyright holder's rights unless she has specifically granted you permission to use the work (preferably in writing, no matter how friendly you are with the copyright holder). There are, of course, exceptions covered under the Fair Use provisions of copyright law, but that's a whole other discussion. The litigious rampages of Metallica and the Recording Industry Association of America (RIAA) aside, most infringement lawsuits filed in the United States involve derivative (or perceived derivative) works rather than exact duplicates.

With the sheer number of Earthlings creating, innocuous replication or derivation of creative work is inevitable. Short of not creating (gasp!), there's nothing we can do to avoid accidents. But, if you intentionally derive your work from someone else's—for example, if you used Lacey's photograph or my drawing deriving from it beyond a practice project following along with this lesson—you would (now knowingly) be infringing upon the rights of another creative.

Copyright Myths

Just for the record, and just in case you need to be dissuaded from this particular commonly believed fallacy, artwork—graphics, text, page code, designs, and so on—on the Internet *is* as protected by copyright laws as this book you're holding or the CD you have blasting in the background. Just because something appears in a global public medium like the Web does not mean it is in the public domain. Lawsuits are filed

every day by huge corporate and individual copyright holders alike to protect their rights from online infringement.

 TIP

Public domain is a term specifically applied to work whose copyright protection has expired—for example, the music of Beethoven and the sonnets of Shakespeare are so old that they are no longer protected by copyright law and may be used without restriction or license by anyone.

Another myth that it's important to disabuse you of is that copyright infringement only counts when it's for a commercial use. Yes, whether you got paid or in some other way profited from an infringement upon another's copyright is indeed a factor considered by federal judges in such cases. It is, however, a relatively minor consideration; you can still be sued, fined (as of this writing $50,000 per instance of infringement), and possibly imprisoned for copyright infringement regardless of whether you profited from it. By the same token, you have the ability—many say the obligation—to protect your rights in and to your work with litigation should someone infringe upon them, regardless of whether the other party profited from the infringement. Copyright protection is literally *protection against copying*. How much was made from an infringement is only relevant to the severity of penalties and what you would receive or pay in damages (moola) upon successfully proving infringement.

According to United States copyright laws in effect at the time of this writing, any work created after January 1, 1978 is protected for the life of the author plus 70 years. It can, however, be renewed in 28-year increments by descendants of the creator after her death. Works created anonymously, pseudonymously (under an alias), or that qualify as work made for hire, are protected for the shorter of 95 years from the date of first publication or 120 years from the date of creation.

Losing Your Rights for Profit or Slothfulness

"Made for hire" is a special term that *every* creative professional and part-timer *needs* to know and be able to define. The "work made for hire" provisions were written into the 1976 Copyright Act expressly for the sole purpose of protecting creatives (like you and me) who were, prior to that time, ignorantly and constantly losing our rights—either accidentally or by coercion or deception. If your contract with an employer or client includes the phrase "made for hire," any work you create under that contract is automatically the copyright-protected property of the employer or client—*you* have no rights in and to your own work. Vigilantly look for that or similar phrases in any contract, and be in full control of your faculties when you agree to it. Assuming you do agree to a made-for-hire agreement, unless the employer or client specifically grants you permission, you will have no legal right or ability to use your own work—even in your portfolio.

Additionally, United States copyright and civil law typically holds that any work created while on the job during regular employment ("regular" often defined as the kind for which you fill out a W-2 and the employer withholds a portion of your taxes) is automatically made for hire even without an explicit agreement to that effect. So, if

you work for an ad agency, for instance, all your designs created on the clock and/or using agency equipment and resources, are owned by the agency, not you.

Every day creatives get a raw deal when they are taken advantage of over copyright, losing some or all of their rights as a result of ignorance or poor planning. Let's face it, we're grown-up kids who just want to sit and color all day. We hardly want to recognize what we do as a business, much less deal with the boring and unpleasant chores of sales (sigh), management (ugh), billing (gawd), and, least of all, the legalities (eek) of being creatives. We aren't out to harm anybody or step on them to get where we want to go, so we try to do business on a smile and a handshake. Regrettably, some people who are more business- and legal-savvy than ourselves *are* happy to step on anybody to help further their own agendas. In addition, we, the amiable, trusting, Birkenstock-wearing, crayon wielders are easy targets.

Protect yourself and your children—your creative work—with knowledge. *Learn* about your rights, and what others can and cannot do with—and to—you and your work, *before* they do it.

Using Stock Photography

If you use stock photography for a project, keep in mind that it too is protected by copyright law. Make sure you have the proper licensing to use the stock photo(s) before you use it. Among stock photo agencies are three main types of licensing: royalty-free, rights-managed, and editorial.

Royalty-free licensing means that, after you've paid the licensing fee for the photo (or photo collection), you may use the image as often and in whatever manner you see fit. There are, of course, specific rights withheld in royalty-free licensing. For example, to protect their investment, most stock photo agencies disallow distribution of their images unaltered (or reasonably unaltered). In other words, they won't allow you to compete with them by using their own inventory. Consult the licensing agreement on the agency's website or CD-ROM (preferably before you plunk down cash) for limitations to an image's use.

The second most common type of licensing is rights-managed. Rights-managed imagery is licensed on a per-project basis; it can only be used in a single project without paying another licensing fee. Moreover, pricing is based on the use of the image. At the time of licensing you will typically be required to provide the size of the print run, or the number of copies to be printed, where and how the image will be used, where and how the final piece will be distributed, and for how long the work incorporating the image will circulate.

Editorial licensing is the third common form, and is usually reserved for editorial content usage. Images licensed under editorial are most often time-sensitive news and sports photography, though older "archive" photos are often licensed as editorial as well. This form of licensing is very similar to rights-managed in that photos (or footage) may be used only for the specific use, in the media, and for the duration communicated at the time of licensing.

Model Photography

Another important consideration when using photography for any creative project is the model. I don't mean how to select and ego-manage the model; that changes with every project (swing by one of my book signings and I'll be happy to regale you with wacky tales of selecting, hiring, handling, and shooting models for a Playboy product line campaign). No, I mean whether you have the rights to use the model.

In addition to copyright protection for creators, each of us in the United States and countries with similar laws has certain inalienable rights. "We the People of the United States, in Order to form a more perfect Union, establish Justice, insure domestic Tranquility, provide for the common defence, promote the general Welfare, and secure the Blessings of Liberty to ourselves and our Posterity," do possess the right to control on which cereal boxes our faces appear.

Called "likeness rights," our faces and any identifiable physical representations of us are prohibited from use in commercial imagery without our consent. Like copyright-protected material, Fair Use trumps likeness rights in some situations. For example, any of us may be photographed in a public setting and that photograph published or broadcast for journalistic purposes. Again, Fair Use is too broad (and gray) an area to go into here.

Generally speaking, in order for my face or yours to be used by someone else, we have to give that right to someone. Models are people too (the jury's still out on Super Models, though), so they also have control over how their likenesses are used. Just because someone appears in a photograph doesn't necessarily mean that she has consented to allow her image to be used for any particular purpose. A common stipulation in model release forms, for example, is that the model's likeness may not be used in promotion of, or in connection with, material of an explicitly adult nature, or material that promotes or implies endorsement of alcohol, tobacco, or non-pharmaceutical drugs.

Before you use a model's photograph for any purpose, be absolutely sure you know the model consented—in writing—to allow her likeness to be used for your purposes. Every couple of months I hear about some model suing a company, creative, or photographer because she never signed a model release allowing her likeness to be used as it ultimately was.

If you purchase model stock photography online, look for the phrase "model released." Do the same for any model stock photography you buy in a collection (such as on a CD-ROM). If you buy directly from a photographer or studio, either request to see the model release form or mandate that the licensing agreement you sign with the photographer state that the photography is model released *and* that the photographer is responsible in the event of a dispute over likeness rights. If you set up and direct a photo shoot yourself, either from behind the camera or directing a photographer you've hired, *you* need to be the one to have models sign model release forms granting you (and your client, if applicable) likeness rights; in such cases, hang onto the forms until at least seven years after the last use of a relevant photograph ceases circulation.

Know Your Rights—For Yourself

As a creative, you already deal with copyrights every time you initiate and finish a project. Copyright is automatic—it takes significant effort or a tiny bit of ignorance to lose it. After that protection is lost, it's almost impossible to get it back. On the other side of the coin, infringing upon someone else's rights takes far less effort and even less ignorance. Protect yourself, your work, your reputation, and your future by knowing your rights and at least the important basics of copyright law.

Every week I find myself in various forums (online and off) fielding questions about copyright issues for creative professionals. More often than that, I hear or read passionately ignorant ranting about what copyright law "really means." Never has there been so much misinformation about any one topic as that bandied about by self-proclaimed copyright experts. I'll tell you a little secret: Most of the people spouting copyright law and rules—especially on the Internet—are preaching what they believe copyright law *should* say, not what it does; the vast majority of them have never read even the friendly pamphlets the U.S. Registrar of Copyrights puts out.

Don't believe the morons on the Internet who claim to know what they're talking about—more often than not, anyone who says "I know what I'm talking about" doesn't know anything except that he's desperate to feel important. Don't believe any copyright advice until you check it out for yourself—and I include in that my own advice here. Don't believe *me*, either. If you don't have a degree in intellectual property law on your wall, you're not an expert in copyright law. I'm no exception. I am neither an attorney nor an expert in intellectual property; I know much more than the average layperson, but that is only because I listen to the genuine experts and I read for myself the facts from the authority—copyright law makers and regulatory agencies.

If you find yourself defending against a copyright infringement suit, ignorance of the law will *not* be an affirmative defense. Worse, ignorance of your rights could prevent action to protect you and your work in the event of infringement. And, worst, you could irrevocably lose your rights simply through ignorance or laziness.

I've given you a primer, one creative pro to another. I pointed you in a few directions any creative veteran knows are critical considerations every creative should explore. Nevertheless, don't believe what I've written just because it's in print. Go read for yourself, straight from the horse's mouth: **http://www.copyright.gov**.

Project: (Almost) Photo-Realistic Portrait

In eight easy steps we'll draw an (almost) photo-realistic vector portrait:

1. **Preparing to Draw**
2. **Drawing the Major Color Areas**
3. **Drawing the Sections of the Mouth**
4. **Creating, Coloring, and Modifying Gradient Meshes**
5. **Coloring Gradient Meshes from Photograph Colors**
6. **Preparing for Tracing**
7. **Live Tracing the Hair**
8. **Converting the Live Trace to Editable Paths**

Creating an (Almost) Photo-Realistic Portrait

While you were kicked back reading the U.S. Copyright Office's *Circular 40*, on a break between projects for REV Creativity Drink, a different kind of job came in.

The latest pop singing sensation Allyson needs advertising and promotional materials—posters, t-shirts, key chains, lunchboxes, temporary tattoos, doll packaging, the works. Her first single skyrocketed to the top of the Billboard charts, and her album is about to go double-platinum. The record company wants to use the album cover shot of Allyson on everything, all the promo items, magazine advertisements, highway billboards, bus signs, even a 40-foot mega-poster that will drape a building on Los Angeles's Sunset Strip.

There's just one little problem: The original album cover shot is a digital photograph; blowing it up and shrinking it down to fit all the different applications will annihilate the quality of a pixel-based, resolution-dependent image.

Your reputation as an Illustrator expert has grown, and the record company has hired you to bail them out of this predicament. Because vector is resolution-independent and may be scaled up or down to infinity without loss of quality, they want you to take Allyson's album cover photo and redraw it in vector as close to photo-realistic as possible.

STEP 1 ▼
Preparing to Draw

No matter what else you may use Illustrator to create—corporate identity material, packaging, 3D mockups, websites—its highest calling is *illustration*. No matter how much you may enjoy working on those other projects, you will never feel more creative, more satisfied in your work than you will after drawing something beautiful. Although I sincerely *hope* you feel a great sense of accomplishment upon completing each of the other projects in this book, I *know* that, when you've finished this project, you will be proud of yourself.

Although it is certainly possible to draw realism of any depth from scratch in Illustrator, if this is your first time drawing for realism, work from a photograph. Use Allyson's photo, a stock photo you've licensed, or something from your digital camera (any one of those three dozen photos of your cat sleeping will do).

Let's prepare the workspace and the source material.

1. First, prepare your photograph. Though some changes are quickly made while drawing in Illustrator, others are easier in advance in Photoshop. Because the original photo wasn't ideal for the situation (see Figure 5.1), I cleaned it up in Photoshop CS2.

After selecting the white background with Select > Color Range, I used the same to select and then dye her hair (auburn with red highlights) and lips (a deeper, but still natural pink) with Hue & Saturation. Then I removed her earring (and piercing hole to imply innocence) and the microphone obscuring her lips and cheek by working with the Clone Stamp, Healing Brush, and Patch tools. I left the spaghetti straps on her shoulders so that we can take them out in Illustrator.

 TIP

If I were going for sex appeal (as most advertising model photography does), I would have made her lips fuller, flared her nostrils, and added a slight flush to her cheeks, ears, and chin; if her eyes had been showing I would have also dilated the pupils and cleaned and lightened the scleras. Regardless of the intent of the photo, I would have whitened her teeth if they weren't already nice and pearly.

FIGURE 5.1   The original photo (left) and touched-up version (right).

2. If you will not be drawing the photograph's background in Illustrator (as in this case), take it out, leaving the area transparent in the Photoshop document. Save as a PSD and quit Photoshop.

3. Open Illustrator and begin a new document from the Welcome screen or by selecting File > New. For a project like this, the size of the artboard is irrelevant. Besides, it can always be changed later. So let's just set it to the default Letter size in the RGB color space to give us the wider color gamut, and name it **Portrait**. We're not going to use rulers, so the units setting is moot.

4. Choose File > Place, and select your photograph or, to work with Allyson's picture, navigate to **Chap05\Assets\model.psd**. The photo should wind up right about the middle of your artboard; if not, don't worry about it. Rename the layer to **Photo**.

5. Choose View > Hide Artboard to make your artboard disappear.

6. Let's set up your workspace to be uncluttered and conducive to drawing. Select Window > Workspace > Save Workspace. Give it a name like **Normal** or **General**. This is your, uh, normal or general arrangement of palettes; we're saving it so you can easily get back to it.

7. Now, let's pull out the needed palettes and divest our working space of those unneeded for this type of project. From the Window menu show: Tools, Color, Swatches, Layers, Appearance, and Navigator. If any of those palettes are grouped or docked with other palettes, tear them away by dragging their *tabs*, not the title bars of the palette group. Close all the other palettes.

8. Arrange the Tools, Color, Swatches, Layers, Appearance, and Navigator palettes on the screen so that they are comfortable for you—you will want Layers to be as tall as possible, and Swatches to have several blank rows visible beneath the existing swatch rows. If you have an extra wide screen (such as an Apple Cinema Display) or multiple monitors (as I do; see Figure 5.2), arrange and resize your Navigator palette to be as large as you can manage.

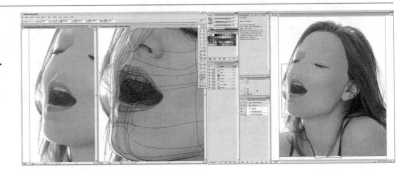

FIGURE 5.2 The author's typical illustration workspace (dual-monitor), showing this chapter's project file in-progress.

9. All set? Save this workspace (Window > Workspace > Save Workspace) as **Drawing**. When you need to work on general types of projects, select the Normal or General workspace from the bottom of the Window > Workspace menu; when you want to draw, restore these palettes and their arrangement by selecting the Drawing workspace.

> ◎ **TIP**
>
> You may decide to use other palettes such as the Links or Info palettes in your drawing projects, or even to rearrange palettes. Just save the workspace as before, and give it the same name as an existing workspace to overwrite.

10. Choose File > Document Setup. Check the box beside Show Images in Outline Mode. Save your document.

STEP 2 ▼
Drawing the Major Color Areas

If you've ever taken a non-computer painting or drawing class, you probably remember a particular phrase drilled into you over and over again: *Draw what you see, not what you think*. Well, it's been running round and round in my head the whole time I've been preparing the artwork for, and writing, this chapter. I just thought I'd share.

Oh! Wait! I *did* have a point to make by mentioning that. Quick: What color is Caucasian human skin? <Buzz> Wrong! It's *mostly* that, but depending on lighting and shadows, Caucasian skin can be white, yellow, pink, red, brown, gray, even (and often) green. Darker complexions like those belonging to Latino- or African-Americans,

can have all of those plus blues, blacks, and even violets. YOU LEFT OFF HERE. Did that help? That all-caps sentence was to assist your short-term spatial memory find your place again in this paragraph 'cause I know you looked away to stare at your own skin. I *know* you did. And, next time you find yourself out on the street or lying beside your significant other, you *will* catch yourself studying the color shifts in other people's faces, hands, and other parts.

Until you train your eyes to notice all the genuine tones and hues present in objects, you will interpret casually observed color as most people do: blending a kaleidoscope of shades and hues together to create the impression of one overriding color with highlights and shadows composed mostly of lighter or darker tones of the core color. This is the color you *think*, not the color you *see*. To paint realism, we need to forget about what we think is the correct shape or tone and simply paint what we see.

1. With the Selection tool, click once on the photograph to select it. Choose Object > Transform > Rotate, and set the rotation to 180°, which should spin your photograph upside down. We're no longer working with the photo of a beautiful girl—or Mr. Whiskers, Aunt Mable, or whatever you happen to be drawing; now we're tracing over areas of color. This is how to work with what you see, not what you think.

2. Lock the **Photo** layer and make a new layer with the New Layer button at the bottom of the Layers palette. Select View > Outline. In Outline mode, you'll see only the paths of your objects—without fills. We will, however, need to see the photo. So,

double-click the **Photo** layer and check the Preview option in the Layer Options.

3. Grab the Pencil tool and draw a close contour around the model's face, from forehead to jaw, excluding the hair, neck, and ear. Go ahead and overlap into her hair a bit to account for the scalp visible between roots. Make sure you close the path by returning to the exact point at which you began.

> ◎ **TIP**
>
> ✒ You may find some of the drawing tasks in this section easier to accomplish with the Pen tool than with the Pencil. It's up to you.

4. If you couldn't get a precise contour outline, work with the Direct Selection tool and other Bézier editing tools to clean it up. Your contour path should look very much like mine (see Figure 5.3).

5. Rename the layer to **Face**; then lock the layer and create a new one.

6. Continuing with the Pencil tool (or Pen, as you prefer), move around the image, drawing close contours around each of the major color areas—places like the neck, shoulders, nose, ear, eyes, and so on. Put each on a new, appropriately named layer, locked after drawing. Don't draw the model's hair, spaghetti straps, or mouth yet. Check your progress against Figure 5.4.

One thing that may help you discern what qualifies as a "major color area" and what doesn't is to think of the painting as a three-dimensional sculpture. If you were building a bust of the model in clay, which features could you sculpt as a single piece, and for which would you use separate pieces of clay? Her entire face, for example, including cheekbones, chin, forehead, brow ridge, and eye orbits could be molded easily into shape with your fingers and various scraping tools. To create the nose, however, would almost certainly require a separate piece of clay stuck on and blended in after forming.

FIGURE 5.3 The first contour path, surrounding the major color area of the face.

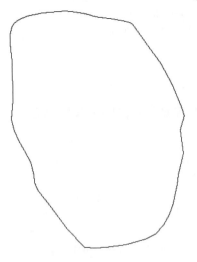

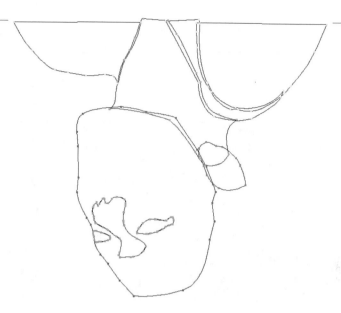

FIGURE 5.4 Missing a mouth and hair, the major color areas of the photo are contoured.

STEP 3 ▼
Drawing the Sections of the Mouth

Gradient meshes have a couple of limitations. Although it is possible to paint the entire portrait in a single gradient mesh (I've done it with other illustrations), overly complex meshes cause color banding during print output. U-G-L-Y. You'll get better results by using multiple mesh objects—thus the reason for drawing the portrait in major color areas.

Two other limitations are directly relevant to this stage of the project. Meshes cannot be made of compound paths; a donut, for example, is a compound path because, though it's one object, its outer rim is one path and the hole a second. If you were to draw the model's mouth as a single path defining the exterior edge of her lips, and then another path for the interior, relying on the Pathfinder palette to knock out the empty space, you'd be shooting yourself in the foot. That would be a compound path.

There are two ways to get around the compound path issue. Looking closely you may notice that the pink of her lips does not completely encompass her mouth, which leads to the temptation to draw a horseshoe-shaped contour path opened at the corner. Of course you wouldn't do that because it would run you smack into the final limitation I want to mention.

When you have a complicated shape like the entirety of this model's pink lips, your gradient mesh lines are going to start out so complicated as to become unwieldy. The mesh grid, you see, forms from the shape of all sides of the path. With a path the shape of Allyson's lips… Oh, the mess!

The best way to handle areas of color as distorted as the mouth is by using multiple mesh objects.

1. Zoom in on Allyson's mouth and create a new layer called **Mouth**.
2. Her lower lip (at the top of your screen) is a relatively basic shape, so draw a

tadpole-shaped contour that includes the tail end at the corner of her mouth all the way to the bulbous edge on the other end, including the highlight (see Figure 5.5).

FIGURE 5.5 The contour for her lower lip.

FIGURE 5.5 The contour for her lower lip.

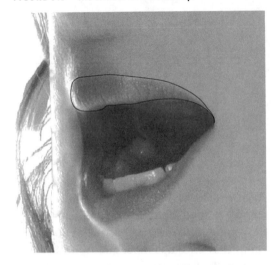

FIGURE 5.6 Drawn in three sections, her lips are now contoured.

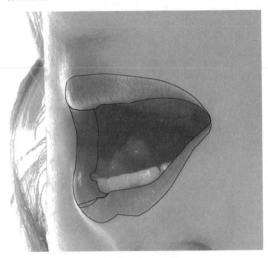

3. On the Layers palette, spin down the Expand Layer arrow to expose the paths on the **Mouth** layer. At this point, there should be only one. Double-click it to rename it to **Lip Lower**. Now lock that path—not the whole **Mouth** layer—by clicking in the center column between the layer name and the visibility indicator.

4. Draw the rest of her lips in two separate parts, one for the side and one for her upper lip (see Figure 5.6). Try to overlap the contours just a tiny bit. Rename these paths to **Lip Side** and **Lip Upper**, respectively, and lock them.

5. Draw a contour for her tongue and a separate one for the interior of her mouth. Because the lips will be in front of all other mouth paths, these two and the teeth (next step) can and should overlap the lips. Rename the paths accordingly and lock them.

6. Now finish up the mouth contours by drawing the teeth. Though it would be fairly easy to create realistic gradient meshes from just two or three paths encompassing a few teeth each, I opted to create separate paths for each tooth (see Figure 5.7). It's your choice how you would like to do it with Allyson's teeth or with similar color areas of your own image.

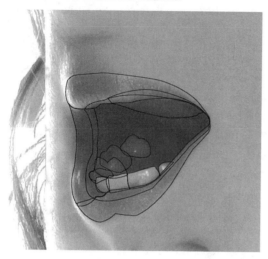

FIGURE 5.8 My layers so far.

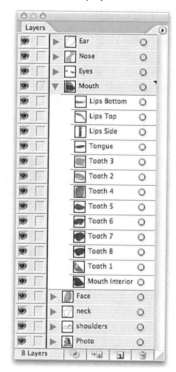

7. In Outline mode the fills of our objects are hidden (so are their strokes, for that matter). In the final artwork, though, the stacking or Z-order of the paths is critical. So take a moment with the Layers palette to order the paths in your **Mouth** layer. Each sublayer (path) may be dragged above or below any other; just drag its Layers palette entry until you see a bold line appear between any two other sublayers. In the end, your Layers palette should be pretty close to mine (see Figure 5.8). Save your document. Save it twice, just to be safe.

Working with Meshes

I know this is not a book about how to use tools. However, I'm breaking protocol just this once because, in order to complete your gradient mesh projects—and this project in particular—and to do so without tearing out your hair, you *must* know how to create and use the tools of gradient meshes. So, let's just get through it and never speak of this incident again—not even when we're alone.

Included in this chapter's resource files, in the Extras folder, is the **Monster Mesh.pdf**, a handy chart showing the tools, cursors, and—everyone's favorite—keyboard shortcuts that you will use constantly as you work with meshes—both gradient and distortion.

STEP 4 ▼
Creating, Coloring, and Modifying Gradient Meshes

There is no more beautiful art produced with Illustrator than that painted with gradient meshes. Coloring realism or any other style of painting is the product of time, patience, and an artistic eye.

The first time you try to use a gradient mesh it will likely be as confusing as quantum physics. That's why I'm here, to demystify this elegant and amazing technique. After the first mesh, each one is a little easier and makes a little more sense. Shortly, working with gradient meshes will become as intuitive and familiar to you as preparing ramen noodles was to you in college.

Don't scoff. It really is as intuitive and enjoyable as I describe. Trust me. I, too, was once flustered and frustrated, pumping my fist and lobbing obscenities like a drunken sailor in a brawl. When Illustrator first incorporated the gradient mesh tool (in version 8), that's exactly what every session was like, a brawl. The first few times I walked away spitting teeth. Now look at me—I'm writing about gradient meshes in Illustrator CS2 for not one but two books. Moreover, I'm going to teach you all the ins and outs and ways around the frustrations that no one was around to show me.

For that reason, this section is going to be a bit longer and much heavier on the expository and even the hypothetical than other sections of this book. Most of the tips, notes, and cautions are inline, as part of the main text flow (feel free to highlight; you'll never want to part with this book anyway). Some

of these steps may feel a little contrived. They are. But I want—nay, I feel a responsibility—to show you the frustrating and infuriating things that you will encounter while working with gradient meshes, to explain what and why they are, and to show you how to deal with them elegantly. So, if, in this next section, I ask you to do something that doesn't seem relevant to your drawing or even logical, humor me. It's to your benefit.

1. Let's start simply. Unlock the Mouth Interior or a similarly uncomplicated path in your drawing and select it with the Selection tool. Fill the Mouth Interior path with a bright color like yellow that contrasts with the photo beneath. Because we're still in Outline mode, the fill will be invisible—that's okay.

2. ◎ There are two ways to begin a gradient mesh. The first and often easier way is to choose Object > Create Gradient Mesh. If this option is grayed out: Check to make sure you have only one path selected. Look for more than one outlined target circle in the Layers palette; make sure you don't have a compound path (you may have to redraw); and ensure that you actually have a path selected, not the picture. If you can't access the Create Gradient Mesh menu option, make a quick shape path just to follow along.

🚫 CAUTION

After you convert a path to a mesh, you can't change it back to a path again. Though it's not perfect, there is a workaround: Select the mesh object, choose Object > Path > Offset Path. Enter 0 for the offset value. Now choose Object > Expand and Object > Ungroup. Delete the resulting mesh and keep the path.

3. In the Create Gradient Mesh dialog, you specify a number of rows and columns into which to divide your grid initially. Below that, Appearance offers the options to automatically begin with a white highlight, and whether the highlight should radiate from the center outward, or from the edges inward. The Highlight percentage controls the intensity of the white highlight. For our purposes, leave Appearance set to Flat, and begin with two each of Rows and Columns. Click OK. Your path should divide into quarters as in Figure 5.9.

FIGURE 5.9 Beginning with just two rows and two columns, my path is now a gradient mesh (shown in Preview mode for clarity).

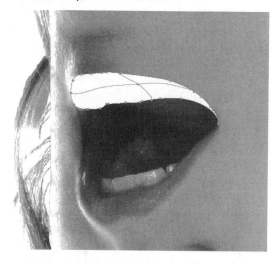

What you're looking at is this: a mesh (a grid) containing *mesh points, mesh lines, mesh patches*, a path, and anchor points. The path and its anchor points, corner or smooth, define the shape of your mesh *object* (no longer a path). By contrast, the mesh constructs (points, lines, and patches) determine the shape and flow of the *color* of that object. Like anchor points to path segments, mesh points define and control the length, angle, and curvature of mesh lines. On your path you have both anchor points and mesh points now, the latter terminating mesh lines and functioning as points of color.

Because your path was asymmetrical, your mesh lines probably are as well. New mesh lines follow the logical transition between path segments to either side; the closer to one side of a path the mesh line appears, the more it approximates the shape of the path segment(s) on that side.

4. Choose Select > Deselect All. We should still be working in Outline mode such that the outline of the mesh object is all you see. Although we need to work in Outline, we need to see in Preview. Impossible, you say? Pshaw! Nothing's impossible for Illustrator! (Except launching maximized under Windows. Grrr!)

5. Select Window > New Window. You should see a second view on the same document. Choose View > Preview. Now arrange this and your previous window on screen simultaneously. If space is at a premium, make the Preview window shorter or narrower than the Outline window. Switch back to your Outline window by clicking on its title bar. Now you can work in Outline view *and* see in Preview!

6. With the Direct Selection tool, click on the intersection of the two mesh lines to select the mesh point there. On the Swatches palette, select a highly contrasting color like Fresh Green Grass or Squash. Do you see in the Preview window what happened? Each mesh point holds a color, and the color radiates out from the mesh point in all directions—horizontally, vertically, and diagonally—to blend smoothly with the color assigned to the next mesh point in that direction (see Figure 5.10). When you created your mesh, all the mesh points filled with whatever color was selected as the fill at the time. Try changing the fill color on the other mesh points; experiment a little to get comfortable with the way mesh points blend.

FIGURE 5.10 **Smooth color transitions occur between mesh points.**

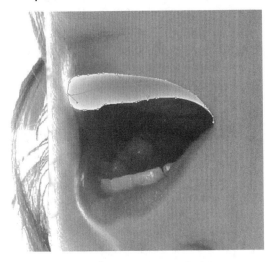

The further apart two mesh points are, the more subtle their color blending.

Anchor points on the outside of your path have also been converted to mesh points capable of holding color. With our mesh thus far, each of the points you see can be colored differently to affect the entire mesh's flow of color. Had we entered 1 for the columns and 1 for the rows in the Creative Gradient Mesh dialog, we would still have a paintable gradient mesh, just without the mesh lines in the middle.

7. Once again, like anchor points, you may select mesh points one at a time by clicking on them with the Direct Selection tool or Mesh tool (we're getting to that). You may also select multiple mesh points at once by dragging a selection area rectangle around one or more points with the Direct Selection tool or by using the Direct Selection Lasso, which enables you to draw an irregularly shaped selection area to highlight or select any choice of points (anchor or mesh). After you've selected multiple mesh points, you may color them simultaneously with a single swatch click. Give it a try by using the Direct Selection Lasso to wrangle all the mesh points on one side of your mesh object. Then pick a swatch to color them all instantly.

8. As you may have noticed, the blending between colors has something to do with the angle and curvature of the mesh lines. If you did notice, give yourself a pat on the back for being so astute. Mesh lines control the four primary directionals (up, down, left, and right) as well as the angle and curvature of the diagonals. Each mesh point has curve handles that, just like anchor point curve handles, affect the angle and curvature of mesh lines attached to the mesh point.

Curve handles on mesh points behave exactly like their counterparts on anchor points. They can be manipulated with the Direct Selection tool to change their curvature and depth, and they can be decoupled—so manipulating the mesh line on one side of a mesh point is independent of the mesh line on the other—by using the Convert Anchor Point tool directly on the curve handle itself. Switch to the Convert Anchor Point tool by pressing Shift+C and releasing. Now drag a curve handle to change the curvature of one of the segments (see Figure 5.11).

FIGURE 5.11 Mesh line
segments can be manipulated
independently with the Convert
Anchor Point tool.

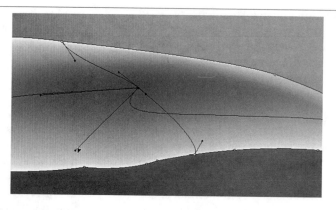

9. Mesh patches are delineated by the mesh lines and formed by mesh points. Mesh patches are what fill with color and, because they are effectively only fill areas, they cannot be altered directly. In Outline mode you can't even see them, but in Preview mode clicking on a mesh patch with the Direct Selection tool will select all the mesh points defining it, thus enabling you to color all the points simultaneously and create a large area of color. Switch over to the Preview window and click on a patch with the Direct Selection tool. Now choose a color swatch. See the result? This is a time-saving way to fill in large areas of color. Even if only the majority of the mesh points bordering a mesh patch are to receive the same color, I often use this method. After all, it's faster to color the majority at once and change the exceptions than to select and color every one separately.

10. Clicking and dragging a mesh patch with the Direct Selection tool will move the patch intact, causing any connected mesh lines and mesh points to accommodate. Of course, this only works in Preview mode. Give it a try!

11. If any of your mesh lines have kinks, immutable curves, or even loops (see Figure 5.12), it can ruin your whole mesh painting—and leave you incredibly frustrated. It's very common, especially with asymmetrical or odd shapes. Almost as common is the confusion and frustration associated with it. Fortunately, the reason such things happen is logical (the mesh line is following the contours of the path), and the way to fix it is easy—when you know the buried secret.

FIGURE 5.12 Sometimes, being kinky can ruin your whole day. Fortunately it's an easy fix.

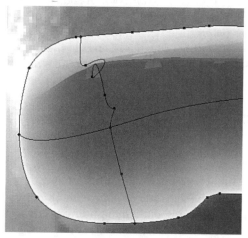

If you don't have a kink, loop, or weird curve now, come back to this part when you do. Leave yourself a sticky note if need be, 'cause, man, dealing with one of those in a mesh will seriously tick you off.

All of a path's secrets are revealed when the Direct Selection tool is active, right? Right—all except the secret kinks of mesh lines. They're hidden from the Direct Selection tool as well as the Pen, Selection, and even Mesh tools. Only seemingly unlikely tools like the Liquefy (Warp, Pucker, Bloat, Crystallize, and so on) and Add and Delete Anchor Point tools will reveal that kinks and so on in mesh lines are really caused by anchor points in the mesh lines. Therefore, if you have a kink, press the minus key on your keyboard to activate the Delete Anchor Point tool. With that tool, you can see the mesh line's points, and delete them if desired. Or you can hold the (Cmd) [Ctrl] key on your keyboard to temporarily switch to the Direct Selection (without turning the anchor points invisible again), and modify the point.

Add Anchor Point of course allows you to insert additional points for any level of control over a mesh line, whether interior to the mesh object or along its perimeter. Take note, however, that these points cannot be colored.

12. Although the Mesh tool may appear to be the tool for everything to do with meshes, it is actually only a part of the process. With it you may select mesh points to color or move them, add or remove mesh points (and corresponding mesh lines), and work with curve handles. Still, you'll find yourself using the Direct Selection tool at least as often as the Mesh tool.

The Mesh tool is how you add additional mesh points and mesh lines, and it's the other way to turn a path into a mesh object. In Outline mode, you may only add new mesh points (with corresponding lines) by clicking on an existing mesh line. Find a place in your mesh where you would like to initiate a new color for blending, and then, with the Mesh tool, click on the closest mesh line. It will create new mesh lines perpendicular to the source line and new mesh patches to match (see Figure 5.13).

Switching for a moment over to the Preview window, click with the Mesh tool on a mesh patch, *away* from a mesh line. New mesh lines are created both horizontally *and* vertically. Because mesh patches are invisible in Outline mode, this only works in Preview (but does work in Pixel and Overprint preview modes).

To remove a mesh point, hold (Opt) [Alt] and click the point with the Mesh tool. Holding (Opt) [Alt] while clicking a mesh *line* with the Mesh tool removes only that line, not the intersecting mesh line as well.

13. The Mesh tool has a couple of other functions you can't get with the Direct Selection tool. Back in the Outline window, click and drag any mesh point. Notice how it moves, taking with it all four attached mesh lines? Undo with (Cmd-Z) [Ctrl+Z]. Now repeat the move procedure while holding the Shift key. This will slide the mesh point along the mesh line in the direction of travel instead of distorting the mesh line.

FIGURE 5.13 A new mesh point, with corresponding mesh lines, inserted with the Mesh tool.

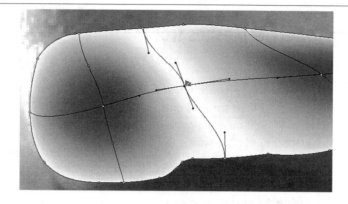

The other nifty function it has is the ability to twirl the mesh point. Select a mesh point with the Mesh tool. Now, while holding the Shift key, drag one of the mesh point's curve handles. Instead of altering the curves of the corresponding mesh line, the mesh point rotates, twirling all four mesh lines.

14. Because color flows smoothly between mesh points, hard transitions may seem difficult. (This one is both a how-to and a gotcha, so read carefully.) If you need a sharp line of color inside a mesh—or if you have one and can't figure out how to get rid of it—the way is through very close or overlapping mesh lines.

Create a new mesh point with the Mesh tool and assign it a contrasting color. Then drag one of the curve handles until you've forced one mesh line to overlap another (see Figure 5.14). When working with odd shapes and adjacent mesh lines, accidental overlap can easily create hard lines or even blotches or holes of color (or the absence of color) where smooth transitions are wanted.

FIGURE 5.14 An overlapping mesh line can create interesting—or undesirable—effects.

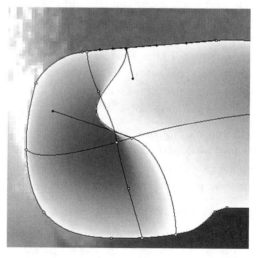

15. That's it for the introduction to working with gradient meshes. Now let's put that knowledge to good use coloring Allyson!

Unless you like what you ended up with, let's return your drawing to the pre-experimentation stage by choosing File > Revert.

STEP 5 ▼
Coloring Gradient Meshes from Photograph Colors

Now that you know how gradient meshes work, as well as some of their ins and outs, painting with them should be as enjoyable and relaxing as watching Bob Ross.

As with an oil painting, how you go about coloring a gradient mesh is different with every drawing. I could write detailed step-by-step instructions that walk you through creating an exact duplicate of my portrait of Allyson, but what good would it do? This is an intricate and involved illustration process; hopefully you're working with your own image. Even if you are working with the Allyson photo, you don't want to read pages of "apply this color to that mesh point" repeated over and over in numbered paragraphs.

Today, on the "Joy of Painting with Gradient Meshes" we'll go through a little of that, just enough for you to get the hang of it; then I'll leave you to paint your own masterpiece.

Let's make some happy little trees.

1. The key to successfully painting photo-realism is to—can you guess?—paint what you see, not what you think. A boon to working that way is to isolate—don't think of this as a portrait of a human being; think of it as areas of color you're trying to paint over. Toward that end, lock all the layers in the Layers palette except the Face layer. Because the face mesh is the background of the eyes, mouth, nose, and so on, we'll work **upward** from the face.

2. In the Outline mode window, zoom in or out until you can see the entire face path, and then select it with the Direct Selection tool. Convert it to a gradient mesh with Object > Create Gradient mesh; set a minimal number of columns and rows, such as 2 or 3 each. All your mesh points should be selected (hint: they're solid, not hollow, when selected). If not, drag around the face with the Direct Selection tool to select them all.

3. Grab the Eyedropper tool from the Tools palette. Look over the face and find an area that defines the predominant color in the rest of the face (in Allyson's case I'd probably go with the median shades that appear in the forehead, cheek, or chin). Click on one of those areas.

Nothing happened, right? Of course not—you're in Outline mode. Check the preview window. The whole face mesh should have filled with the selected color. Starting with all mesh points filled with the dominant color will not only save you time filling mesh points that should be that color, but it will also help other tones blend more believably—making your progress easier to gauge.

> ## ✖ NOTE
>
> Using the Eyedropper tool in Outline mode is the most effective technique to gradient mesh coloring. With it, you can click directly beside a selected mesh point to pick up the corresponding color of the image. Trying to do this in Preview mode is an exercise in futility.

4. If you didn't get quite the color you wanted, double-click on the Eyedropper tool on the Tools palette. In the Eyedropper Options dialog you can choose what attributes the tool picks up from other objects and what it applies to selected objects. This will come in handy with your other projects, but for painting gradient meshes all we really need the Eyedropper to pick up is Appearance > Focal Fill > Color, which should already be checked.

The reason for this trip into the Eyedropper Options is that easily overlooked drop-down box in the bottom-left, the Raster Sample Size. You have three options: Point Sample will pick up (and subsequently apply) only the color of the pixel directly beneath the Eyedropper cursor when you click; 3 × 3 Average will average together the color values of the pixel you click on plus the 8 pixels surrounding it on all sides (3 × 3 = 9); and 5 × 5 Average does the same thing, with a larger sample area (see Figure 5.15).

If you zoomed in very close on the photograph you'd see that each area is not a smooth color. There's plenty of *noise* there. Moreover, none of the noise pixels is actually the hue we would choose for Allyson's flesh. As with the red, green, and blue phosphors of a computer monitor or TV screen, our eyes blend the different colored pixels together to form an average hue. Therefore, using the Eyedropper tool in Point Sample mode is almost useless in this type of work. Whether you choose 3 × 3 Average or 5 × 5 Average depends on your particular photo, the area you're working on, and the colors in that area.

Be prepared to change the Raster Sample Size frequently as you work. Try 3 × 3 mode to choose the dominant color again. How did it work? See if 5 × 5 gives you a better or different result.

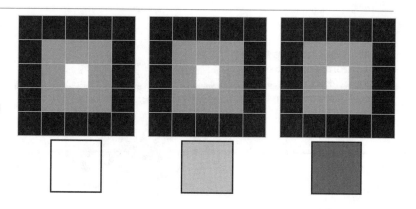

FIGURE 5.15 Clicking the Eyedropper tool on the center pixel in each of these blocks—raster sample size set to Single Pixel (left), 3 × 3 Average (center), and 5 ×5 Average (right)—will yield the shades in the lower squares.

Still not perfect? Click in a slightly different area. Remember, either of the average settings will mix the colors of the one pixel you click on, as well as those surrounding it. Sometimes clicking just one or two pixels away will yield very different results.

5. Let's isolate our attention even further. Zoom in on the chin until you can only see from the bottom lip downward (or upward, because we're working with an upside-down picture).

6. Examine the chin area. Everywhere there's a pronounced change in color— for example, where the highlight meets the mid-tone flesh hue along her chin— create a new mesh line with the Mesh tool. Remember that colors flow smoothly between mesh points and mesh lines. Don't divide the mesh for each shade; rather, insert a mesh point at the beginning and another at the end of blended areas. For example, in Figure 5.16, I've inserted a mesh line in the darkest part of the shadow under

Allyson's lower lip, and another at the top of her chin, where a completely new color begins. Between them the gradient mesh automatically fills in the subtle shades.

7. Using the tools and techniques you learned in the "Creating, Coloring, and Modifying Gradient Meshes" step, adjust the position, angle, and curvature of mesh points to manipulate the mesh lines to flow along with the colors in the photograph.

8. Deselect any undesired points, and, one or a few at a time, select the mesh points to be colored. Then, with the Eyedropper tool, click just beside the selected point(s) to pick up the color of the underlying photograph. Click as close as possible to the mesh point without clicking directly on it because that will grab the blue, red, or other color Illustrator uses to show you the points (that's the color assigned to the layer, by the way).

FIGURE 5.16 Mesh lines define the start and end colors for the shadow blending beneath her lip (left), and the gradient mesh fills in the intervening tones (right), creating a realistically subtle transition of color.

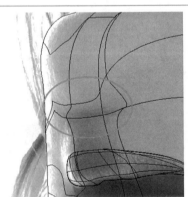

TIP

New mesh points automatically inherit the color of their location. For example, creating a new mesh point midway between a point filled with black and one filled with white will create a gray (50% black) mesh point. This behavior is extremely useful, and can be used to great effect with a little strategic thinking.

9. With one eye always in the Preview window, and working in isolated sections, color the rest of the face mesh, and then move on to the other mesh objects. Remember to lock each object as you finish with it.

Use the Monster Mesh file to help you, and, of course, feel free to examine my handiwork in the Portrait.ai file in this chapter's resource files. If you do use my drawing as a guide, view isolated areas—looking at a gradient mesh drawing this complex as a whole can be intimidating. If you look at each section (like the chin, an eye, the lips, and so on), however, the drawing can answer many questions for you.

Note that it's highly unlikely that your drawing will look photo-realistic when zoomed in. It's not meant to. Zoom out, to 100% at most, to see the realism. Figure 5.17 shows my progress on Allyson so far.

Remember, draw what you see (accept the color the Eyedropper gives you) not what you think (the color should be).

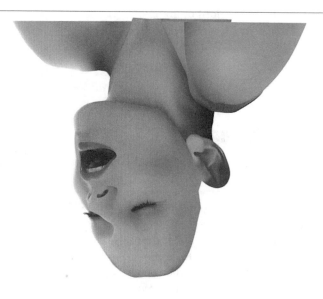

FIGURE 5.17 My gradient mesh illustration so far.

Live Trace the Hair

It certainly *is* possible to draw Allyson's hair by hand, but c'mon—do you *really* want to? Just look at all those strands, the hard lines between them, the colors and tones within them… Drawing her face (and all its features), neck, and shoulders in gradient meshes took me around 20 hours. Re-creating her hair by hand in vector paths would take at least three times as long. Fortunately, there's another way.

Illustrator CS2 introduces to the world's greatest vector drawing application Live Trace, a native, automated tracing technology previously available only in external programs. If you remember the Adobe Streamline application, which stopped production after the 1997 release of version 4 (but which continues to sell well today), you will feel right at home in Illustrator's Live Trace. Live Trace is, with some seriously cool improvements, the Streamline tracing engine.

STEP 6 ▼
Preparing for Tracing

An ounce of Photoshop is worth a pound of antacids.

1. Because we want to trace only Allyson's hair and eyebrows, we need a copy of her photograph showing only her hair and eyebrows (see Figure 5.18). Bring your photo into Photoshop and erase or mask out (with a layer mask) the areas you intend to draw as gradient meshes. Leave only the hair or other area to be traced. Save a *copy* of the photo from Photoshop's File menu with the Save As command and select the As A Copy

checkbox. When saving the copy, make the format Photoshop (*.PSD, *.PDD), which will preserve the transparency for Illustrator. If you don't have Photoshop, see the "Raster Masking without Photoshop" sidebar.

FIGURE 5.18 Allyson's hair and eyebrows only.

If you're following along with this chapter's resource files, I've already done the masking work in Chap05\Assets\Model's Hair.psd.

2. Save your drawing and lock all of its layers. Duplicate your **Photo** layer by dragging and dropping it atop the Create New Layer button at the bottom of the Layers palette. Drag the duplicate layer to the top of Layers palette, above all other layers.

3. Double-click the duplicate layer to access the Layer Options dialog. There, rename it to **Hair** and unlock it. Click OK.

When you click Place, your existing photograph should be replaced with the new one. If you don't see it in your main document, switch to Preview mode.

6. If necessary, move the new image until it lines up perfectly with the previous one on the locked layer (hide the gradient mesh layers if needed). Save your document.

STEP 7 ▼
Live Tracing the Hair

We'll now do in 30 seconds (well, 10 minutes because you have to read while you do it) what it took weeks to do before Illustrator CS2.

1. **Live Trace** Select the hair (or other image to be traced) with the Selection tool. Doing so will reveal the Trace button on the Control palette (by default docked to the top of the screen just below the menu bar). It appears whenever a placed image is

4. Back on the artboard, select the photograph with the Selection tool. Choose File > Place.

5. Navigate to the location of the image isolating the area(s) for tracing (**Chap05\Assets\Model's Hair.psd** if you're using the resource files). Before clicking the Place button, ensure that both the Link and Replace options are checked.

selected. Clicking the Live Trace button will perform an instant trace utilizing the last used settings—which we haven't set yet, so don't click the Live Trace button. Instead, click the black arrow to its right—the Tracing Presets and Options button—and choose 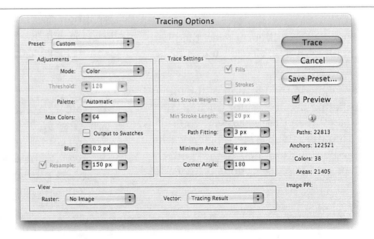 Tracing Options from the pop-up menu.

2. With all of its measurement boxes and sliders, the Tracing Options dialog may look intimidating (see Figure 5.19). Don't let it frighten you. When you start playing, it becomes a lot of fun. On the Presets menu choose any item. Now turn on Preview (far right). See what it's doing? Try a different preset.

Watch the different settings change and try to see in the tracing preview what they mean, how different Max Stroke Weight or Minimum Area settings affect the tracing and the info on the right—the number of paths, anchors, and areas. Configure the View section to Original Image and Outlines to see the raster image overlaid with the trace. Here's what all of those boxes, menus, and checkboxes mean:

▶ **Mode**—The color mode of the desired tracing—color, grayscale, or black and white. All other options in the Adjustments section (and some in the Trace Settings section) are enabled or disabled depending on the mode.

▶ **Threshold**—Available only in Black and White mode, Threshold determines the maximum range of tonal value to remain white before converting to black. Pixels with tonal values lighter than the threshold will be white; higher values will become black.

▶ **Palette**—Available in Color or Grayscale mode. These are the colors Illustrator will use for filling or stroking paths created by Live Trace. Automatic, which gives Illustrator full reign over color choices within the document's color mode, is the only option available unless other swatch libraries (for example, Pantone Process Coated) are opened prior to initiating a Live Trace.

FIGURE 5.19   **The Tracing Options dialog.**

- **Max Colors**—Available in Color or Grayscale mode. Limits the maximum number of colors Illustrator may use when tracing. More colors create more detail and depth at the expense of more paths, creating a more complicated tracing.

- **Output to Swatches**—Available in Color or Grayscale mode. This option creates swatches from the colors Live Trace uses in tracing the image.

> ◎ **TIP**
>
> Here's an immensely useful trick: When you need Illustrator color swatches from a raster image, don't make them manually with the Eyedropper tool. Instead, Live Trace the image and check Output to Swatches. The colors in the image will be added to the document's Swatches palette. Then just delete the traced image—the swatches will remain.

- **Blur**—This is the amount of blurring to be applied to the *image* prior to tracing. Higher values make tracing easier, and often eliminate noise and artifacts in the photo.

- **Resample**—Available only on embedded images, Resample will change the resolution of the source image prior to tracing.

- **Fills**—Determines whether to fill traced paths.

- **Strokes**—Determines whether to stroke traced paths.

- **Max Stroke Weight**—If Strokes is checked, this determines the maximum weight of strokes in traced paths before they are converted to fills or to separate objects.

- **Min Stroke Length**—Also dependent on Strokes being checked, this setting determines the shortest allowable stroke. Higher values equal fewer paths but less detail.

- **Path Fitting**—The measurement here is how closely the traced vector paths should follow the pixels of the image—within how many pixels. In other words, if the setting is 2px, a traced path will jump over single pixel indents in a color but follow the contour of an indent 2 or more pixels in depth, width, or height.

- **Minimum Area**—Similar to Path Fitting, Minimum Area defines not how closely the path follows contours, but rather the smallest color area in pixels to draw as a path. With the default setting of 10 px, any area of the raster image smaller than 10 pixels will be incorporated into a larger path.

- **Corner Angle**—By default, Live Trace attempts to create smooth points (curves); this setting specifies the angle threshold of smooth points before they must be converted to corner points.

- **Raster**—Whether and how the original raster image should be made visible after tracing.

- **Vector**—Whether and how the vector paths resulting from the trace should be made visible after the tracing.

When Preview is checked, the Live Trace information section on the bottom right propagates with facts about the traced drawing—how many paths, anchors, colors, and areas result. And, of course, any changes you make cause the trace to update.

 TIP

If you create custom Live Trace options that you may use again, save a preset that can be instantly applied from the Control palette's Tracing Presets and Options button without even entering the Tracing Options dialog.

3. Start with a preset. What kind of image are you tracing? Is it a photograph with low detail or a lot of detail? Is it a hand-drawn illustration? A black-and-white line drawing like a logo or blueprint? Choose the preset most like your particular image; then customize from there. If you're working with the Model's Hair.psd file, start with the Photo High Fidelity preset and customize to taste.

How close to the original are you able to get? Table 5.1 shows my settings.

TABLE 5.1 Tracing Options Settings

Adjustments		Trace Settings	
Mode:	Color	Fills:	on
Threshold:	[disabled]	Strokes:	[disabled]
Palette:	Automatic	Max Stroke Weight:	[disabled]
Max Colors:	128	Min Stroke Length:	[disabled]
Output to Swatches:	Off	Path Fitting:	3 px
Blur:	0.2 px	Minimum Area:	4 px
Resample:	72 px	Corner Angle:	180°

In the View section, set Raster to No Image and Vector to Tracing Result.

4. When ready, click the Trace button and check out your new tracing. The original image will disappear, leaving only the tracing, which should look something like mine (see Figure 5.20).

  If you care to see the original image again, look to the Control palette. The upward-pointing solid triangle is your original image view settings, and the hollow triangle is the trace view settings. Set the one to Original Image and the other to Outlines. Remember to set them back to No Image and Tracing Result, respectively, before moving on.

FIGURE 5.20   Traced hair.

STEP 8 ▼
Converting the Live Trace to Editable Paths

Live Trace did a good job of drawing the hair and eyebrows, but it also filled in the empty areas with white. We need to fix that.

1. The "live" part of Live Trace comes from the fact that the trace is not committed to immutable paths; editing the Live Trace options or even updating the linked image or exchanging it for another will cause Illustrator to retrace dynamically. To edit the individual paths we must first *un*-live the trace.

 TIP

After tracing, choose Object > Live Trace > Tracing Options to access and change the tracing options again.

Set the raster preview mode (via the solid triangle on the Control palette) to Transparent Image. Then choose Object > Live Trace > Expand As Viewed, which converts the Live Trace to paths we can work with as well as leaving a template of the raster image beneath.

Back on the Object menu choose Ungroup. This separates the traced paths from the original image. Click Ungroup once more to give us direct access to the traced paths. Deselect all.

2. With the Selection tool, click once in the white area of the background or Allyson's face to select it. Now delete it. You should be left with the other paths intact. You might also have other white or background color paths (see Figure 5.21); they must also go.

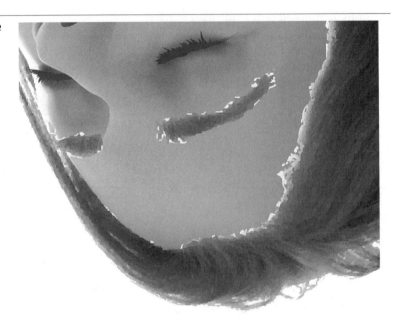

3. Select one of the white bits, and then choose Select > Same > Fill Color. Now *all* the paths filled with white are selected simultaneously. Press the Delete key. Tell me *that* isn't neato mosquito!

 NOTE

If you see white gaps between colored paths only at certain zoom levels, ignore them. They're screen arti-facts that don't really exist. They won't print or export.

4. At this stage it's all about cleanup.

   Eliminate any other paths that, like the white, don't belong in the final drawing. Select and delete (or lock if you want to keep it around for the time being) your original raster image—you may find it easier to expand the **Hair** layer and delete (or lock) the Model's **Hair** (raster image) sublayer at the very bottom.

If you want to change the tint of Allyson's hair—maybe to give her a dye job or just highlights—select each of the colors to change one by one, employing the Select > Same > Fill Color command to select all instances of the color. Then use the Filters > Colors menu commands or the Colors or Swatches palettes to change or adjust the fill of those areas.

 TIP

Saturate and desaturate colors by holding Shift while moving any slider in the Colors palette. This moves all the sliders proportionally at once until any one color slider reaches an end.

Use the Direct Selection tool and other path editing tools to modify paths as needed, and, if you find areas better suited to gradient meshes than multiple paths, convert them. Just Shift-select all the paths that make up the area for the gradient mesh, and, on the Pathfinder palette, Opt-click (Alt-click) the Add to Shape Area button. This will create one merged path from the individual paths, which can then be turned into a mesh object.

Figure 5.22 shows my finished portrait of Allyson.

Final Thoughts

If you're saying to yourself, hey, why not just Live Trace the whole portrait and be done with it? Sure, that's an option—a good one for some photos. But, before you make that decision, try it in a new document. Live Trace, and then click the Expand button. Notice how the whole thing is obscured by colored anchor points? Open the Document Info palette from the Window menu. From that palette's flyout menu, select Objects and Selection Only. Your results may differ

slightly, but when I use the same settings I applied to the hair on the entire Model.psd, my Document Info palette tells me the trace result contains 18,566 closed paths, 98,090 anchor points, and 367 compound paths. I *dare* you to try printing something that complex. After about an hour of chewing your printer will come back with a "no freakin' way, man" error message.

Your service bureau's RIP would do the same.

Using Live Trace to create photo-realistic vector is a trade-off. Yes, it can be done. Yes, it can yield great results. However, with detailed images the result is thousands of paths and tens of thousands of anchor points, generating an extremely complex document that will tax the memory of just about any output device. By contrast, using gradient meshes for the bulk of the drawing creates much less work for the output device, and generally creates better, more realistic artwork.

FIGURE 5.22 **The finished portrait, with traced hair and all other parts created with gradient meshes.**

Live Trace, when used judiciously, is a valuable addition to an illustrator's toolbox. It is not, however, a substitute for talent and skill.

If your document is still too complex to print—which is not terribly unusual—use it as a master plate for rasters instead of trying to print the vector document directly. For each printed project to be created from your artwork—Allyson's t-shirts, posters, and temporary tattoos, for example—scale the original vector artwork (or a temporary copy to be safe) in Illustrator to the desired dimensions. Then use the Object > Rasterize command to rasterize that particular instance of the drawing at the required resolution. Export it to a raster format like PSD, TIFF, or PDF, and send it to press. In such a workflow, you needn't worry about RIP or printing time—or clogging or choking an output device—while retaining the freedom and resolution-independence inherent in the vector artwork.

In the "Live Trace the Hair" section is a tip about automatically creating Illustrator swatches from the colors in any raster image. *It's not just for Illustrator.* Because Illustrator CS2 can create swatch libraries for use in Photoshop, InDesign, and other CS2 products, use Illustrator as the intermediary to create swatches from and for *any* application and any document—even an InDesign layout exported to TIFF, PDF, or another format Illustrator will place! When you have

the swatches created, just choose Save Swatches for Exchange from Illustrator's Swatches flyout menu. The resulting swatch exchange file can be loaded into the Swatches palette of any CS2 application.

Add a background to your artwork. In Allyson's case, the record label wanted to let its graphic artists insert media-specific backgrounds, so our job is done. Working with your own illustration, however, you will most likely want to insert some kind of background—even a subtle gradient—to give your illustration context. That's another golden rule from art class: never leave the background white.

Incidentally, I have no idea if the model's name is really Allyson. Giving her a name seemed more respectful and more eloquent than simply referring to her as "the pretty singing woman with nice teeth."

If you want people to think you drew it from scratch, leaving the photo in will blow the ruse; delete it. *Then* you can tell people that you drew this portrait all by yourself, from your imagination, with neither a photo nor a sitting model to look at. If you want to spite your art school teachers who snidely proclaimed that you'd never amount to anything, say that you drew your gradient mesh portrait from what you *thought* instead of what you saw (or just write a book and dedicate it to those naysayer art school teachers, as this one is).

CHAPTER 6: Designing Product Packaging

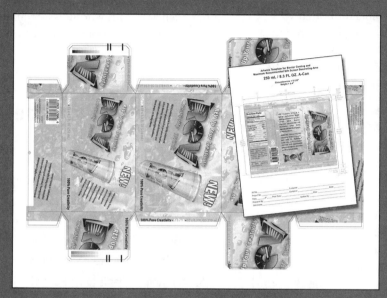

About the Projects

While you're designing the labeling for a liquid container and an exploded box, you will learn to work with press-ready packaging templates. You will work heavily with clipping masks, and learn a bit about the legal considerations of packaging design.

Prerequisites

It would be helpful if you had a basic operational knowledge of selecting and modifying paths with the Selection, Direct Selection, and Pen tools. You should have the ability to draw basic shapes with the Pen and Rectangle tools, be able to set and change fills, strokes, type, and type-styling options, and open swatches from other Adobe Illustrator documents.

@work resources

Please visit the publisher's website to access the following Chapter 6 project files:

- ▶ Chap06 (Can Label.ai, 12-pack case.ai, template-250mL Can.ait)
- ▶ Chap06\Assets (Logo.ai, bg_box.tif, bg_can.pdf, barcode.eps, Recycle Logo Circle.ai, Drink Can.psd)
- ▶ Chap06\Finished Project

Planning the Projects

Packaging is not merely about designing a label. It entails choosing the right container materials, selecting a container type and shape, and picking colors that often vary from ink colors. Of course, packaging must also clearly communicate vital and often regulated information—particularly if the container holds food or hygiene products.

What sort of container or package is right for your—or your client's—product? *Look around.* There are thousands of types of bottles, boxes, cans, tubes, vials, bags, and so on available to you. Thumb through manufacturers' catalogs, investigate materials, and scope out the competition. A good package designer typically spends the bulk of her time roaming store aisles and scrutinizing retail catalogs, whether examining what her client's competition is up to, or on the prowl for fresh ideas. In such a designer's studio are shelves filled with products she bought but never used. Boxes in the corner overflow with container samples.

What material is right for your product container? Is the product corrosive to metal? Will the plastic tube need to be lined? Is tamper-proofing necessary?

The printing process differs between the various types of packages and their materials. Adhesive labels generally are printed on an offset press, affording very high resolution and special processes such as *varnishing* or *foil stamping*. Some types of packages, like cans and tubes, are screen-printed—a medium-resolution process. Still others require very low-resolution stamping. Whichever process your package uses will determine the detail possible in your design.

Usually product packaging is regulated by a governing body; in the U.S., the agency that oversees all consumable and topical products is the Food and Drug Administration. Other types of products fall under the purview of other agencies. With what laws, regulations, and guidelines must your design comply?

Project:
Wrap-Around Can Label

We'll create a wrap-around can label in seven easy steps:

1. **Opening and understanding a packaging template**
2. **Placing and masking images**
3. **Setting type with paragraph styles**
4. **Setting type with character styles**
5. **Applying gradients to type and stroking outside the path only**
6. **Repeating formatting with object styles**
7. **Setting tabs while building the required nutrition facts box**

Designing a Wrap-Around Can Label

REV is a creativity-enhancing drink marketed toward creative professionals under the tagline "REV Up Your Creativity." Armed with a logo and corporate identity material, and with promotional items already sent to the manufacturers, the client now needs a container for the REV drink.

Rather than differentiate themselves with a new container shape and risk the market misperceiving the function of the product, the client has chosen to can their beverage in the 250 mL/8.3 oz. aluminum cans that have become a hallmark of energy drinks. Because the container itself won't be distinctive among the competition, the client is counting on us to design a label that grabs attention, effectively communicates their brand, and inspires consumers to choose it over the other energy drinks in the cooler. Of course, it must also comply with FDA regulations for such products.

The production team at the outsourced canning plant has just sent over the template we need, so let's get to work.

STEP 1 ▼
Opening and Understanding a Packaging Template

If this is your first time designing packaging, it's worth taking a moment to examine and understand a typical package template.

1. Choose File > New From Template, and navigate to where you saved the Chapter 6 resource files. Select Template-250mL Can.ait. Because this file is an Illustrator CS2 template file rather than a document, Illustrator will not open it directly; instead it will open a *copy* of it as a new document, leaving the original absolutely safe from accidental changes.

> ### ◎ TIP
> To edit an Illustrator template, open it via File > Open, make your changes, and Save. With templates, Illustrator will force you to perform a Save As, so just overwrite the original.

2. You should now see a template similar to any you might receive from a manufacturer (see Figure 6.1). Because this particular one is a can template, it has a single continuous artwork area and

relatively few markups. Other containers' templates—heat-sealed tubes common in cosmetic or hygiene products, for example—are somewhat more complicated in that they have more production marks and notes, front and back panel areas, and more non-artwork areas (for example, the shoulder that tapers into the cap, the heat-seal area, and so on).

FIGURE 6.1 A blank template typical of cans, bottles, and similar containers.

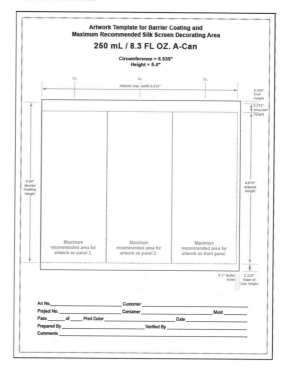

3. Palm-sized energy drink cans have seal rings where the cap attaches, a slightly tapered shoulder beneath and leading into the seal, long narrow bodies, and, finally, tapered bases. Due to the characteristics of printing and manufacturing of such containers, seals and bases are generally unprintable, and shoulders are difficult to decorate. Depending on the container and the labeling

process, they often can be printed, but avoid putting critical information there. For that reason, correctly produced templates will indicate the recommended areas for artwork. In this case, that is the 6.435 × 4.815-in. area suggested by the arrows.

4. Because this is a tall, slender, cylindrical can, its artwork will wrap sharply. The manufacturer (in this case, me) has courteously divided the label into dotted-line panels (aren't I nice?) to help the designer (you) build an optimized design that doesn't force the consumer to rotate the can in order to read left-to-right copy. Readability of— and consumer interest in—the product is negatively impacted if she has to turn a container to read its label. The "CL" notations indicate the centerlines of the panels.

> ◎ **TIP**
>
> Most manufacturers will provide templates in either EPS or PDF format, making them accessible to many applications, including Illustrator.

5. On the Layers palette you will notice a locked **250 mL template** layer and the currently selected **Artwork** layer. As long as you don't unlock the lower layer, and your artwork stays within the indicated area, you can't make a grievous mistake.

STEP 2 ▼
Placing and Masking Images

Stop me if you've heard this one: A monotone PDF, a vector logo, and a barcode walk into a layout...

1. Draw a box that outlines the combined artwork and shoulder areas with the Rectangle tool.

2. From the File menu, choose Place and import the monotone bg_can.pdf file from the Assets folder in this chapter's resource files. When the Place PDF dialog comes up, crop to Art.

3. The image will be too big, so scale it down to fit the label without distortion or leaving any part of the box you drew visible—hold Shift as you drag to constrain the proportions of scaling.

4. Send the image behind the box by pressing Cmd-[(Ctrl+[), and then, with the Selection tool, Shift-click the box. You should now have selected both the box and the background image.

5. Select Object > Clipping Mask > Make. Any overhang on the image should disappear, clipping it to fit within the artwork and shoulder area—though the bounding box of the full-sized image will still be accessible should you need to manipulate it (see Figure 6.2). Lock the background image with (Cmd-2) [Ctrl+2].

6. Now place the REV logo (logo.ai), barcode (barcode.eps), and the recycle logo (Recycle Logo Circle.ai). Position those as you see fit.

7. It might help to hide the background image so you can see the template beneath. To do that, click the arrow beside the **Artwork** layer in the Layers palette, which reveals the content of the layer as individual entries. Using the thumbnails, locate the background image—it will be titled <Group>—and hide it by clicking its eyeball icon.

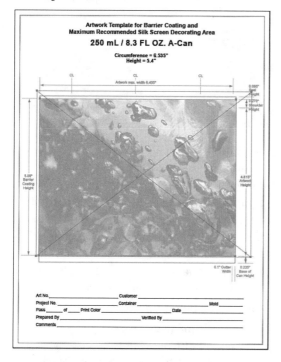

Artwork Template for Barrier Coating and
Maximum Recommended Silk Screen Decorating Area

250 mL / 8.3 FL OZ. A-Can

Circumference = 6.535"
Height = 5.4"

Art No._____ Customer_____
Project No._____ Container_____ Mold_____
Pass____ of____ Print Color_____ Date_____
Prepared By_____ Verified By_____
Comments_____

  TIP

Check out Appendix B, "Resources," for pointers to barcode fonts and barcode generators.

STEP 3 ▼
Setting Type with Paragraph Styles

Working efficiently is all about reducing repetitive tasks. Whenever possible, automate repetitive tasks. Clicking fewer menus, tools, and palette options will save your wrist from carpal tunnel syndrome and your artistic mind from Repetitive Brain Stress Injury. You won't find that one in a medical dictionary;

it's a term I coined to describe how mind-numbing it is working without styles (aka style sheets), symbols, defaults, and other automation or reuse tools. Let me help you fend off Repetitive Brain Stress Injury.

1. With the Text tool, click and drag out a rectangle to define your first area of text—the marketing copy on the back of the can. Don't merely click—click and drag, or you'll wind up with *point* text line, not a paragraph text *area* (also known as a text frame or text box, especially in layout software like InDesign or QuarkXPress).

2. Type, paste, or place your marketing copy in this new box—resize the box if needed.

3. Now style it however you like. Keep in mind this is a screen-printed can, so don't choose too delicate or small a typeface.

4. Open the Paragraph Styles palette (Window > Type > Paragraph Styles).

5. With your cursor still somewhere inside a paragraph of text, click the Create New Style button at the bottom of the palette. A new entry, Paragraph Style 1, should appear in the palette. Double-click it.

6. In the Paragraph Style Options dialog, give your style a name—something like **Copy** would be ideal. If you set all your character and paragraph level formatting, no other changes should be necessary here (see Figure 6.3). Just click OK.

  TIP

When building styles, give them descriptive names that will mean something to someone else who might work on your files—or to you if you have to go back to this design six months or a year down the road.

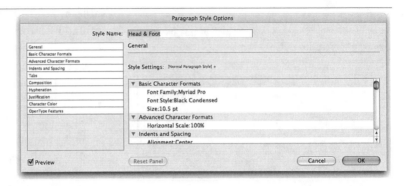

FIGURE 6.3 **Illustrator's Paragraph Style Options dialog—in this case showing a paragraph style we'll build in a moment.**

7. Highlight all the text in the marketing copy block and click on the Copy style entry in the Paragraph Style palette. Now all your text is tied to that style; any changes you make to the Copy style will automatically affect all the type assigned to it—automation and efficiency at its finest.

8. Set your ingredients list and other block copy following steps 1–7, creating or reusing paragraph styles for each block. Don't forget to save.

STEP 4 ▼
Setting Type with Character Styles

Paragraph styles apply to paragraph-level formatting—leading, indents, hyphenation, and so on. They also include character

formatting like typeface, styling, color, and so forth. But a paragraph style applies to all the words from the beginning of the paragraph until the end, until the invisible ¶. By contrast, a *character* style controls formatting of letters, numbers, and punctuation, individually, in whole words, or as far as you want. Character styles are a way to override a paragraph style without breaking the association to the paragraph style.

1. Find some place in your design where text of different colors or styles will appear on the same line. In my design I did this atop colored rectangles that wrap around the top and bottom of the can (see Figure 6.4). If you haven't already created such a text area, make one.

2. Set your type, style it with a *single* dominant style, and create a paragraph style from that. I named mine **Head & Foot**.

FIGURE 6.4 **The wraparound tri-tone text is colored by two character styles to override the paragraph style, which determines one color and all the other formatting.**

3. Now style the *exception* to the paragraph style. As you saw in Figure 6.4, I used two exceptions: My paragraph style is based on the green text, with the white text and black bullets overriding it. Highlight the overridden text, and open the Character Styles palette from Window > Type > Character Styles.

4. Just as you did when making a paragraph style, click the Create New Style button at the bottom of the palette. In the Character Style Options dialog, note that it looks very similar to its mother, the Paragraph Style Options dialog, but only contains a subset of the options there. Give your character style a name—setting a name based on the paragraph style name is usually the best practice. I chose **Head & Foot White** for white text in my Head & Foot paragraph style. Don't click OK.

5. Switching to the Basic Character Formats tab, reveals that the Font Family, Font Style, and so on are all filled in. We don't want them to be.

Character styles work because they override paragraph styles with *only* the formatting that must be different (in my case just color). Everything that is the same between them—for example, the Font Family, Size, Leading, and so on—should be left *out* of the character style definition. Otherwise, a change to a common setting like the typeface requires altering multiple styles, thus defeating the purpose of using them.

6. Click Reset Panel at the bottom. All the options should go blank (see Figure 6.5). To erase settings one at a time—such as when the override you want is on the current tab—either reset and then choose your override again, or highlight the content of a field and press Delete on your keyboard (this doesn't work in some fields, like Font Family and Font Style). When you've stripped out all the overrides you don't want, click OK.

7. Repeat the last two steps for any other character- or word-level overrides in your text. Save your document.

Now, if you need to change a common attribute of the entire paragraph—the tracking or typeface, for instance—change it just once in the paragraph style, which will automatically apply to all text assigned to that paragraph style, even if the text is also assigned to a character style. You can even apply a different paragraph style without losing the overrides created by the character styles. In Figure 6.6, you can see that the character styles kept the text white and black while accepting replacement of common attributes from the paragraph style, like the typeface and type style.

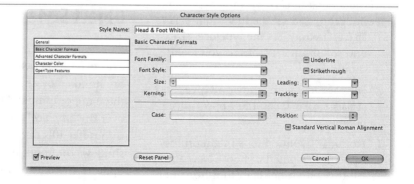

FIGURE 6.5 **Between the Basic and Advanced Character Formats tabs, all the options from the Character palette are available—but not mandatory—for character style definition.**

100% Pure Creativity • **Creativity Drink** • **100% Pure Creativity** • (

100% Pure Creativity • Creativity Drink • 100% Pu

STEP 5 ▼
Applying Gradients to Type and Stroking Outside the Path Only

Let's take a brief intermission from our crash course in reusable styles to dispel a couple of myths.

First, there are no alligators in the sewers. And, Elvis *is* dead; Jim Morrison, however, is not. Now then...

Among novice and intermediate Illustrator users are two unifying myths about, and complaints against, Illustrator: First, gradients cannot be applied to type without first converting the type to outlines. Second, though the Illustrator CS2 Stroke palette finally has buttons to control the placement of strokes relative to the path, they don't work on text; thus strokes will always fall half inside and half outside type.

Both are, of course, wrong. To paraphrase Copernicus, the world ain't flat, folks.

1. Make a new point text instance (remember to *click* with the Type tool, not drag) and set the REV tagline: **REV Up Your Creativity**. Set the typeface, size, and so on until it looks as you feel it should.

2. Fill your text with white and give it a **2 pt black** stroke. Open the Appearance palette.

3. From the flyout options menu on the Appearance palette, choose New Fill. Fill this with a gradient that transitions

evenly from white to DS 294-3 (from the `logo.ai` file in this chapter's resource files). Rotate the gradient **90°**. If your text is still white, drag the Characters entry in the Appearance palette beneath the Fill. Misconception number one dispelled.

4. Grab the Stroke entry in the Appearance palette and drag it beneath the Fill entry but above Characters. Misconception number two dispelled (see Figure 6.7).

FIGURE 6.7   See? A picture of the Appearance palette, with gradient-filled text and strokes only on the outside. Let's see photographic evidence of alligators in the sewers.

STEP 6 ▼
Repeating Formatting with Object Styles

Paragraph styles control text formatting. Character-level overrides to that formatting are handled by character styles. Adjunct to these are graphic styles, which hold domain over the *graphical* formatting and styling, things like fills and strokes, effects like drop shadows and path offsets, and transparency options. If your noodle is baking from all this talk of styles, take a break. Go out and get some sun; you spend too much time at the computer anyway.

When you're ready, let's learn how to reuse complicated graphical styling as easily as we reuse text formatting.

1. Select your tagline text object with the Selection tool, and open the Graphic Styles palette (Window > Graphic Styles).

2. Click the New Graphic Style button at the bottom of the palette, which should create a new green–white gradient thumbnail (see Figure 6.8).

FIGURE 6.8 The thumbnail in the Graphic Styles palette shows the appearance attributes defined within it.

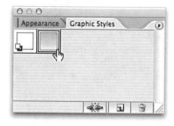

3. Create a new point text object and type in **Creativity Drink**. Set its text styling (not the fill or stroke) similar to the tagline, but maybe not as heavy (I used 21 pt Myriad Pro SemiExtended, while my tagline is 23 pt Myriad Pro Black Condensed).

4. With the text object selected, click on the new thumbnail in the Graphic Styles palette. Instant gradient fill, instant stroke. In fact, it has the exact same appearance as the tagline. Note, however, that the graphic style had no effect on the type style—which is, of course, handled by paragraph and character styles.

Try making a rectangle and applying the same graphic style. It works for every native Illustrator object, be it type, drawn object, or embedded image. Anything done to an object that creates an entry on the Appearance palette can be saved in—and applied by—graphic styles.

STEP 7 ▼
Setting Tabs While Building the Required Nutrition Facts Box

In the United States, the Federal Drug Administration (FDA) mandates the inclusion of a nutrition information block on the packaging for every edible manufactured product. Creating the nutrition label gives us the perfect opportunity to learn about setting tabs.

1. Create a new text area approximately **1.35 × 2.25 in.** to begin creating what the FDA officially calls a vertical label for packages with 40 square inches or less. If you are working with your own package design rather than the REV drink can, choose the FDA-approved nutrition label format appropriate for your package.

◎ TIP

See **http://www.fda.gov/ora/inspect_ref/igs/ nleaattb.html** for full specifications on the formats and content of nutrition labels, and the Resources section of this book for additional labeling resources.

2. Type in the label information, including required elements like the **Nutrition Facts** header, serving size, **Amount Per Serving**, number of calories, and so on.

If you are working through this chapter without an actual project, grab the nearest soda can, water bottle, candy bar, or bag of chips to use as a source. Don't worry about formatting the type just yet.

⊘ CAUTION

The information in this section is current as of this writing, but may be outdated at any moment. FDA regulations and requirements are in a constant state of change. In fact, as of the date of this writing, the FDA is actively seeking public commentary on how to improve the appearance and content of the nutrition label. Always consult the latest FDA bulletins before sending a packaging project to press.

3. The FDA regulates not only the content of the nutrition label, but the presentation of the content as well. It wouldn't do if some people couldn't read the information. So, set all your type at a minimum of **8 pt.** and build a paragraph style for it. **Amount Per Serving**, **% Daily Value**, caloric conversion footnote (if included), and Daily Value footnote (* **Percent Daily Values based on a 2,000 calorie diet**) may be as low as **6 pt.** Build new paragraph styles for these items.

The header, **Nutrition Facts**, must be bold and at least **8 pt** (10—12 pt is recommended).

4. Consult the FDA regulations about what must and can be bold, and build a character style whose only attribute is styling type bold, and use that to apply bold to the words that need it.

5. Insert tabs between the words and percentages of the core nutrients (calories, total fat, sodium, total carbohydrates, and protein) and vitamin and mineral information. Highlight all the

lines with tabs in them, and then open the Tabs palette (Window > Type > Tabs).

6. The Tabs palette will appear above your text area (see Figure 6.9). It is the width of the box, with the 0 point aligned to the text area's left edge. Conveniently, Illustrator allows setting tabs in the most intuitive manner possible—visually. Click the Right-Justified Tab button to select it, and then click once in the white area above the ruler. Your text should snap into place, with the percent symbols all lined up neatly. If they don't fall exactly where you want them, click on the tiny arrow you created and drag it into place.

◎ TIP

If you know the exact placement for the tab (for example, 1.5 inches from the left edge), click on the tab indicator to select it, and then type the coordinate in the X: box above the ruler.

FIGURE 6.9 Setting tabs is easy because the Tab Ruler appears above, and sized to fit, the text area.

7. With the Line tool, draw rules separating all the lines of text in your **Amount Per Serving**, nutrients, and vitamin and mineral sections. Each rule should be **0.5–2 pt** between items in the same section, and double-thick rules between sections.

 TIP

If you find the FDA documentation difficult to interpret, or it doesn't answer a specific question, talk to your package manufacturer or printer. They usually know the ins and outs of labeling requirements.

8. Finally, the nutrition label must be as visible and legible as possible, with a high contrast between its type and background. On dark backgrounds, the type may be reversed. If you use a background image on the package, as I did for the REV can, draw a white (or other contrasting color) box behind the nutrition label.

Project:
Exploded Six-Sided Box

In four easy steps we'll create a ready-for-production six-sided box:

1. Defining the box's panels
2. Shaping non-rectangular flaps
3. Creating bleed guides from the box panels
4. Laying out sectional box faces efficiently with symbols and clipping masks

Designing an Exploded Six-Sided Box Template

More common than any other type of packaging is the six-sided box. Nowadays everything comes in a box—even wine and brewed coffee—not just Cadillacs.

Therefore, we are going to design an *exploded* box—a folded and three-dimensional piece designed flat—which is how any folding or three-dimension project with two or more printed surfaces must be laid out. For four-dimensional packaging projects, please see *Time Warps @ Work: Projects You Already Did on the Job*, by H.G. Wells (Sams Publishing, 2525).

STEP 1 ▼
Defining the Box's Panels

Creating a box with six visible sides involves building more than six sides or panels. One box made from a single continuous piece of board or other *substrate* typically has at least a couple of folded (and possibly glued) flaps. The 12-pack of REV Creativity Drink we'll design in this step has 15 panels.

1. Begin a new CMYK document that is **26 × 18 in.** Title it **12-pack case**.

2. Draw 15 rectangles arranged in five columns and three rows (see Figure 6.10), and size them according to Table 6.1. It may help to number them as I have. If you do, place the numbers on their own layer so that their visibility can be toggled without hindering your work.

FIGURE 6.10   Refer to this
numbered panel arrangement as
you work through the next few
sections.

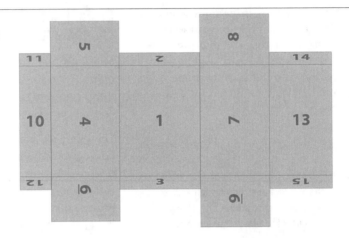

TABLE 6.1   Box Panel Measurements

Name	Panel	Width	Height	Angle
Top Face	1	6.50	8.65	0
Flap	2	6.50	1.00	180
Flap	3	6.50	1.00	0
Left Face	4	5.50	8.65	-90
Flap	5	5.50	3.50	-90
Flap	6	5.50	3.50	-90
Right Face	7	5.50	8.65	90
Flap	8	5.50	4.00	90
Flap	9	5.50	4.00	90
Bottom Face 1	10	2.50	8.65	0
Flap	11	2.50	1.00	0
Flap	12	2.50	1.00	180
Bottom Face 2	13	5.00	8.65	0
Flap	14	5.00	1.00	0
Flap	15	5.00	1.00	180

3. Utilizing the Selection tool and the Transform palette's X and Y coordinates and Reference Point proxy, make sure all panels are precisely positioned to begin where the previous one ends. For example: If the top-left corner of panel 1 is positioned at coordinates X: 8.4861 and Y: -4.675 in., the bottom-left

corner (not counting rotation) of panel 2 should also be at X: **8.4861** and Y:**-4.675 in.**

 TIP

Several panels can be positioned at once. First, align the bottom edges of all panels in the top row. Then, if the top of panel 1 sits at the **-4.675** Y-coordinate, select panels 11, 5, 2, 8, and 14, and simultaneously set their common bottom reference point to Y: -4.675. The same can be done for the bottom row, and each column of panels.

4. If you numbered your panels, rotate the numbers to indicate the way artwork will need to be angled to assemble correctly. Select the number and use the Rotate box on the Transform palette. Refer to Table 6.1 for the required angles.

TIP

To rotate multiple objects at once all in place (without rotating them as a group), select the objects to be rotated and go to Object > Transform > Transform Each.

5. Select all objects in the layout—panels and numbers—and on the Transform palette, set the whole aggregate center point to the center of the paper—X: **13 in.** and Y: **-9 in.** Lock the numbers layers for safety.

If you've lost as many design hours due to inadequate safety practices as I have (earlier in my career), you already know at this point that it's a wise idea to make a copy of the panels layer. So, rename your panels layer to **Panels** by double-clicking on it. Then, from the Layers palette flyout menu, select Duplicate Panels. Hide the copy. Of course, save your document.

STEP 2 ▼
Shaping the Non-Rectangular Flaps

Even though the REV 12-pack box will be constructed of thin chipboard, if we left all the panels as perfect rectangles, the volume of the chipboard would make assembly nigh impossible. We need to alter the outer edges of most of the construction flaps to make construction more feasible.

1. I'm going to teach you a tip that will prove *very* helpful in a number of situations, including this one. Zoom in on panel 2 and grab the Line tool. Starting at the intersection of panels 2, 1, 4, and 5, hold Shift to constrain the angle and draw a line approximately **1.5—2 in.** tall. On the Transform palette, set the reference point to the bottom-left corner of your line, and then angle it **-20°**.

> ## ⊘ CAUTION
>
> Before determining the amount of overlap needed by your panels for gluing and assembly, talk to your printer or production house. Typically, thinner boxes that will contain light items require less overlap; heavier contents demand more strength and overlap areas from their containers.

2. Now, with the Direct Selection tool, carefully click on the top-left corner point of panel 2. Use your keyboard arrow keys (or the mouse with Shift held down) to move the control point to meet the -20° line. Because individual control points cannot be rotated via the Transform palette, this trick enables alignment of control points very quickly and without guesswork.

3. Repeat this trick to angle the other side of panel 2 as well as both outside edges of panel 3. On panels 11 and 12, angle only the right corners—top-right and bottom-right, respectively. Angle only the *left* corners on panels 14 and 15. Because 11 & 14 and 12 & 15 will overlap each other, they should not be angled on their overlapping edges. Your flaps should mirror mine (see Figure 6.11).

4. The remaining construction flaps—5, 6, 8, and 9—also must be reshaped, but there's another consideration: Applying a simple 20° angle to all the flaps would result in gaps between them, gaps that leave openings in the ends of the box. The ends can't have openings.

Rather than trying to visualize how the flaps come together to seal the end, let's work with the flaps as they will be constructed. Select all the flaps on the top row and copy them (and their corresponding numbers).

FIGURE 6.11   All 20-degree
flaps finished.

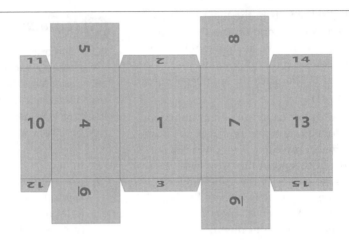

FIGURE 6.12   Tinting each flap
panel will enable easy identification and differentiation.

5. Scroll over to the empty pasteboard and paste the flaps. Color or tint each flap to differentiate it from the rest (see Figure 6.12), then group each with its corresponding number. Use the (Cmd-G) [Ctrl+G] shortcut to group.

6. Assemble your flaps as they will be in the printed chipboard box, at the same time utilizing the Object > Arrange menu commands to set their *z-order* as follows: panel 14 on the bottom, followed by 11 just above it, 2, then 5, and, on top, panel 8.

Using the Transform palette, arrange each panel with the rotations and coordinates in Table 6.2, all relative to their top-left reference points (rotate first, and *then* set the coordinates):

TABLE 6.2   Box Panel Locations

Name	Panel	X	Y	Angle
Flap	2	-14	0	180
Flap	5	-11	0	90
Flap	8	-14	0	-90
Flap	11	-10	-4.5	0
Flap	14	-14	-4.5	0

When all the panels are in place, their total combined area will be 6.5 in. wide × 5.5 in. tall. They will overlap, which is necessary for gluing, and look like the assemblage in Figure 6.13.

FIGURE 6.13   If everything went well, your panels will assemble like this (shown at 50% opacity to demonstrate construction).

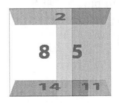

7. Lock panels 2, 11, and 14; no changes will be made to these. Panels 5 and 8 must be reshaped, however, to accommodate folding and gluing, while maintaining no less than **0.25 in.** overlap on the smaller panels and **1 in.** overlap on each other (these amounts may vary depending on the project). A simple angling of the panel borders will not do here.

8. Using Illustrator's path modification tools—Direct Selection, Pen, Add Anchor Point, Delete Anchor Point, and Convert Anchor Point—add and manipulate points until you achieve the desired shapes in panels 5 and 8 (see Figure 6.14).

FIGURE 6.14 My completed panels 5 and 8 (shown at 75% opacity to demonstrate construction).

9. Select the five panels you've assembled. In the Layers palette make a new layer called **End Assembled Guide**, and paste your panels to this layer. Hide the **End Assembled Guide** layer until later.

◎ TIP

Trim the surface area of the flaps as much as possible without impacting assembly. Although more angles beget more cuts, which require additional cutting dies, the upfront cost of production is recuperated by the savings in shipping resulting from the weight reduction.

10. Using the original panels 5 and 8 as positioning and rotation guides, return the newly reshaped panels to the exploded box. Delete the original, plain rectangles. Make copies of 5 and 8 and use them to replace 6 and 9 as well. This is the trim shape of our exploded box (see Figure 6.15). Note: I inserted circles for reference to represent the product as held by the container. Save your document.

FIGURE 6.15 The final trim shape of the box.

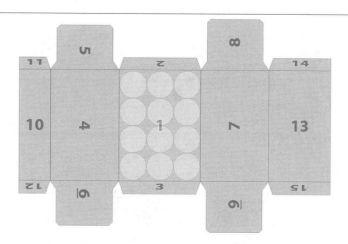

STEP 3 ▼
Creating Bleed Guides from the Box Panels

If the package artwork will run to any edge, we need to set up a bleed area outside the panels to account for potential misregistration. Because an exploded box is not a simple rectangle, setting up our bleed guides is a little more involved than simply dragging from the rulers.

1. Duplicate the **Panels** layer and name it **Bleed Panels**.

2. One at a time, select each panel (except the interior 4, 1, and 7 panels) and increase its dimensions by **0.125 in.** in all directions. The fastest way to do this is to ask Illustrator to do its math magic. Making sure to select the center reference point for each panel, add **.25 in. (0.125 × 2)** to both the width and height.

TIP

Illustrator's measurement boxes can all do math. Instead of breaking concentration to hunt for a pencil and paper or reach for the calculator, try this: In any measurement box (dimensions, positioning, sizing, and so on), type your numbers and the appropriate math symbols. Illustrator understands addition $(x + y)$, subtraction $(x - y)$, multiplication $(x * y)$, and division (x / y).

3. What happened to the panels? The rectangular ones like 4, 1, 7, and 13 all look good, but it didn't work perfectly for the non-rectangular panels, did it? It's time to grab the Direct Selection arrow and hand-tweak the paths of each bleed panel. Any place where one panel's bleed area overlaps another panel's trim area—panels 10, 4, 1, 7, and 13 especially—adjust the control points to obviate any such overlap (see Figure 6.16). For instance: Panel 11 extends down into panel 10, while 10 also extends upward into 11 and to the right into panel 4.

FIGURE 6.16   After initial resizing, panel 10 overlaps the trim areas of panels 11 and 4 (left). After fixing, the overlap is gone (right).

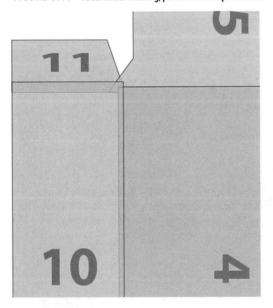

4. Duplicate the **Bleed Panels** layer and name it **Bleed Guides**. Hide **Bleed Panels**.

5. Select all objects on the **Bleed Guides** layer. In the Pathfinder palette, click the Add to Shape Area button to merge the boxes, and then Expand to expand their paths into a single merged shape.

6. On the View menu, choose Guides > Make Guides. Now you should have a single, continuous cyan line surrounding your panels at 1/8-inch out. This is the bleed guide, to which all bleeding artwork must extend. Lock this layer but leave it visible. If you hid the **Panels** layer, unhide it. Save.

STEP 4 ▼
Laying Out Sectional Box Faces Efficiently with Symbols and Clipping Masks

With the template finished, it's time to begin designing. Because faces like the ends (top and bottom rows) and the box bottom (panels 10 and 13 combined) are multiple panels that combine to form a single face, artwork for each of these faces must be sectioned corresponding to the panels. To avoid frying our brains, we'll design each face assembled, and then divide it using the incredible ease and stunning efficiency of symbols and clipping masks.

1. Remember the **End Assembled Guide** layer? Turn it on and lock it. Using these five pieces as placement guides, copy and assemble their corresponding flaps from the **Bleed Panels** layer into a new layer named **End Assembled**. Check your assembly against Figure 6.17.

FIGURE 6.17 The box end, assembled from the bleeding flaps.

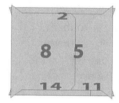

2. Using either File > Place or drag and drop from the Can Label.ai file, bring in the bg_box.tif background image, logo, Creativity Drink text, and tagline. Lay them out as you see fit atop the assembled construction flaps. If anything overhangs the box end, don't worry about it for the moment. If it helps, make the flaps semitransparent so that you can see through them to the trim area flaps beneath.

3. When you are happy with your design, open the Links and the Symbols palettes from the Window menu. If you placed any images as links (or dropped linked images from another file), select their entries in the Links palette and embed them with the Embed Image command on the Links palette flyout.

> **⊘ CAUTION**
>
> This action breaks the link to external files. If the source image is edited, those changes will *not* be reflected in Illustrator.
>
> Also watch out for issues with placed files like the logo becoming multiple and/or uncropped paths. Under some circumstances, a technical issue in Illustrator can cause this and other strange behaviors when placing or embedding. If you experience any such behaviors at this stage, instead of placing and embedding drawings, try either dragging and dropping the artwork from the original AI files into your current document, or rasterize them (Object > Rasterize command) in their original files prior to placing.

4. Select the logo or another reusable element and, while holding Shift, drag and drop it over an empty area of the Symbols palette. The logo will immediately become a symbol—you will no longer be able to work with the individual objects and paths. In the Symbols palette, double-click the new symbol and change its name to **Logo**. Do the same for each of the other elements that will appear on multiple flaps (including background, if any), naming each symbol appropriately. When these have all been turned into symbols, select all the elements of the box's side face artwork, and, make a new symbol called **End 1** incorporating all of them. Note on the Transform palette the position of the End 1 symbol on the pasteboard.

5. Send the End 1 symbol instance backward with Object > Arrange > Send Backward until it is behind your first flap, panel 8. Select both the End 1 symbol instance and panel 8, and choose Object > Clipping Mask > Make. The End 1 symbol instance should clip to fill only the area defined by panel 8. Send panel 8 to the back.

6. Drag End 1 from the Symbols palette and drop it near its placement in the assembled face. Use the Transform palette to precisely align it to the coordinates you noted in step 4.

> **◎ TIP**
>
> Symbols, like styles and graphic styles, are reusable automation elements. Modify the original symbol, and all instances of that symbol in the current document will mirror the adjustments to the original. In a layout such as this, that means changes will instantly roll across all five flaps that combine to form a single face—without the need to even touch the masked and in-place flaps.

7. Repeat the last two steps for all five flaps, sending each to the back after applying the clipping mask. When finished, you should see a fully assembled end artwork (with overlap, of course). Position each of the artwork panels where it belongs in the box template (see Figure 6.18).

8. Go ahead and lay out the rest of the box design, repeating the workflow from steps 1–7 to design, create symbols from, and mask all elements and assembled artwork to the required shapes. If the side panel has any elements in common with other panels, drag instances of those elements from the Symbols palette rather than placing or dragging in new copies. At the same time, make symbols from any new assets you do import.

Remember there are two other multi-flap, sectional faces—the other end formed by panels 3, 6, 9, 12, and 15, and the bottom face of the box with panels 10 and 13. Somewhere on the box exterior should also be included the barcode, nutrition label, and other required elements. There's no need to make symbols of panels that will only appear once. Check out Figure 6.19 for the finished REV 12-pack case.

FIGURE 6.18 Disassembled, my end construction flaps are now in place.

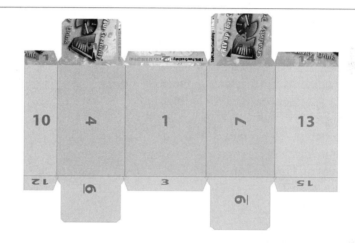

FIGURE 6.19 The final exploded design for the REV 12-pack, including glue areas and printers' marks.

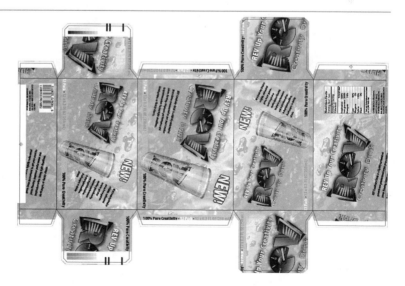

Final Thoughts

When designing any type of packaging, always print a proof and build a physical mockup to check for construction errors—particularly with folding packages like our exploded box. For presentation to your client, consider virtual mockups like a 3D box built from your exploded design or a 3D labeled can such as the one I used in my box design. Of course, if you have a good proof printer and the means, nothing will knock a client's socks off like putting a physical mockup of her conceptual product in her hands.

Where panels of a box overlap, they needn't contain artwork because they will be glued. Prior to that use, they are ideal for holding vital printing information like color scales and registration and other marks. Though your print provider will often prefer to define the glue areas and marks himself, he may ask you to do it—ask.

CHAPTER 7: Creating 3D Product Packaging Mockups

About the Projects

Armed with brand new package designs, we will employ Illustrator's 3D effects tools to create three-dimensional mockups of those products. With a little transparency wizardry, we'll even make the 3D can design photo-realistic.

Prerequisites

It would be helpful if you had the ability to draw basic shapes with the Pen and Rectangle tools, and to set and change fills and strokes.

You should have a working knowledge of creating symbols, and the ability to make and release clipping masks.

@work resources

Please visit the publisher's website to access the following Chapter 7 project files:

> ▶ Chap07 (12-pack case - 3D.ai, Can Label - 3D.ai)
>
> ▶ Chap07\Assets (12-pack case - artwork.ai, 12-pack case – artwork (rasterized).ai, 12-pack case - symbols.ai, Can Label - artwork.ai, Logo.ai, bg_can.pdf)
>
> ▶ Chap07\Finished Project

Planning the Projects

The very first question you should answer is: Why are you making 3D mockups? Concepting? Proofing a design to a client? Final output—as in the case of making a virtual box for a product that will not have a physical box? Or are you making 3D packaging mockups as a proof of concept to write an Illustrator book?

Moving on… The techniques in this project are excellent for conceptualizing a product idea or just a package design. When you are designing a flat label template or exploded box, it can be difficult to visualize the finished look. Sometimes it helps to see it in action.

If your goal is to proof the client, consider making a physical mockup. Although few clients are imaginative enough to fully grasp the final look of a flat package design, and a digital mockup is a tremendous help, nothing will compare to the impression made by putting the physical package in the client's hands. If your design uses a special material or container, get a sample of that container from the manufacturer and apply your label to it. Don't use 3D mockups to substitute for ink, X-Acto blades, and spray adhesive. Illustrator is *one* of a graphic designer's tools, but not the *only* one.

Project: 3D Labeled Box

In three easy steps we'll turn an exploded six-sided box package design into a 3D mockup suitable for presentation:

1. Making symbols from the exploded box design
2. Extruding the box into 3D
3. Applying the artwork in 3D

Creating a 3D Six-Sided Box

Starting with a standard exploded box layout, we'll create a fully 3D mockup viewable from any angle. Of course you can use your own exploded box design, but if you haven't got one ready, employ your REV 12-pack case design from the previous project, or the copy of that project in this chapter's resource files.

STEP 1 ▼
Making Symbols from the Exploded Box Design

Before building the box, we have to work with the exploded box template a little to create symbols we'll use as decals for each side of the mockup box.

1. If you already made symbols of your box faces while constructing the design in the first place, check out the "Rasterize *This*, Buddy!" sidebar, then pass Go, collect $200, and skip the rest of this entire section. Otherwise, open your box design. The 12-pack case - artwork.ai resource file is already fully symbolized.

2. If you built multiple-piece faces as symbols, pick one symbol that fills the entire area and copy it to a new layer. Release its clipping mask with Object > Clipping Mask > Release, and delete the mask path, which will be above the artwork symbol but devoid of fill or stroke. Now pat yourself on the back for doing things efficiently and skip down to step 5.

3. If you did *not* build multiple-panel box faces as symbols: Reassemble any faces composed of multiple pieces like construction flaps and other glued edges. It will probably be easier to do

this on a new layer via copy and paste. Use Object > Clipping Mask > Release to release any clipping masks you may have used. Delete the mask path(s), which will be above the artwork devoid of fill or stroke.

4. Remove any redundant pieces left over from releasing the clipping masks. Do anything else necessary to get your design for that face of the box finished; in a few moments we're going to fix the design in that state.

5. Because we built the exploded box artwork to run to the bleed edge on all panels, and the 3D box doesn't need

(and can't use) the safety net of the 0.125-inch bleed edge, we need to trim off the excess. If your design doesn't include a bleed area, skip this step.

You have a choice with how to do this. Depending upon your design, it may be reasonable to trim the bleed area off the artwork; if not, use a clipping mask to do it. If you're working with the REV 12-pack case design, the trim size of the end panels should be 6.5 × 5.5 in.

6. Select all the pieces of your fully assembled end panel and make a new symbol by Shift-dragging onto the Symbols palette (Window > Symbols).

Rasterize *This*, Buddy!

Live effects (drop shadow, Gaussian blur, or anything from Illustrator's Effects menu) can make working in 3D fiendishly slow. The rendering and re-rendering will slow Illustrator to a crawl for every single little niggling step you take, causing render times of *minutes* instead of seconds.

Although on a decent system vector artwork without live effects works quite well as mapped 3D artwork, if your artwork contains live effects, do something about it now, during the symbol creation phase. You can either expand or rasterize.

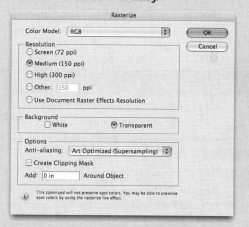 Expanding the appearance of objects with effects has the equivalent result of using the effect's corresponding non-live filter from the Filters menu. Select the relevant box panel. If it's already a symbol, place it and click the Break Link to Symbol button at the bottom of the Symbols palette. Then choose Expand Appearance from the Object menu.

Alternatively, you can rasterize the artwork, fixing its resolution as a flat raster image. Select the panel artwork (or symbol whose link has been broken) and choose Object > Rasterize. In the Rasterize dialog (see Figure 7.1) choose the Color Model, desired output

resolution, and set the background to Transparent. Leave the other options at their defaults.

FIGURE 7.1 The Rasterize dialog.

After appearance expansion or rasterization, make new symbols or update existing symbols. To do the latter, select the panel artwork on the artboard, and in the Symbols palette highlight the appropriate symbol. From the Symbols palette menu, choose Redefine Symbol.

CAUTION

If, while attempting to make a symbol, you receive the error "A symbol definition cannot contain a linked image," then you have linked images in your design. Go to the Links palette (Window > Links), highlight any entries on the list, and, from the Links palette flyout menu, select Embed Image before making the symbol.

7. Repeat this process for the remaining five faces—the other end, top, bottom, left, and right sides—making a separate symbol for each one.

TIP

If any faces are identical, make one symbol to represent all of them.

8. In the Symbols palette, double-click each of your new symbols and name it according to its face—you'll thank yourself later (see Figure 7.2). While you're at it, write down the measurements of the box's three dimensions—width, height, and depth. Note that many of the symbols shown in the figure are pieces of artwork used in other symbols—the logo and background image, for example, are symbols contained within all the face symbols.

9. Delete any extraneous symbols from the palette by choosing Select All Unused from the Symbols palette flyout menu, then clicking on the Delete Symbol trash bucket. And, also from the flyout menu, choose Save Symbol Library. Give your new symbols library a meaningful name (I named mine 12-pack case - symbols.ai), and save it somewhere (I heartily endorse saving it in the project's folder). Save

the document as a new file (in case of needed changes) and close it.

FIGURE 7.2   After making symbols of the faces, your Symbols palette should look something like this.

STEP 2 ▼
Extruding the Box into 3D

You are now entering a dimension not only of height and width, but of depth.

1. Begin a new document sized to hold the largest single face of your box (with a few inches to spare).

2. With the Rectangle tool, draw a rectangle the width and height of the box's largest or most prominent face—with REV's 12-pack case, that would be the 8.65 × 6.5-inch top panel. Use the Transform palette to get precise sizes. Fill the rectangle with a color that matches or approximates the dominant color of the design; remove any stroke.

3. Select your box and go to Effect > 3D > Extrude & Bevel.

4. In the 3D Extrude & Bevel Options dialog, set the Rotation to Off-Axis Front. Set Preview to on. The cube you see in the center is the track cube, and it represents your object in three-dimensional space. Click and drag on any face of the track cube to rotate it around any of the three axes. To the right of the track cube, the measurement boxes will change accordingly. Hold the Shift key while dragging the track cube to constrain rotation to a single axis.

For extra drama, try playing with the Perspective slider. Don't take too long deciding on your rotations, though— my editor is waiting for this chapter, and I'm waiting for you. These options will always be editable, so you can come back later.

⊚ TIP

Hold (Opt) [Alt] to change the Cancel button into a Reset button that restores all options to their defaults without leaving the 3D Extrude & Bevel Options dialog.

5. In the Extrude Depth measurement box, enter the depth of your box (you did write it down, didn't you?). Don't fret that Extrude Depth wants measurements in points; just type the depth in inches or millimeters or whatever you used, followed by the appropriate measurement notation ("in" for inches, "mm" for millimeters, and so on).

6. Leave the Bevel set to none, and the Surface to Plastic Shading. Make sure the solid end cap is selected. Click OK. You now have a 3D box (see Figure 7.3).

FIGURE 7.3 Quick and easy 3D box.

STEP 3 ▼
Applying the Artwork in 3D

The symbols you created in STEP 1 (Making Symbols from the Exploded Box Design) are our decals. Let's apply them to the faces of the box.

1. Save your file before going any further.

2. From the flyout menu on the Symbols palette, select Open Symbol Library > Other Library. Navigate to the box faces symbols library you saved a few minutes ago. Upon clicking the Open button, you will see a new floating palette named after your symbol library. Click on the first symbol, and then Shift-click on the last, which should select them all. Drag them from your library into the main Symbols palette, thus adding them to the current document.

⊠ NOTE

If you're working with the **12-pack case – symbols.ai** file in the **Chap07\Assets** folder in this chapter's resource files, those symbols are rasterized at 150 dpi.

3. Select your 3D box. On the Appearance palette (Window > Appearance), double-click the 3D Extrude & Bevel attribute to reopen the 3D Extrude & Bevel Options dialog. Turn Preview on and click the Map Art button.

4. Map Art is the way to decal 3D objects—be it Extrude & Bevel or Revolve. Top left is the Symbol drop-down containing all your decals. Top right is the surface to which they will be applied. You should have six surfaces; the arrows allow you to navigate between them. Dominating the dialog is a preview of the object's surface. A light surface is showing in the current view; a dark rectangle denotes a surface that is not currently visible.

If you peer around the Map Art dialog, you will see on the 3D box an outline denoting which surface is currently selected (see Figure 7.4). With the top face (currently our front-directed face) selected, choose the FACE Front symbol from the Symbol drop-down.

5. When the symbol appears, note that it has a bounding box. Use the bounding box to move, resize, and/or rotate the decal until it completely fills the rectangle of the face. To rotate, hover your cursor just beyond a corner control point. When the cursor becomes a curved, double-headed arrow, click and drag to rotate (Shift-drag to constrain to increments of 45°).

 TIP

Turn off Shade Artwork and/or Preview to speed positioning. Leave Invisible Geometry unchecked so that the can itself remains visible.

6. Using the arrows at the top, which cycle through the various faces of the box, apply the decals to each visible face. Just before you click OK, turn on Shade Artwork (see Figure 7.5). If you want to change the rotation of the box, go for it. Just apply decals to any new surfaces that become visible.

FIGURE 7.4 Note the outline (left side) showing which face of the box corresponds to the surface in the Map Art dialog, and the bounding box (right) that reveals the actual shape of the path.

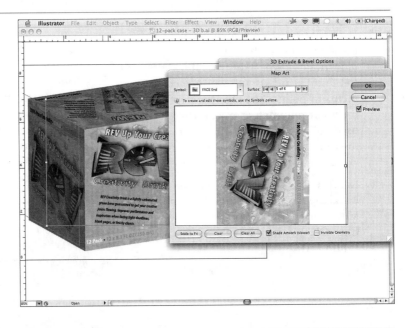

CHAPTER 7: Creating 3D Product Packaging Mockups

FIGURE 7.5 With decals in place and Shade Artwork turned on, the REV 12-pack is finished.

Project:
3D Drink Container

We'll build a 3D photo-realistic can with wraparound label in five easy steps:

1. Drawing the can contour
2. Revolving the can into 3D
3. Making symbols from the label design
4. Applying the labels and setting multiple light sources
5. Adding photo-realistic highlights

Building a 3D Photo-Realistic Can with Wraparound Label

Working from the container label design of REV's 250mL can, we'll see how easy it is to make a photo-realistic can (or bottle, glass, jar, and so on) complete with lighting and a wraparound decal.

STEP 1 ▼
Drawing the Can Contour

From humble beginnings comes great art—or at least, cool 3D.

1. In a new document, drag guides from the ruler to define on the artboard a rectangle equal to the height of your can (or other container) and exactly half the width. If you're working with the REV 250mL can design from the Can Label - artwork.ai resource file, the dimensions are 1.041 × 5.4 inches.

2. With the Pen tool, draw a single path that defines the shape of the left half of your can—including the seal ring and tapered shoulder and base. Use the guides to help you, and leave the path opened, with unconnected points at the top- and bottom-right corners of the path (see Figure 7.6).

3. Zoom in on your path and check it carefully. Are the opening and closing anchor points in line with each other— if not, one end of your can won't close; it will become a cup. Are all the curves accurate? Do they behave like an aluminum can? Is the fill an aluminum gray with no stroke? Save your document.

STEP 2 ▼
Revolving the Can into 3D

Round and round we go, whirling out of the 2D world into the third dimension.

1. Select your path and go to Effect > 3D > Revolve. If you created the 3D six-sided box in the first project, the 3D Revolve Options dialog should look quite familiar. It's very similar to the 3D Extrude & Bevel Options dialog, but with a few key differences.

2. Turn on the preview. Do you see something like the twisted wreck of Figure 7.7? If so, choose the opposite edge in Offset From. Revolve 360°, with a solid end cap and **0 pt** offset. Set the X, Y, and Z axis rotations and the perspective as you like. I used: **-22°**, **-13°**, **-10°** and Perspective set to **123°**. Let's leave the project here for now and click OK.

FIGURE 7.7   Horrific, twisted wrecks (or happy accidents) result when revolving from the wrong edge.

> **TIP**
>
> Setting the Angle to anything less than 360° results in a partial revolve, making for easy *cutaways*.

3. Scrutinize your now can-like construct. Does it have the shape of a can? If there are too-sharp edges or unrealistic curves, switch into Outline Mode (View > Outline), and massage the path. To see your progress, flip back into Preview Mode (View > Preview); Illustrator will update the 3D Revolve in real time.

4. Save your progress and copy your can contour to the clipboard.

STEP 3 ▼
Making Symbols from the Label Design

If you have a simple container like the REV can, make the whole label design a single symbol. When you get to the map art stage, just carefully align multiple instances of the same symbol. If, however, your package contour is a little more complicated—a bottle with a tapered neck, for example, or negative areas in the label where the container will be unlabeled—making symbols for each individual face would be the more efficient way to work. For this latter method, work through this section. Otherwise, just make a symbol from your label and skip to the next section.

1. Open the `Can Label - artwork.ai` file (or your own package design), and paste the contour path onto a new layer.

2. If the contour is in 3D, strip it down to the base path by dragging the 3D Revolve attribute on the Appearance palette to the trash icon at the bottom of that palette. Now align the contour to your label design so that the top and bottom are flush with their respective guides in the template.

3. Zoom in on the contour path until all its anchor points—overall or in a section—are plainly visible. Drag guides from the horizontal ruler down to meet each point on the contour path. Move around until you have guides on all points (see Figure 7.8). Count the number of rows you created with the guides. This is the number of faces in your 3D container.

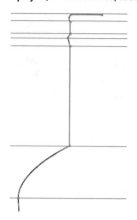

FIGURE 7.8 Rows created from guides aligned with the anchor points of a bottle contour path (not used in this project). When revolved, each row becomes a new surface.

 TIP

A great way to move around while zoomed in is to hold the spacebar, which temporarily turns all but the Text cursor into the Hand tool, allowing you to click and drag your view.

4. Lock the contour path layer.

5. Back in the label layer made visible again, select the label design and make it a symbol by Shift-dragging it to the Symbols palette. Now duplicate the label symbol instance once for each face by copying the first instance and using Paste in Front.

6. Over each face row, draw rectangles to define the face's area. Each rectangle should be the height of the row between any two guides and the width of the label.

7. One at a time, select a rectangle and a label symbol instance. Select Object > Clipping Mask > Make to mask the label symbol to the area of the rectangle. From this masked symbol create a

---

new symbol named after the face, an ascending number (working from the top down), or some other logical name.

8. Repeat the last step until all faces have been symbolized, then save the symbol library as you did for the box. Leave the seal ring unlabeled; if the can was filled with a light or medium gray, it should look like aluminum when revolved and lit in 3D.

STEP 4 ▼
Applying the Labels and Setting Multiple Light Sources

Realism begins with proper lighting.

1. Back in your 3D document, open your symbol library (or open the label document as if it were a symbol library), and drag the symbol(s) into the Symbols palette of your document.

2. Select your contour path and, on the Appearance palette, double-click the 3D Revolve appearance attribute to edit it.

3. Click Map Art and add the symbol decals to each surface as you did for the box. Because you're working with decals designed to fully wrap a container, and the revolved path will only show one face, the majority of each symbol will hang outside the viewable area.

⊘ CAUTION

Seams, jagged edges, and other screen *artifacts* may appear in your 3D objects—particularly if they have mapped artwork. These artifacts are *only* onscreen, and will not appear in the final artwork when printed or saved for Web.

4. When you've finished mapping the decals, return to the 3D Revolve Options dialog and click the More Options button. The lighting controls area will appear (see Figure 7.9). Set the Surface drop-down to Plastic Shading, which makes the surface glossy and reflective.

FIGURE 7.9 Lighting controls in the 3D Revolve Options dialog begin the process of photo-realism.

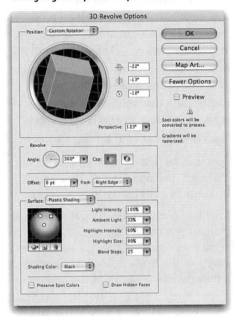

◎ TIP

For matte surfaces like cloth, set the Surface to Diffuse Shading. No Shading makes the 3D object the same color as the original 2D (fill and/or stroke). No Shading and Wireframe, the latter of which creates a transparent mesh of the object, have no lighting controls.

5. See that orb? It represents the viewing plane on which your container resides. The little white circle is the light source. Click and drag it around in three-dimensional space to set the best location for the primary light source.

6. On the right, set your lighting controls—*Light Intensity, Ambient Light, Highlight Intensity, Highlight Size,* and *Blend Steps.* To add additional light sources, click the New Light button and position the light source. To place a light source behind the 3D object, click the first button below the lighting orb.

So just what are these controls? Glad you asked!

> ▶ **Light Intensity**—The brightness of the selected light source—0% is off, 100% is the brightest possible setting.
>
> ▶ **Ambient Light**—Diffuse illumination that does not shine directly on an object but rather is an overall atmospheric illumination affecting all surfaces of all objects uniformly.
>
> ▶ **Highlight Intensity**—The amount of light reflected by the object, its shininess.
>
> ▶ **Highlight Size**—The size of the highlight shining on the object, from a pinpoint at 1% to a flood-light at 100%.
>
> ▶ **Blend Steps**—The number of steps or color of light bands between lit and unlit areas.

Because this object is not transparent, and we won't see any back surfaces through the front, leave Draw Hidden Faces turned off.

◎ **TIP**

Adding a soft light source or two behind a 3D object lends realism.

---

7. When you're satisfied with the lighting, click OK and lock the container's layer. Save your progress so far.

STEP 5 ▼

Adding Photo-realistic Highlights

Lighting controls in the 3D Revolve and 3D Extrude & Bevel Options dialogs are an excellent start on realistic lighting and shadow, but achieving genuine realism requires hand-drawn reflections.

1. On a new layer, draw a long, narrow rectangle the height of the can's face (not including shoulder and base). Because the can is revolved, you will probably need to use the Pen tool to match its shape. Position the rectangle just off the center of the can's face. Remove any stroke and fill it white.

2. On the Transparency palette, set the white rectangle's blending mode to Screen, and the opacity to somewhere around **25–50%** (see Figure 7.10). You may be happy leaving the light reflection as it is, but begrudge me one more step? Thanks.

FIGURE 7.10 The Transparency palette settings of the main reflection strip.

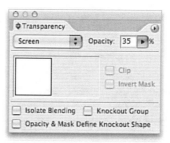

---

3. With the reflection strip still selected, go to Effect > Blur > Gaussian Blur. Using the slider at the bottom, give it a slight blur that looks good to you. For the REV can, I would recommend keeping an almost sharp edge, so try a Gaussian Blur setting around **1.4** or **2** (see Figure 7.11).

4. Make a few more reflection and highlight objects on the label face, shoulder, seal ring, base, and end(s) if visible (see Figure 7.12). For longer areas like the can body, use shapes that are primarily rectangular; for other areas, try oval shapes. Vary the opacity and Gaussian Blur intensities of reflection and highlight objects. Also consider adding shading shapes (blending mode set to Multiply) and possibly even non-white reflections.

FIGURE 7.12   The finished, photo-realistic REV can.

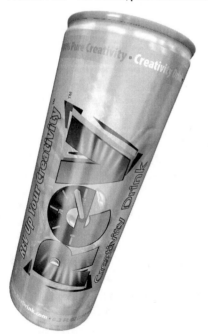

Final Thoughts

A part of Illustrator since version CS, Bevel & Emboss and Revolve are excellent medium-grade 3D tools. Their results will wow a client and any audience. However, if your needs extend beyond basic extruding, beveling, embossing, and revolving, investigate robust 3D applications like ZBrush, Cinema 4D, 3D Studio Max, Bryce, Poser, Maya, and LightWave 3D.

Working in Illustrator's 3D tools is extremely RAM-intensive—especially with complicated designs or live effects. If you have difficulty with rendering time or out-of-memory errors, try rasterizing your labels prior to making symbols of them. Another technique is to use symbols within symbols: Anywhere an element might repeat, make it a symbol and simply use instances of that symbol in all the necessary places—even inside other symbols. Examine the `12-pack case - artwork.ai` file to see how I reduced a 48MB file to 6MB just by using symbols instead of duplicated objects.

3D objects created in Illustrator are live effects and will not export as paths to other programs. To export your 3D work to other programs like Macromedia Flash, either rasterize or, better, choose Expand Appearance from the Object menu. Expand Appearance will convert the 3D effects and other appearance attributes to individual paths and objects that can be saved or exported to formats compatible with other vector programs.

If the top of your can will be visible, map a photo or drawing of a can lid, with tab and opening, to that surface.

When building realistic or photo-realistic lighting, shading, and reflections, consider using a gradient mesh. Although the light/reflection technique with shapes works well for an object like REV's drink can, a shading and lighting gradient mesh (blending mode set to luminosity, screen, or multiply as appropriate) would also work. Objects with more curves or angles to their shapes would definitely benefit from the superior control and smooth color transitions of a gradient mesh (for more on gradient meshes, see Chapter 3, "Adding Logos and Artwork to Non-Flat Objects," and Chapter 5, "Illustrating an (Almost) Photo-realistic Poster").

Objects on a plain white artboard appear to be floating in space, and they look fake no matter how well the objects are themselves shaded. Realism requires context, so, before supplying the client with her new 3D digital mockups, give the drawing a background. If you have the means, slap a photo in there— a shot of a grocery store shelf or checkout counter prominently featuring the product would be ideal. However, even something as simple as a cast shadow can complete your packaging mockup.

CHAPTER 8: Designing a Tri-Fold Brochure

About the Projects

In this project we will design a tri-fold brochure using external source files, as would be common in a team environment, and learning how to organize and automate repetitive styling tasks to make the work go much faster. We'll also make this notoriously one-page-only application do multiple pages.

Prerequisites

You will need to have installed Adobe Acrobat or a printer capable of handling custom page sizes. It would also be helpful if you had a basic understanding of drawing basic shapes, setting and styling type with the Character and Paragraph palettes, creating guides, positioning and resizing objects using either the Selection tool or Transform palette, using the Transparency palette to change opacity and blending mode, defining clipping masks, and creating basic gradients.

@work resources

Please visit the publisher's website to access the following Chapter 6 project files:

- ▶ Finished Project
- ▶ Project Files (Brochure.ai, Logo and head.ai, Logo.ai, tachometer.ai, Drink Can.psd, model 3F1142.psd, bg.tif, Copy - Inside - Right.doc, Copy - Bacover.doc, Copy - Inside - Bottom.doc, Copy - Inside - Main.doc, Copy – Inside – Headline.doc)

Planning the Projects

Is Illustrator the right tool for this job? Because Illustrator is effectively a single-page drawing tool, a two-sided brochure should typically be created in a page layout application like InDesign, QuarkXPress, or even PageMaker. However, when those applications don't have the level of drawing ability you need, or if Illustrator is the only tool in your belt, Illustrator will do the job with a little extra work. A little-known secret is that Illustrator indeed *does* have multi-page features—they're just hidden.

Consider the paper stock you will use. Is it thick paper or thin? Thinner paper typically cannot support full coverage ink without the ink cracking, flaking, or smearing to the touch; thick paper may have issues folding, and costs more to ship. Is the paper color white, off-white, or colored? Anything but a neutral white paper will tint the semitransparent cyan, magenta, and yellow inks. Are you going with a matte finish or glossy? That choice affects a number of factors including spot color choices.

If at all possible, prior to the inception of design, get the client to approve the copy—all of it, from the main story inside to the cover lines, tagline, and even the copyright notice that should appear on the back. Get the client to sign a copy proof, thus affirming that the client—not you—is responsible for any errors or inaccuracies in the copy.

Make sure the client has approved all the relevant constituent elements of the design, too. It's a waste of time to build an entire brochure keyed off the logo and colors of a brand identity that hasn't yet been decided on.

Is PDF-based review a reasonable expectation? If so, what version of Acrobat, Acrobat Approval, or Adobe Reader does the client have? Full versions of Acrobat 4 through 7 (Standard and Professional) have varying review and commenting abilities; Acrobat Approval 5 (the only version ever made) has comparable capabilities, but recent versions of Adobe Reader (formerly Acrobat Reader) have no such reviewing and commenting tools. Additionally, each subsequent version of Acrobat and PDF has added security and creative features not compatible with prior releases; deliver a new model year PDF to someone running a classic application and the file may not open—at the very least, the client will receive confusing and distressing error messages.

Ask the client about his PDF viewing and reviewing software, but be aware of one important caveat: Most people whose only often-used Adobe product is Acrobat typically confuse the company with the product, referring to all versions of Acrobat, Approval, and Reader as simply "Adobe." Get the client to *open* the application and *read* the title and version from the Acrobat/Approval/Reader menu > About [application] (Macintosh), or from Help > About [application] (Windows).

How will you transmit PDFs to the client? Using many fonts or a complex design grows the PDF quickly—often well out of the range of email delivery (mail servers vary, but try to avoid sending attachments in excess of 2MB). Additionally, the larger the file attachment, the more likely it is to be corrupted by one or more of the servers it will pass through between your mailbox and the client's. If you intend to email a large PDF, consider zipping it. Better yet, upload it to your FTP server; the client can then download it or even open it directly from his familiar web browser.

Who will work with the print service provider—you or the client? Who pays the service bureau and/or press house? If it's to be you, when will the client reimburse you?

Project: One-Page, Multi-Page Template

We'll build a one-page, multi-page template in two easy steps:

1. **Defining guides**
2. **Setting page tiling**

Building the One-Page, Multi-Page Template

This technique has been part of Illustrator for a number of versions now, but it's surprising how few people know about it—and how many who *have* heard of it have no idea how to do it right. Here's how to get multiple pages from Illustrator—whether for a multipage layout or a single page too large to print.

STEP 1 ▼
Defining Guides

Without guides to steer us as we work on this particular layout we'd be constantly lost. To keep the guides from becoming overwhelming, we'll actually draw rules and labels to use as guides.

1. Begin a new CMYK document entitled **Brochure**. We're going to build a typical **8.5 × 11 in.** tri-fold brochure, so set your document's initial measurement to **11.25 × 17.5 in.** If you had to read the last line twice, rest assured it's not a typo. (Wouldn't I be embarrassed if a typo *did* make it through in this step!) No, the measurements are accurate. Trust in your sensei, Grasshopper. Enlightenment will soon be upon you.

2. Show the rulers with (Cmd+R) [Ctrl+R] and press (Cmd+0) [Ctrl+0] to fit to window. Drag a guide down from the horizontal ruler to the vertical center of the page—**8.75 in.** For now, we'll focus entirely on the area above that line.

3. Grab the Rectangle tool, and draw a rectangle exactly **0.125 in.** from the top and left edge of the page, and sized to the width of the page minus **0.25 in.** (**11 in.** in this case). The height should be **8.5**—half of the artboard height minus **0.25** (17.5 / 2 = **8.75 – 0.25 = 8.5**). Remove the fill and give it a **1 pt red** stroke.

> ## ✖ NOTE
> If your brochure won't *bleed*, change the stroke color on the red rectangle to green and skip Step 4.

4. Make another rectangle with a **1 pt green** stroke **0.125 in.** smaller on all sides than, and **0.125 in.** inside, the red rectangle (see Figure 8.1). For fastest results, copy the red rectangle, paste in front, and use the Transform palette to shrink its width and height **0.25 in.** from its center point.

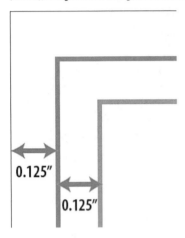

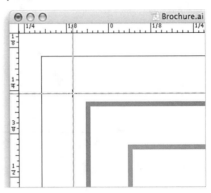

5. Select both rectangles; copy, paste, and position them in the bottom half of the artboard to match the top (that is, **0.125 in.** from all sides). The red rectangle defines the trim area of the outside (top) and inside (bottom) faces of your brochure, and the green rectangle defines the live areas. Beyond the red rectangles are the bleed areas. Now, Grasshopper, does the odd page size make sense?

⊙ TIP

Instead of copying and pasting, drag the object with the Selection tool while holding Opt and Shift (Ctrl and Shift) to create a duplicate aligned with the original.

6. Deselect all objects (Select > Deselect All). Click and drag the vertex of the two rulers (see Figure 8.2) to meet the upper-left corner of the top red box. This will temporarily change the rulers' zero points to that coordinate, making the next step much easier.

7. With the top-left corner of the trim area as the new zero point, divide the trim area into vertical thirds. How? Elementary, my dear Watson: How wide is the trim rectangle? Divide that into thirds, and set a vertical guide at the 1/3 mark (11 / 3 = **3.667 in.**). Set another vertical guide at the **2/3 mark** (11 / 3 = **3.667 in. * 2**). The guides are the fold points of the brochure (see Figure 8.3). If you double-click in the little square where the horizontal ruler meets the vertical, it will reset the zero point to its correct location.

8. Optional: The upper half of the artboard is the outer panels of your tri-fold brochure, with the right panel as the front of the folded brochure, the center panel as the back, and the left panel appearing inside. You might find it helpful (I often do) in keeping track of which panel is which face by creating text labels above the artboard. In a moment we'll define this entire layer as non-printing, so setting type here will not appear on your final layout.

FIGURE 8.3   My template, with panels, labels, and divided artboard.

STEP 2 ▼
Setting Page Tiling

Here's the crux of the whole multiple-pages-from-one technique. As you work through the following steps, you'll see it is much easier to accomplish than it is to *describe* in print.

1. Select File > Print. Set the Printer to Adobe PDF (if you have Acrobat 6 or 7), Acrobat Distiller (for earlier versions of Acrobat), or whatever printer you may have. For this technique to work with a for-press brochure, you will need Acrobat or a physical or *virtual printer* driver installed that is capable of handling custom page sizes.

2. On the General tab, set Media Size to Custom, which automatically jumps the Width and Height measurements to the full dimensions of the artboard. Change these to **11.25 × 8.75** (for full bleeds, **11 × 8.5** for non-bleeding), and the orientation to portrait. In the Options section, the Print Layers setting should be Visible & Printable Layers, with the Do Not Scale radio button selected.

3. Switch to the Setup panel and choose Crop Artwork to Artboard. Set Tiling to Tile Full Pages, **0 in.** overlap, and the Placement origins both to **0** (with the top-left corner of the Placement reference point proxy.

4. Turn off all marks and set the bleeds to **0 in.** on the Marks and Bleeds tab. Your print preview panel should look like the one in Figure 8.4.

5. Click Save Preset and give it a name like **2X 8.5 × 11 w Bleeds**. Click Done—*not Print*.

6. On the Toolbox, click and hold on the Hand tool to reveal the Page tool.

7. When you double-click on the Page tool (the button itself in the Toolbox), dotted lines will appear on your document along with numbers in the lower-left corner. These are your page numbers. If you did everything correctly so far, you should have two pages with the first on top (see Figure 8.5). If not, go back to the Print dialog and check your settings; the preview in the Print dialog should show two pages stacked, no more. Clicking the Done button should divide your document into the two pages.

FIGURE 8.4 With all settings correct, the preview in the Print dialog shows an evenly divided document.

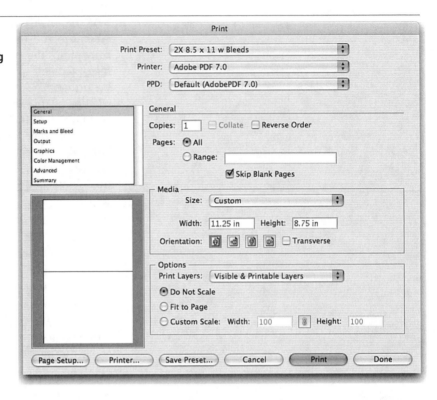

Print

Print Preset: 2X 8.5 x 11 w Bleeds

Printer: Adobe PDF 7.0

PPD: Default (AdobePDF 7.0)

General
Setup
Marks and Bleed
Output
Graphics
Color Management
Advanced
Summary

General

Copies: 1   ☐ Collate   ☐ Reverse Order

Pages: ● All
       ○ Range:
       ☑ Skip Blank Pages

Media
Size: Custom
Width: 11.25 in   Height: 8.75 in
Orientation: ☐ ☐ ☐ ☐   ☐ Transverse

Options
Print Layers: Visible & Printable Layers
● Do Not Scale
○ Fit to Page
○ Custom Scale: Width: 100   ☐   Height: 100

(Page Setup...) (Printer...) (Save Preset...) (Cancel) (Print) (Done)

FIGURE 8.5 The tiled artboard with guides and labels.

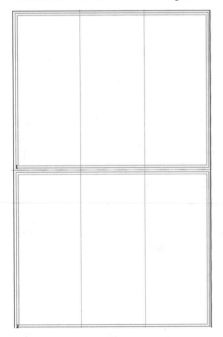

🚫 CAUTION

If you accidentally click somewhere with the Page tool, it will give you many more tiles/pages. Use (Cmd+Z) [Ctrl+Z] to undo it, double-click the Page tool again, or reset everything in the Print dialog.

8. On the Layers palette, double-click **Layer 1** to access the Layer Options dialog box. In the dialog box, change the name of **Layer 1** to **Guides** and uncheck the Print box. Click OK. Now this layer categorically will not print. Lock it and save your document.

Project: Brochure Design

We'll design the brochure in five steps:

1. Placing and organizing graphical elements
2. Using graphic styles and symbols to finish the outside panels
3. Setting type stories in threaded text areas and columns
4. Improving readability with paragraph options and the Adobe Composer
5. Using the advanced typographic controls of OpenType

Designing the Brochure

With the multi-page template created, we can get down to the fun and really interesting part of this project: setting type and image elements to build a brochure.

STEP 1 ▼
Placing and Organizing Graphical Elements

Organization is important in all but the simplest of documents for a number of reasons. First, without proper organizational skills, changing even the smallest thing a few months down the road could become a game of hunt and peck trying to locate and isolate the object(s) requiring edit. Sending the file to someone else will force that person to play detective unless you organize well. Second, well-organized files also typically have smaller file sizes, which not only saves disk space but RAM and processor overhead, improving rendering and working time.

1. Set your top-tier layer organization scheme by creating new layers for each page and its foreground and background layers--for example **P1 FG, P2 BG**, and so on. As you work, place or create each element on the appropriate layer. Leave the **Guides** layer alone and on top of all other layers (so you can see the trim and live guides).

2. Place your images. If you're working through creating the REV brochure, place bg.tif, Drink Can.psd, and model 3F1142.psd. If you have the full Creative Suite 2, the easiest method to place all three images simultaneously would be to drag them into your document from the Adobe Bridge. Position and scale them as you like. Use clipping masks if need be.

3. If the bg.tif isn't the only background your brochure will have, go ahead and build the remaining backgrounds. Though I used the *bg.tif* file unchanged for the inner panels, I overlaid it with a gradient mesh blended in Hard Light on the front panel. For the back and fold-over flap I employed a simple black-to-green gradient (see Figure 8.6).

4. Open—don't place—the files logo and head.ai and tachometer.ai. Copy or drag the contents of both from their respective documents into the brochure.ai document (paste onto the pasteboard to work unhindered by other objects). After copying, you can close the source files.

5. Focusing on the logo and its accompanying elements, you should note that the REV logo itself is not editable; it's linked to the logo.ai file in this chapter's resource files. For our purposes, that works quite well. Grab all three elements—the logo, the

tagline, and the Creativity Drink deck below the logo. Position and scale them to fit one of their intended placements.

FIGURE 8.6   **My brochure so far.**

6. ![icon] Select the **REV Up Your Creativity** tagline and, on the Paragraph Styles palette (Window > Type > Paragraph Styles), click the Create New Style button. Double-click the new paragraph style and rename it to **Wavy Deck**. With the tagline still selected, do the same on the Graphic Styles palette (Window > Graphic Styles)—create a new style with the New Graphic Style button, double-click the swatch, and rename it to **Wavy Deck**.

7. Select the tagline and the little **TM** text box to its right and drag them to the Symbols palette (Window > Symbols). Before dropping onto the Symbols palette, press and hold Shift. This will create a new symbol while simultaneously converting the selected objects

into an instance of that symbol. Repeat for the **Creativity Drink** deck. Shift-click on both new symbols, the logo, and the logo's **TM** text box to select them all, and then group the four objects by pressing (Cmd+G) [Ctrl+G].

> **NOTE**
>
> The logo cannot be turned into a symbol without embedding it, thus breaking the link to the external **logo.ai** file. Avoid embedding whenever possible because it increases the number of files you must edit to make a change to a common asset like the logo.

8. Returning our attention to the tachometer, let's make a symbol from every part except the needle—include the tick marks, numbers, and the highlight implying the dial. Remember to drag and Shift-drop into the Symbols palette.

9. With your dial now a symbol, select it and the needle, and make it another new symbol. Why nest symbols? Good question! Because we're going to use the dial in multiple symbols, but the needle position will change between them. And, on that note…

10. ![icon] Keep the dial and needle selected and click on the Break Link to Symbol button at the bottom of the Symbols palette. As the name conveys, you've now broken the link to the symbol, returning the tachometer face to its state of a moment before. Note that the tachometer face is still its own symbol.

11. ![icon] Zoom in on the needle and dial to which it's attached. Select only the needle itself. Locate the center point of the imaginary dial. With the Rotate tool, click once on that

center point to define the rotation axis, and drag the needle around until it's somewhere close to the 140 tick on the tachometer. If it doesn't line up perfectly, either undo and reposition the center point, or move the needle around with the Selection tool.

12. Make a new symbol from the tachometer face and the repositioned needle.

13. With our symbols and graphic styles defined, it's a good time to rename them so we know what we're doing. I renamed my symbols to **Tagline**, **Logo Deck**, **Tachometer Face**, **Tachometer Front**, and **Tachometer Inside**, respectively (see Figure 8.7).

FIGURE 8.7   **Set to Large List View (from the palette flyout menu); my Symbols palette contains easily identifiable symbols I will use more than once.**

STEP 2 ▼
Using Graphic Styles and Symbols to Finish the Outside Panels

Here, the organization from the preceding step sequence begins to pay off by saving a few minutes and more than a few clicks.

1. If you're making the REV brochure to match mine, set your logo group, drink can, model shot, and Tachometer Front symbol to match. Note: I blended the Tachometer Front symbol with a Hard Light blending mode and used Effects > Transform > Free Distort to put it on the same *plane* as the model (see Figure 8.8).

2. Import the REV colors by clicking on the Swatches palette's flyout menu, selecting Open Swatch Library > Other Library, and navigating to the logo.ai file.

FIGURE 8.8   **Among other effects, the Free Distort dialog allows you to create the illusion of objects residing on planes not perpendicular to the viewer.**

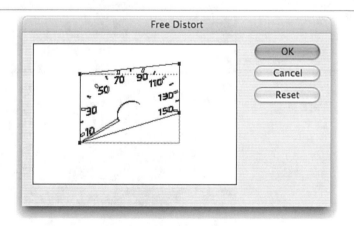

3. To create the vertical tagline, set the tagline in a wide text area. With the Rotate tool, rotate the text box **-90°** and use the Character palette (Window > Type > Character) to size the text up until it fits well. With the Selection tool, click on the text area box and select the **Wavy Deck** graphic style from Graphic Style palette. Looks good but for the wave, right? Just drag the **Warp: Flag** entry from the Appearance palette (Window > Appearance) to the trash bucket on the bottom of the palette.

4. Go ahead and make a new graphic style from this modified **Wavy Deck** style named merely **Deck**.

5. At the top of the middle panel (the back of the brochure), create a small text area and type in REV's website address, **www.REVDrink.com**. Click on the **Wavy Deck** paragraph style in the Paragraph Styles palette, then the **Wavy Deck** graphic style. See how fast working with styles makes things? The **Wavy Deck** graphic style contains three fills—two of them offset—a gradient, and a warp. Doing it by hand would take five minutes each time, and then more time to set the type options stored in the paragraph style.

6. Each line of the cover copy is a different text area with one of two graphic styles applied. The styles include an outer glow, a Free Distort, and a gentle warp that alternates direction between the odd and even lines. Because graphic styles apply to the entire content of a text area and not to individual characters, creating the differing styles in the **inspire my creativity** line requires three separate text areas.

Inspire and **creativity** need the **Wavy Deck** paragraph style and the new **Deck** graphic style you created from the vertical tagline. Then, grouped with the **my** text area, they get the same graphic style as the other odd-numbered lines.

Examine the Appearance palette in my finished brochure file to pick apart each style option and setting.

7. Before calling the outside panels finished we need to set the back cover copy. With the Type tool draw a type area to fit comfortably between the URL and logo. Rather than typing the information, go to File > Place and bring in the Copy - Bacover.doc file. In the Microsoft Word Options dialog, check Remove Text Formatting. Season to taste using the Character and Paragraph palettes (see Figure 8.9).

FIGURE 8.9 **The finished outside panels (page or tile one) of REV's new brochure.**

STEP 3 ▼
Setting Type Stories in Threaded Text Areas and Columns

The outside of a brochure is the hook. It has to be simpler (in structure and copy) and somewhat flashier to grab attention and make a reader pick up the document. The inside three panels (four if you count the fold-over from the outer page) are the meat of any brochure, where you give readers the full story. Thus, our outside panels are a simple three-column *grid*, but the inside is set on a six-column grid to accommodate the comfortable presentation of much more information.

1. Operating from a basic six-column grid, draw with the Type tool boxes 1 and 2 (see Figure 8.10), which are **3.5556 in.** wide (shy of a 1/3 page each by the **0.125 in.** live area).

2. Click once inside box 1 with the Type tool and place the file Copy - Inside - Main.doc, which we would have already had the client approve in a copy proof. For the time being, don't bother styling the text; just click on the text area with the Selection tool.

3. The red plus sign in the lower-right corner of the text area (see Figure 8.11) indicates the presence of *overset* text. We have more copy than will fit in the single column, so we need to make it flow into the next. So click once on the red plus sign (which is the *out port* of the text area), and move your cursor to the general vicinity of the top-left corner of box 2 (its *in port*). When your mouse changes to a cursor with chain links, click. Your overset copy should flow into the second box. The text boxes are now *threaded*.text:

FIGURE 8.10 Diagram of the four text areas. With a six-column grid, text areas can easily be set to fill a panel by occupying two columns while other text areas align perfectly to their centers.

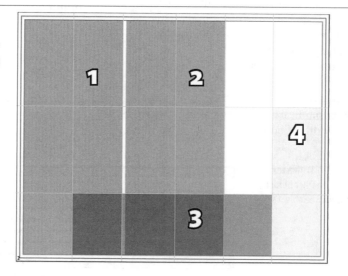

FIGURE 8.11 A red plus sign in a text area's out port denotes overset text.

pit rabat-

:quat. Duis

: in vulpu-

4. Select both threaded text areas and choose Type > Area Type Options. In the Offset section, change the *Inset Spacing* to **0.125 in.** When you click OK, your text will push back from the edges of its boxes and create a nice *gutter* between columns. Lock boxes 1 and 2.

5. Now draw text boxes 3 and 4, and fill them with `Copy - Inside - Bottom.doc` and `Copy - Inside - Right.doc`, respectively. Note that box 4 is a single column, and box 3 runs from the center of 1 all the way out to flush with four. If the text oversets, don't worry about it for the moment.

6. Select box 3 with the Selection tool and go to Type > Area Type Options. This time we're going to leave the inset spacing alone and change the number of columns to 2, with a **0.15 in.** gutter. Click OK. Your bottom copy should now partially fill two columns in the same text box. Resizing the box would adjust the width of both columns equally.

7. We're still left with the issue of box 3 overlapping boxes 1 and 2. Let's fix that now. With box 3 selected, choose Object > Text Wrap > Make. Click OK on the warning. If nothing happens, bring box 3 to the front with Cmd+Shift+] (Ctrl+Shift+]). The text in boxes 1 and 2 should wrap around 3 (see Figure 8.12).

The default outset for text wrap is **6 pt**; use Object > Text Wrap > Text Options to change that if necessary.

8. The headline is simply a four-column wide text area that, like the REVdrink.com box on the back panel, has been styled with the **Wavy Deck** paragraph and graphic styles. It has the same text wrap settings as box 3. You will find the text of the headline in the `Copy - Inside - Headline.doc` file. Place it in now.

FIGURE 8.12 With a text wrap applied, another border appears around the object's bounding box.

9. Hmm. With sentence case (initial capital letter and the rest lowercase), it doesn't have quite the impact we were hoping for, does it? Let's fix that with Type > Change Case > Title Case. Ah! Much better.

10. Now would be a good time to add the logo above box 4 (copy and paste it from the back panel above), then unlock boxes 1 and 2.

STEP 4 ▼
Improving Readability with Paragraph Options and the Adobe Composer

Although we haven't the space to go into all the best practices of typesetting and the rules that define them—that's a whole book unto itself—it behooves us to take a look at some of the easiest-to-implement—and most powerful—paragraph composition tools built into Illustrator CS2.

1. Style the type in your three stories (four type areas) to fill their respective spaces. Be careful to choose OpenType fonts or the rest of this section won't do you much good. I used different faces from Adobe's Myriad Pro family for boxes 1, 2, and 3, and Adobe Minion Pro for box 4 (both are bundled free with Illustrator CS2 and Creative Suite 2).

> **◎ TIP**
>
> OpenType fonts from Adobe are identified in a font family list by the "Pro" or "Std" suffix.

2. Select boxes 1, 2, and 3 with the Selection tool. On the Paragraph palette, set their alignment to left (or justified, if you prefer) using the top row of buttons. Set box 4 to flush right alignment.

3. With all four boxes selected, activate hyphenation on the Paragraph palette. Do you see any lines of box 4 ending in hyphens? If so, zoom in on one until you can clearly see it and the live area guide it abuts. If none of the lines in your box 4 hyphenate, zoom in on the opening quotation mark in box 2.

4. To separate paragraphs, don't press Enter twice. That's a fallacious practice left over from the days of typewriters when the limitations of the hardware necessitated hacking paragraph spacing with multiple carriage returns. Professionally set type uses spacing before and/or after a paragraph. Add, say, **15 pt** of spacing before the paragraphs in boxes 1 and 2 on the Paragraph palette's Space Before Paragraph box (you might need to show options from the palette menu).

5. You're still on the Paragraph palette, so go ahead and select Roman Hanging Punctuation from the palette menu—watch the hyphen (or quotation mark) as you do this. Did it move out into the margin beyond the text area (see Figure 8.13)?

of course, a fict-

ct and brand. It

ited by Pariah S.

e in tutorials he

The *correct* way to set type is to try to achieve an overall evenness of tone between the ink of the text and the emptiness of the spaces around and inside it. This is called the grayness or *color* of type, and it should be consistently even from one glyph to the next, one line to the next. Punctuation marks like hyphens, commas, quotation marks, and so on typically create more white space than black (or any color) ink. This causes slight optical indentations in the flush edge of the text. To maintain an overall even color, punctuation marks—indeed, many glyphs— are properly hung out into the margin. At close zooms, this looks awkward; when viewed zoomed out, however, in the context of the column as a whole, the color of the type is more even— improving readability thereby.

6. Go ahead and select Adobe Every-line Composer from the flyout as well. The Every-line Composer makes decisions on how to hyphenate, wrap, and space words and glyphs—how to compose—in

a paragraph by examining all lines in the paragraph. It actually looks at the lines above and below, ascertaining the effects of each potential hyphenation, wrapping, or spacing decision on the rest of the paragraph. With the Every-line Composer, Illustrator's text-rendering engine strives to achieve a more even *rag* edge and reduce *rivers* to improve the appearance of the entire paragraph with every decision. By contrast, the Single-line Composer looks no further than the current line when choosing how to hyphenate, wrap, and space. *Usually* the Every-line Composer creates more readable and better-looking text paragraphs (it does little for single lines like the cover).

STEP 5 ▼
Using the Advanced Typographic Controls of OpenType

Before the D*esktop Publishing Revolution* put the power of bad design into the hands of anyone who could afford a computer, professionally set type was beautiful, properly punctuated, and easy to read. Professional typesetters used dedicated and proprietary computer systems—and before them, lead block or "hot metal" type—to *properly* set type in ways that creative software programs like Illustrator have taken 20 years to implement. Yes, sad as it is, it wasn't until the release of Illustrator CS in late 2003 that the world's greatest vector drawing program finally achieved the level of typographic control that typesetting software possessed in the 1970s and 80s.

1. Zoom in on and select (only) box 4. If it isn't already, change the type family to Minion Pro, Adobe Garamond Pro, Adobe Jenson Pro, or Adobe Caslon Pro—just for now.

> **TIP**
>
> **The ability to underline text (without a dodgy hack involving copying text from Photoshop) didn't appear in Illustrator until CS2 in 2005—the nineteenth anniversary and twelfth version of Adobe's very first application!**

2. 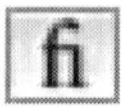 On the OpenType palette (Window > Type > OpenType), turn on the Standard Ligature button. Notice the *fi* in the word "fictitious" (see Figure 8.14)? Many letters, when paired, crowd each other. In this case the dot of the *i* would intersect the teardrop loop of the *f* (people don't say, "what a cute couple" when these two are together). To compensate, most fonts include *ligatures* or combined letterforms for such pairings. In this case, *i*'s sister does much better on a date with *f*. Standard ligatures include ff, fi, fl, ffi, ffl, and ft.

FIGURE 8.14 Which pair makes the cute couple and which argue too much?

fi fi

3. 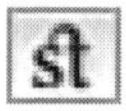 Activating discretionary ligatures can add a touch of typographic style by replacing pairings like *st* (in "illustration") and *ct* (in "fictitious" and "product") (see Figure 8.15).

FIGURE 8.15 Soul mates or an arranged marriage? You decide.

ct st ct st

4. 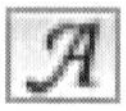 The Swash option varies in effect. Like all OpenType font features, the options are only as available—and extensive—as the type designer has made them. With typefaces like Caflisch Script Pro, swashes add an extra flourish to already stylish glyphs—great shoes to finish off a gorgeous dress. In Minion Pro Italic, however, Swash keeps just the blouse to use as the foundation for a whole new outfit (see Figure 8.16).

FIGURE 8.16 Swash flourishes create an entirely different style of the same Minion Pro typeface.

REV is, of course a fictitious product and brand. It was created by Pariah S. Burke for use in tutorials he writes to

5. Select text box 1 and zoom in on its first paragraph. Set the typeface to something from the Minion Pro family. On the OpenType palette, change the Figure drop-down from the default "Default Figure" to "Proportional Oldstyle." Watch the numbers in the ingredient percentages as you do. See the difference? Zoom out to 100% (Cmd+1) [Ctrl+1] and see if you can pick out the numbers. If it takes longer than one second to spot them among the mix of upper- and lowercase letters, you've got good typography.

Numerals in tables or columns of numerals should be the same size and width to make the data easily readable. In the flow of text, however, numerals are correctly set proportionately, that is, they approximate the variable heights and widths of letters, often with *ascenders* and *descenders* (see Figure 8.17). The numerals we typically see are tabular lining—to be lined up in a table—and are distracting to the eye, drawing a reader out of the flow of text in other sentences or even adjacent columns. The purpose of text is to be *read*—in the *order* it is written. Proportional oldstyle numerals within text fulfill this purpose, whereas in "standard" style, tabular lining numerals are designed for an entirely different purpose.

6. Finish your brochure by performing any text touch-ups and dropping the **Tachometer Inside** symbol into the middle of the panels (see Figure 8.18). I actually used two copies of that symbol, aligned to each other. The obvious one is set to 75% opacity, whereas the copy behind it is 100% opaque, but with a radial blur effect that renders it semi-transparent.

 TIP

OpenType fonts are the first format to be cross-platform—the same font files work on both Mac and Windows—eliminating all the problems created by Type 1 PostScript and TrueType fonts when moving documents between platforms.

FIGURE 8.18 Designed and typeset, my brochure is now ready for proofing.

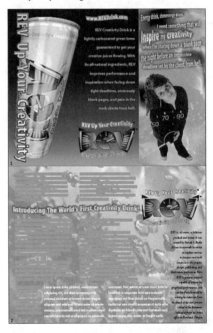

FIGURE 8.17 In which of these samples are the numerals easier to pick out—and be distracted by?

Energy drinks give you energy for a variety of activities, getting the adrenaline pumping to bolster your *stamina*. But they don't help you *create*. With its Recommended Daily Values of 100% Inspiration, 200% Imagination, and 70% Chutzpah, only REV Creativity Drink gets your creative juices flowing.

Energy drinks give you energy for a variety of activities, getting the adrenaline pumping to bolster your *stamina*. But they don't help you *create*. With its Recommended Daily Values of 100% Inspiration, 200% Imagination, and 70% Chutzpah, only REV Creativity Drink gets your creative juices flowing.

Project:
Proofing and Printing

We'll proof and print the brochure in two steps:

1. Previewing transparency flattening
2. Printing the one-page, multi-page document

Proofing and Printing the Brochure

In an ideal world—well, an ideal world would look a lot like Willy Wonka's chocolate factory, but that's a different dream altogether. In an ideal *design* world, what we create in a computer would roll off a printing press exactly the same way. As much as we may want that, Veruca, it is not to be. Therefore we must proof the brochure.

STEP 1 ▼
Previewing Transparency Flattening

In applications like Illustrator that support transparency, objects may be layered atop, and interact with, each other through blending modes, opacity settings, and effects like glows, blurs, and shadows. Presses and printers, however, don't understand stacked objects; printing devices work strictly in two-dimensional areas of color—a document is chopped up into either rasterized (pixel) sections or solid, single-color vector paths. The process of transforming layered objects with any type of interactive transparency into flat areas of color is called *flattening*.

Flattening can beget unexpected results, but historically, there was no way to preview flattening until the document reached the *RIP* at the *service bureau*. Illustrator CS and CS2 (and InDesign CS and CS2) let you see on screen how your design will flatten, affording you not only the opportunity to fix potential problems but also to specify the quality of the flattening.

1. Still got your `Brochure.ai` layout on screen? Open the Flattener Preview palette from the Window menu. Use the lower-right corner to resize the palette until it fills your screen—you won't need to see the original document.

2. If you don't yet see a thumbnail in the expansive preview area at the bottom of the palette, click the Refresh button. You should see your original document. From the Highlight menu choose All Affected Objects, and then click Refresh again. Almost everything is red, isn't it (see Figure 8.19)? Areas highlighted in Rubylithe-like red (if you've been in this business long enough to remember Rubylithe) are going to be flattened.

3. Change the highlight to Outlined Strokes to see strokes that will become filled objects.

 TIP

Maneuvering around the Flattener Preview window is similar to a document window: Click to zoom in, Opt-click [Alt-click] to zoom out, and Space-drag to move around with the Hand tool.

FIGURE 8.19 Previewing all objects affected by transparency highlights nearly the entire document.

4. Tell the palette to show you All Rasterized Regions. Everything highlighted will become raster areas, no longer resolution-independent vectors. Where raster and vector regions share colors there can be—and often is—a discernable color or quality difference in the final output. The picture of the REV can, for example (see Figure 8.20), is going to cause an uneven section of the gradient to rasterize. When you print to a PostScript-compatible printer device, there *is* a noticeable difference in tone between the raster and vector areas of that gradient.

So how do you fix it? In this case the rasterization is caused by the can's transparent background, so I would draw a path the shape of the can and use it as a clipping mask. Other instances, though—the inner panels, for example—can't be helped. Where there is transparency, it must flatten to print.

5. From the Flattener Preview palette menu choose Show Options. You will probably need to resize and refresh again.

6. Choose whether to simulate, preserve (keep without simulating), or discard *overprints*. The Preset offers three choices—low, medium, and high resolution. Often medium resolution provides excellent quality prints. Beneath the Presets, the Flattening Quality Slider determines the quality versus complexity ratio; the more vector objects created to break up colors (see Figure 8.21), the

higher both quality and complexity. Too complex a document will choke a RIP, rendering your job unprintable.

7. If you make any changes in the Flattener Preview that you might use again, save a preset (from the palette flyout menu). You can then employ that flattening preset if you decide to

actually flatten the document from Object > Flatten Transparency.

TIP

All of the Flattener Preview options are explained in detail in Illustrator's help file.

FIGURE 8.20 When printed, the colors in the left panel's rasterized area will be perceptibly different than the same colors on the back.

FIGURE 8.21 In this illustration (left) of the RGB additive color model, each circle overlaps the other two with a blending mode set to Screen. When flattened (right), the overlaps become separate objects of solid color.

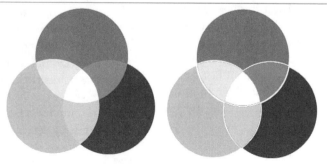

Printing the One-Page, Multi-Page Document

This part couldn't be simpler. We've already done all the work!

1. Go to File > Print.

2. Select the Print Preset you made at the beginning of the project. Click Print. Done.

3. If you want to send a PDF to the client for proofing, *print* to Adobe PDF. Don't *save* as a PDF or the client will see the tiled document exactly as you do; printing is the only way to create the separate pages.

4. After the PDF is printed, open it in Acrobat and use File > Document Properties > Security to limit the client's ability to print or to edit. I recommend allowing the client to comment and sign the document digitally.

Final Thoughts

One drawback to the multiple-pages-in-one technique is that you cannot add crop, registration, and other marks. If you need them, print your document to PDF as usual. Open the PDF in Acrobat 7 Professional, and go to Tools > Print Production > Add Printer Marks.

If you don't have Acrobat 7 Professional, earlier versions of Acrobat can add printer's marks through File > Print > Advanced (button) > Marks and Bleeds. You can add them here for printing to a desktop printer, or you can *refry* the PDF—printing it from Acrobat to the Adobe PDF printer, thus printing a PDF from a PDF. Just remember to adjust the output size to include the space added by the marks.

If you intend to print your brochure solely from a desktop printer or photocopier, start with an 11 × 17 in. document and adjust the measurements set in the "Building the One-Page, Multi-Page Template" section accordingly. Do not include a bleed area, and set your trim area according to the *rebate* imposed by the printer or copier.

There are a lot of subtle things going on in my brochure. On the front cover, for example, keywords that drive home the marketing message (for instance, "blank page" and "deadline") are filled with a 75% tint of the same color the surrounding text uses at 100%. The model herself is a big device. Her left foot and direction her chest faces create *lines of force* that direct the reader's attention toward the right edge—the edge to open the brochure. On the inside, the "introducing…" headline leads the eye through the left and center panels to the logo in the right; the white space above and below-left of the logo helps to emphasize its importance. Also, notice how I allowed the REV can to peek out onto the back flap? If the brochure is seen from the back, that little bit of image may catch a reader's interest and prompt her to open the brochure and have the chance to be drawn in by the marketing copy. There are other subtle devices at work—some designed to convey the reader's eye through the brochure, others to embed the brand name in their minds.

If you are new to the concept of transparency flattening, it can be difficult to fully grasp. To better understand it, print (don't save) to a PDF. In Acrobat, use the Object Touchup Tool to click around areas of your flattened artwork. The borders of each piece will highlight, and the piece can be dragged out of place to reveal the emptiness beneath. Note: Black ink overprints by default, so black fills and strokes will not knock out the ink beneath.

CHAPTER 9: Designing and Color Proofing a Magazine Advertisement

About the Projects

In this chapter we will design an advertisement, then utilize Illustrator's built-in proofing methods to verify how it will print on different proof printers and ultimately separate on an imagesetter.

Prerequisites

It would be helpful if you had the ability to draw basic shapes with the Pen tool, and the ability to set and style type. You should also be comfortable moving, scaling, and rotating objects.

@work resources

Please visit the publisher's website to access the following Chapter 9 project files:

- ▶ Chap09 (Advertisement.ai)
- ▶ Chap09\Assets (Logo and head.ai, New.pdf, Drink Can.psd, Bg.tif, Body copy.doc, Premise copy.doc, Warning copy.doc)
- ▶ Chap09\Extras (copyfit.txt, lorem.txt, 860 ICC MAC/p860std, 860 ICC WIN/p860std.icm)
- ▶ Chap09\Finished Project

Planning the Projects

When planning an advertisement, the first question is one of mechanics: What are its dimensions? Is it a half-page? A quarter-page vertical? An ad fills a predefined space in a periodical or signboard, so what are the dimensions of the ad space in the particular media in which it will run? A full-page ad in a broadsheet newspaper is certainly not the same as a full-page ad in a standard magazine.

Most of the mechanical questions are answered in a publication's ad spec sheet (which may or may not be included as part of a media kit or rate card). Just ask the media sales representative for the specs.

Also in the specs will be the media's digital file specifications—what kind of digital file to deliver (PDF, EPS, and so on), what subformat (PDF/X-1, fonts outlined, and so on), and how to submit it (email, FTP, or a browser-based ad submission system).

Organization and hierarchy are crucial to advertisement design because readers don't seek out ads, and they will quickly leave an ad if it doesn't hold their interest and provide everything they need. Nearly every ad should contain a headline, main visual, body copy, logo, and response area. Give each of these a ranking of importance, and design your ad around the primary goal of promoting that hierarchy.

In the ad's response area, motivate the reader to *do* something. *For a free widget, call... Stop in to our Main St. location for a test drive today! Free gizmo to the first 50 people through the door!* Include a call to action that inspires the reader to do something like purchase, participate, play, or some other

verb. Place your contact information close to the call to action to establish the relationship between the call to action and the means of contact—do *this*, by going/calling/writing *here*.

What is it going to look like? You will have no control over the output process of an ad placed in another entity's publication, and they won't fix for you any problem that doesn't prevent printing. Before sending it out, proof your ad carefully for accuracy, completeness, physical structure, color, fonts, and output capability.

Project: Ad Design

In four easy steps we'll design a full-page advertisement ready for insertion in a monthly magazine:

1. **Setting a layout grid with angled guides**
2. **Placing image elements into the grid**
3. **Importing and setting copy with the Area Type tool**
4. **Making text wrap**

Designing the Ad

Effective designs depend on effective planning (and chocolate, but the publisher just wouldn't go for bundling Reese's Peanut Butter Cups with this book no matter how nicely I asked). Because the average reader is not a fan of advertisements, capturing and holding the reader's interest long enough to present a complete marketing message and inspire action is even more difficult than with other forms of communication. The reader (or viewer) will take any opportunity to leave the ad. Thus, planning an effective ad design becomes crucial to its function.

Setting a Layout Grid with Angled Guides

Information-based layouts rely on logical structure and direction to convey their message. That structure and direction is created with a layout grid. If this is your first time working with grids, don't be frightened; I'm right here with you.

1. Let's begin a new full-page magazine advertisement with a **7.8 × 10.45 in.** CMYK document.

2. Show your rulers and drag out guides to create a **0.125 in.** bleed area all the way around the artboard. Because magazines are either *saddle-stitched* or *perfect bound*, information set too close to the binding edge of a page could get cramped in the *spine*. To avoid this, let's create live area guides **0.25 in.** in from the edge of the artboard rather than the customary **0.125 in.** Name this layer **Master Guides** and lock it.

> ◎ **TIP**
>
> For all but the simplest of ads to work, they must be on a grid; for the grid to work, all (or at least nearly all) elements must adhere to the grid.

---

3. Because the launch ad in the REV campaign will have much less *copy* than imagery, let's build a basic two-column grid with a **0.25 in.** gutter. With an odd page size such as this one, it's easier to let Illustrator do its math magic than to figure out the placement coordinates ourselves.

   Select View > Guides > Lock Guides to toggle the checkmark off and allow us

to precisely position guides as we would any other object.

4. On a new layer, drag a guide from the vertical ruler to roughly the middle of the artboard. Notice that the guide is a different color than the rest (if not, click on it). Unlocked, guides are treated like any object in Illustrator. So, bring up the Transform palette (Window > Transform), and clear the contents of the X: measurement box.

5. We know the artboard is **7.8 in.** wide, but what is its horizontal center minus half of a .25 gutter? Heck if I know. In the X: measurement box, type in **7.8/2** (the width of the page divided by 2). Your guide should jump to **3.9 in.** Click between the **3.9** and the **in** and type **-.125** (1/4 in., or half the 1/2 in. gutter we want; see Figure 9.1). Your first column guide is in position. Repeat this procedure to set up the second column guide, defining the other side of the gutter by *adding* **0.125 in.** instead of subtracting.

FIGURE 9.1 Illustrator's math magic at work in the Transform palette.

6. Setting the horizontal grid guides will be a little different. Because we want six blocks—seven equidistant horizontal guides including the top and bottom margin guides—the math would be tricky, even with Illustrator's help. So let's do things the less cerebrally taxing way. From the horizontal ruler drag down two guides and align them over the top and bottom margin guides that reside on the **Master Guides** layer.

---

7. That's two, so drag five more guides and drop them anywhere in the artboard between the first two. With the Selection tool, click and drag a selection rectangle that touches all seven horizontal guides but neither of the vertical guides.

8. 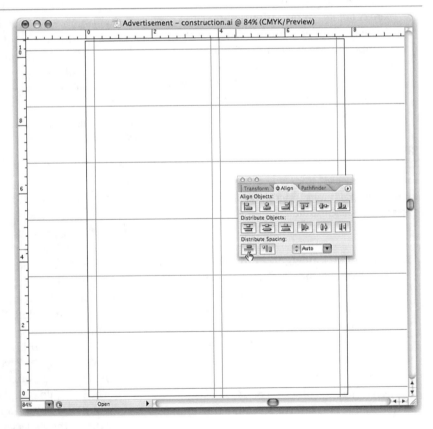 Open the Align palette (Window > Align), making sure Show Options has been selected from the Options flyout. In the Distribute Spacing section, set the drop-down to Auto, and then click the Vertical Distribute Space button. Your guides should now be evenly distributed between the top and bottom margins (see Figure 9.2).

9. For most ads, this would be the end of the grid creation process. However, as you've probably figured out by now, REV likes to do things a little differently. While still adhering to a layout grid, this ad is going to be off-axis. So, select all the grid guides (Cmd-A [Ctrl+A] is the fastest way), and return to the Transform palette.

10. Select the center point in the reference point proxy, and rotate it to **-13°** in the rotate measurement field. The entire grid should now tilt around the center point of the ad (see Figure 9.3). Lock the guides once again from View > Guides > Lock Guides, and save your progress.

FIGURE 9.2 Unlocked, guides are treated like objects and can be easily distributed with the Distribute Spacing buttons on the Align palette.

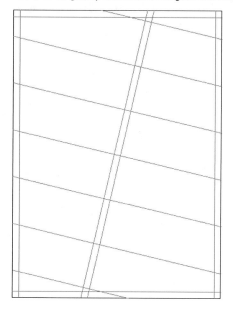

STEP 2 ▼
Placing Image Elements into the Grid

Before moving into setting copy, place and align graphical elements to the grid.

1. From File > Place or the Adobe Bridge bring in your background image. Position and scale it and, if necessary, apply a clipping mask such that the background image (if your ad has one) fills the artboard and bleed area but no further. Lock the background image with (Cmd-2) [Ctrl+2] to prevent accidental repositioning (and copious cursing).

2. Headlines are critical to grabbing interest, so set your ad's headline now with the Type tool. If you are working strictly with the REV ad, place the logo and head.ai file, which integrates a stylized headline into the logo.

3. Next, place the Drink Can.psd main visual and New.pdf blurb images. When

placing these images, remember to check Link in the Place dialog.

4. Position and size the graphical elements as you like, bearing in mind that the logo and headline are crucial, and the **New!** blurb will attract attention.

> ◎ **TIP**
>
> Madison Avenue has known for decades that "new," "sale," and "sex" are the three words most capable of grabbing interest, though overuse has greatly diluted their ability to separate a consumer from his cash. In recent years, changes in the social consciousness have promoted other words to universally command attention. These include "improved," "more," "less," and "low" (as in "low fat" or "low sodium").

5. Align the elements to the grid, rotating each **-13°** degrees to match (see Figure 9.4).

FIGURE 9.4 **See how the grid builds relationships between the elements and creates an order and direction for the viewer's eye?**

STEP 3 ▼
Importing and Setting Copy with the Area Type Tool

A picture is worth a thousand words, they say. After writing this book, I agree with them. Rare ads can exist on pictures alone, but most often it takes a combination of pictures and words to tell a complete marketing story.

1. Decide where your copy will appear, and then drag guides from the horizontal ruler to define a 0-degree° top for each of the text areas. To stay within the grid (modified, slightly), align the horizontal guides to the intersection points of the angled horizontal grid lines and the vertical margins, and/or to the center point of the entire grid (see Figure 9.5).

FIGURE 9.5   **Top off intended copy areas with 0-degree guides that cross existing intersections.**

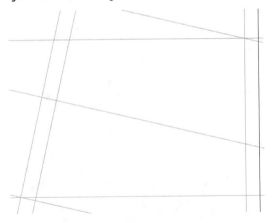

2. Grab the Pen tool and draw shapes that define your copy areas. They should have flat tops and, where they meet a margin, straight edges, but should otherwise follow the

angle of the grid. For the REV ad, you want at least three—preferably four—copy blocks, even if they stack (see Figure 9.6).

FIGURE 9.6   **These odd shapes will become blocks of copy.**

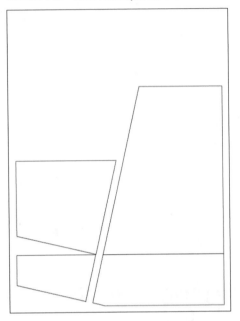

3. When you click and hold on the Type tool in the Toolbox, additional tools will slide out. Among them is the Area Type tool, which is what we need now. Click the Area Type tool somewhere along the path of the response copy block—if you are re-creating the REV ad, use the bottom left block—and start typing. Type in **REV Up Your Creativity now at www.RevDrink.com!**. With the REV ad, this is our call to action, getting readers to visit the website.

4. Again using the Area Type tool, click in the block you've designated to hold your premise copy. When your I-beam cursor is in there and you're ready to type, don't. Instead, go up to the File menu and choose Place. Navigate to where you saved this chapter's resource files,

and open the copyedited and client-approved Microsoft Word document, `premise copy.doc` from the `Chap09/Assets` folder. In the Microsoft Word Options dialog, check Remove Text Formatting (the rest of the options are irrelevant to this document), and click OK. The premise copy will not fill the block.

5. Now import the `body copy.doc` and `warning copy.doc` files to their correct placements. If your ad looks like mine (see Figure 9.7), your text will be bland and overlap the imagery; at this stage, that's expected.

FIGURE 9.7 With all the elements on the artboard, it's time to begin styling type.

STEP 4 ▼
Making Text Wrap

One of the best ways to liven up a layout is to break images out of their usual boxes and make them interact directly with text.

1. Select the REV can image. Then find its entry on the Links palette (Window > Links); it should already be highlighted. As with other techniques and effects, text wrap is only applicable to native or embedded objects. So, from the Links palette flyout menu, choose Embed Image. In the Photoshop Import Options dialog, choose Flatten Photoshop to flatten the layers to a single image. A new icon should appear beside the `Drink Can.psd` entry, and the X across the image's bounding box should disappear.

2. Select Object > Text Wrap > Make. Other than a new outline around the shape of the can, nothing will likely happen. *So what's the point, man,* you might ask. *Bring the can to the front, dude,* I might suggest. *Sweet!* You might exclaim.

   Go to Object > Text Wrap > Text Wrap Options to adjust the offset (more commonly called outset) or to even invert the wrap so that text appears only *inside* the shape instead of outside. In this case, the default **6 pt** offset will suffice.

3. Style your type as you like and finalize the ad. Figure 9.8 shows my finished ad.

FIGURE 9.8   My finished REV ad (shown without bleed).

Project: **Proofing**

We'll proof colors and color separations for our finished ad in two easy steps:

1. **Soft-proofing a specific printer's color support**
2. **Printing hard proof color separations**

Proofing Colors and Color Separation

The most inspired design in the world is for naught if the colors don't print as expected.

Soft-proofing is the process of proofing on-screen, as opposed to *hard-proofing*—which would be...? Anyone? Anyone? Bueller? Bueller? Ri-ight: printing hard copies. In this section, we're going to do both.

STEP 1 ▼
Soft-Proofing a Specific Printer's Color Support

Hypothetically, let's say you plan to save the ad as a PDF to send to the client. You're pretty sure the client will print it out, and you know she has a Xerox Phaser 860 solid ink (aka "crayon") printer. *You* went the Lexmark route and don't have access to a Phaser for printing. There *will* be differences in color between what you print and what your client prints. How do you predict what she's going to see?

Right: Soft-proofing.

1. Close Illustrator. Included in this chapter's resource files, in the `Chap09/Extras` folder, are two subfolders: `860 ICC WIN` and `860 ICC MAC`, containing *ICC* profiles downloaded from the Xerox website.

2. If you are using Windows 2000, XP, or later: Right-click on the file `p860std.icm` in `Chap09/Extras/860 ICC WIN/` and select Install Profile. Or you may simply copy it to `C:\WINDOWS\system32\spool\drivers\color` (note: your system may use a different drive letter and/or folder name for Windows).

3. If you are using Macintosh OS X:: Copy the file `p860std` from `Chap09/Extras/860 ICC MAC/` to *either* [your user name] `Library/ColorSync/Profiles` (accessible only to your account) *or* the system's `Library/ColorSync/Profiles` folder (accessible by all user accounts on the system). Note: The latter requires administrative access to the system.

4. Launch Illustrator and open your advertisement. Select Window > New Window to open another window of the same document, then (Windows only) Window > Tile to line them up side by side. In both windows press (Cmd-0) [Ctrl+0] to zoom them to fit. Press your keyboard's Tab key to temporarily hide all palettes.

5. Select View > Proof Setup > Customize. In the Proof Setup dialog, search the Device to Simulate list for the Phaser 860 and select it. Leave Preserve CMYK Numbers checked, which dims the Rendering Intent. Check Simulate Paper Color (see Figure 9.9). Click OK.

6. Compare the two views of your document. See any differences? They're slight, which is good. This layout should print pretty well on the client's Phaser 860. Try other CMYK printer profiles you might have in the Device to Simulate list; they won't all look this good. The Tektronix Phaser III Pxi might be an interesting test. To turn off soft-proofing and return to a normal view of your document, toggle View > Proof Colors off.

STEP 2 ▼
Printing Hard-Proof Color Separations

Possibly before sending the layout to the client but definitely before sending it to press, print your own color *separations* (colloquially, "seps"). Hard-copy seps will highlight many problems such as color areas that are too small to print correctly at the output *line screen* and accidental use of rich black or registration color (both of which print on all four *plates* instead of just the black plate).

1. Select File > Print.

2. In the Print dialog, choose a Print Preset (if you have one) or your proof printer and its *PPD*.

3. On the Marks and Bleeds tabs, activate any marks you want, and, if you want to print bleeds, set the Bleeds measurement boxes to match the bleed area of your document (**0.125 in.** all around).

4. The Mode setting on the Output tab is the important part here. By default it's set to Composite, which prints as full color. Change this to Separations (Host-Based)—the host being your computer. Leave Convert All Spot Colors to Process unchecked, but check Overprint Black because a real printing press typically *overprints* the opaque black ink, the last of the four inks to run. At the bottom, in the Document Ink Options area, are all the ink colors in use in your document (see Figure 9.10). If you want to print only certain inks, remove the others' print icons by clicking in the first column.

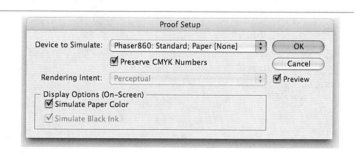

FIGURE 9.9 The Proof Setup dialog.

FIGURE 9.10 In Illustrator CS2's Print dialog, the Output tab shows the inks that are in use and will print.

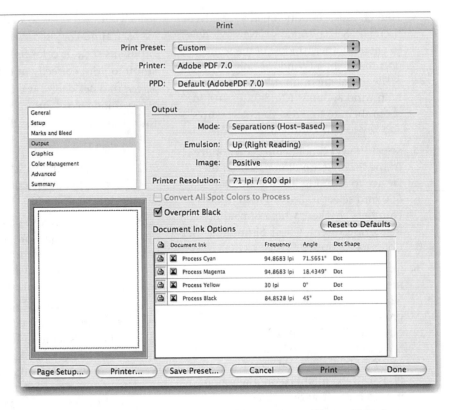

5. Set your printer's ICC profile on the Color Management tab, and review the Overprint and Transparency Flattener Options on the Advanced tab.

6. When you're ready, switch on your printer and click Print.

would separate to *film* or digital press. Look them over for anything broken or out of place—for example, missing or low-resolution placed images, text in the wrong font or "boxes" replacing characters, and whether black objects appear on all the plates.

 TIP

If you might print seps to the same printer again, save a preset to automate the configuration.

 TIP

For an approximation of how the inks will register on-press, hold all five copies together against a lightbox or window. Even better, print seps onto transparencies available in the overhead projector aisle of any office supply store.

7. What should come out of your printer are black-and-white separations, one page for each ink in your document (see Figure 9.11). This is how your document

8. If you don't have a laser printer or a good inkjet available, here's a cool trick: Go through steps 1 through 7 again, but set the Printer to Adobe PDF (Acrobat 6 or 7) or Acrobat Distiller. The resulting PDF will have separate pages for each ink; though not as good as a hard copy, it's not far from it. (You *do* have Acrobat, don't you? If there's any software tool every designer absolutely must have these days, it's Acrobat or a comparable standalone PDF creator/editor.)

Final Thoughts

If there's a secret to the success of good advertising, layout, or graphic design in general, it would have to be grids. Though the uninitiated often view grids as restrictive to creativity, preferring to shoot from the hip, they are exactly the opposite. Adhering strictly to too simple a grid is limiting, yes, but rather than abandon grids, expand them. Add more columns and rows—even if elements span multiple columns and/or rows. You can also vary the size of columns and rows; there's no rule that says grids must be symmetrical. Grids bring order, structure, and direction, three crucial elements in any form of visual communication.

Look at ads and other designs that appeal to you. Then grab a ruler and pencil and discover their grids and hierarchies.

Curious how I created the NEW! blurb—which is live, editable text? Open the New.pdf in Illustrator; it was saved as a PDF with Preserve Illustrator Editing Capabilities checked, which means that it's just an Illustrator file. Hint: How I did it is all in the Appearance palette.

The body copy document is a section of *greeking* that uses Lorem Ipsum, a nonsense selection of scrambled text that has been in use in printing, typesetting, and design industries since the 1500s. Lorem Ipsum is used as placeholder copy when the real copy isn't available, or to force a viewer to focus on the design rather than on reading the text.

Included in the Extras folder among the resource files is a complete copy of Lorem Ipsum in the lorem.txt file. I've also included a file called copyfit.txt, which, like Lorem Ipsum, is used as placeholder text. The difference is that although Lorem Ipsum approximates normal copy with words and paragraphs of varying lengths, CopyFit is composed entirely of five-letter words—the median length of words in Latin-based languages—and every twenty-fifth word is numbered to aid in determining how many words will fit in a predefined space.

As a result of conditioning from a very early age, people will read whatever is placed in front of them. When you proof a layout, you want your client or audience to see and evaluate the *design*. Unfortunately, the fact is, the average person will spend more time reading the copy than looking at the visuals. (This is a valuable fact to keep in mind while designing too, not just proofing). Take the focus off the text and place it on the design, layout, or another aspect of the proof, by using greeking.

I've had a few clients complain about the greeking, some saying that they couldn't understand and critique the layout without seeing their text in place. That assertion, however, only proved the point that they were focusing too much on the copy and not enough on the design. One client even yelled at me, demanding to know where I got the idea that he wanted to advertise his English-language products to Latin speakers! Most of the time, clients will defer to your judgment on such matters if you merely explain to them your motivations.

If you're thinking that my experience is reason enough to not use greeking, let me fill in what sometimes happens if you don't use greeking.

In a few such cases I was unable to convince the client to give me feedback on the design without seeing his copy in place (this was the layout phase, not the copy proofing or final proofing phases). When the clients demanded putting their copy in, I acquiesced. Then I spent several revision cycles with each of them (numerous billable and unbillable hours) working on fixing the language and grammar of their copy to the way they wanted it (post-copy proof phase, mind you). During these revisions, I received little if any feedback on the actual design of their respective projects; it was all about the copy. After the clients finally had the copy the way they wanted it written, *then* they began looking at the design, which they invariably had to change, often forcing more copy changes, which beget more design changes, and so on.

One client (the same one who complained about me trying to market his products to speakers of a dead language) began like the others, but never really did focus too much on the design; every time I gave him a design proof, he would simply read the copy (usually making some minor correction). The day I got back a signed final proof, I was ecstatic— I could finally send the job off to press! However, when the client got his printed pieces back from the press, he was livid. He disagreed with several elements of the design, including overall color choices (the final deliverables matched the colors in the proof he signed). Although his dissatisfaction could be attributed to a change of heart, it wasn't; he hadn't looked at anything but the copy in all my proofs to him—including the one he signed off on—and only really looked at it after he had paid for 5,000 copies of it. (After that experience, the client listened to me and scrutinized every detail of my proofs... They employed greeking, of course.)

About the Projects

We'll design a typical DVD package, including outer package ("Amaray") and disc label, ready for delivery to a DVD production plant.

Prerequisites

It would be helpful if you had a basic understanding of working with the Layers palette and creating, reordering, and naming layers, as well as drawing basic shapes, using the Pathfinder palette, applying fills and strokes, and placing external graphic files.

One portion of the DVD label project uses Photoshop. If you choose to complete this optional section you will need to have Photoshop CS or CS2.

@work resources

Please visit the publisher's website to access the following Chapter 10 project files:

- ▶ **Chap10** (complete projects to use as a reference while you work: DVD label.ai and Amaray.ai)
- ▶ **Chap10\Assets** (Logo - Grayscale.ai, Logo Duotone.ai, Logo.ai, cantop gray.psd, cantop.psd, Drink Can - Multilingual.psd, barcode.eps, bg.tif, DVD-Video 1.tif)
- ▶ **Chap10\Extras** (CompactDisc-DigitalAudio.tif, CompactDisc-DigitalVideo.tif, CompactDisc-Recordable-ReWritable.tif, CompactDisc-SuperVideo.tif, DVD-Audio.tif, DVD-Audio-Video.tif, DVD-Video 1.tif, DVD-Video 2.tif, DVD-Video-R-RW.tif, DVD-Video-RW.tif, RW-Compatible.tif, RW-DVD+ReWritable.tif)
- ▶ **Chap10\Finished Project**

Planning the Projects

I expect a fair number of you reading this will be coming from a video production background. This may even be your first project for print. This section covers planning concerns for video production professionals as well as anyone else working on these projects.

Considerations for Video Professionals

If you are a video pro but unfamiliar with for-print work, there are two critical differences between broadcast and print of which you must be aware: resolution and color. You'll need to plan for them.

If you hope to repurpose frames of your video for printing the DVD package, you have an uphill battle. Not only will you need to correct the pixel aspect ratio to square pixels, but the resolution of your video is also woefully unsuited to printing. Your printed piece will need a resolution of at least 300 *dpi* (roughly equivalent to *ppi*) and must fill the printed space at 100% scale. To fill the approximately 7 × 5 inch front panel of an Amaray insert with a captured frame at 300 dpi, your artwork must be 2,100 × 1,500 pixels. Have you got that in your digital video?

When studios produce printed matter like posters and DVD and VHS packaging, they don't use frames for cover art; they shoot still photographs during or after production, create the artwork from scratch in Photoshop or Illustrator, or generate digitally touched-up prints from the original high-resolution celluloid. Resolution is the reason that stills taken from frames, when they *are* used (as often seen on DVD and VHS back covers), are so small. But even those are cleaned up by photo touch-up professionals. Frames on the back

covers of B- and C-film DVDs, like *Vampire Cheerleaders from Beverly Hills High*, look so bad not just because the original film was low-grade, but also because they haven't got the budget to touch up frame captures for print.

Trying to print frames directly from your film to use as the main art on DVD packaging will produce a look very similar to overcompressing an MPEG and then blowing it up.

High-definition film or video does yield better results when used for print, but not that much better. Even HD frames aren't adequate for professional grade printing. If you want to use imagery from your film on paper, shoot stills or mock it up in Photoshop. If your desired shots are effects-laden frames, see if your compositor or effects application supports rendering frames out to higher resolutions.

 TIP

If you really want to use a film frame for print, Live Trace it in Illustrator (see Chapter 5, "Illustrating an (Almost) Photo-Realistic Portrait"). Starting at any resolution and any size, Live Trace will instantly and automatically trace your raster frame capture into vector artwork. *Vector*, of course, is *resolution-independent*; you'll get perfect prints every time.

In the broadcast world, you're accustomed to working in NTSC-safe *RGB* color. There, your biggest concerns are worrying about high saturation colors fuzzing out on TV sets. In the print world, the concerns of NTSC are laughable—you couldn't get a pure, 100% red if you tried. This world is ruled by the subtractive color model of *CMYK*. RGB is an additive model—the more you increase color, the closer you move toward white. That's light. With ink, the more color you add, the further you move *away* from white (theoretically toward black, but because ink isn't completely opaque, 100% of all four inks is actually a nasty brown).

With only the pigments of cyan, magenta, yellow, and black, your color range is severely hampered. Instead of the roughly 16.8 million colors available in RGB, you have only approximately 65,000 in CMYK. Except for a few shades of yellow outside RGB, CMYK is a subset of RGB (see Figure 10.1). Pure pigment red, blue, and green, as well as many other saturated colors like bright, 50/50 mixed purple and orange—among many other shades—simply can't render in CMYK. When converting RGB imagery to CMYK, most people describe the result as "washed out," referring to the lack of vibrancy in CMYK. This ain't processing by Technicolor, baby.

If you're going to use frame captures or original raster artwork, convert it to CMYK in Photoshop before placement into Illustrator. You have more control over raster image colors—and can more easily adjust them for the best results before converting—in Photoshop than in its older sister, Illustrator.

Burning Your Own DVD

Will the DVD be mass-produced, or will you create one-offs at home or in the office?

DVD technology is still evolving. There are already nearly a dozen formats of DVD— none of them yet an industry standard—and more emerge and gain ground every year or so. Worse, there are even DVD replacement hopefuls yawping from the top of the next hill, just waiting to banish *all* the DVD formats to the distant lands settled by 78 RPM records, 8-track tapes, and 5 1/4-inch floppy disks.

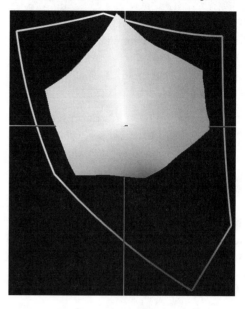

FIGURE 10.1 Though difficult to discern printed in grayscale, this scale comparison of the generic RGB (shown as an outline) and generic CMYK (inner polygon) demonstrates the limits of the CMYK color gamut. At the intersection of the axis lines is the common white point for both gamuts.

I wish I could tell you, *use* this *DVD format*, but I can't. The technology is in such a state of flux that any specific advice I give you is likely to be outdated by the time—*Woosh!* a new DVD subformat was just announced—I finish typing this sentence. The industries concerned with DVD specification and production are still sorting out the standards, trying to find the best technology and DVD format(s) to settle on.

Before buying a DVD burner or settling on the DVD format for your project, talk to the video production community and replication services—even if you will be burning your own disks, replication services can often point you to the best format to choose.

DVD Replication Services

Hiring a replication service to mass-produce your DVD is the less expensive (and vastly easier) route if you plan to burn 100 or more disks. Most replication services provide a full-service DVD production cycle, including replication of your master disk (or disk image) onto blank media, screen-printing the disk, printing packaging and labeling, and then assembling all the pieces.

How do you find a DVD replication service? Check out the advertisement sections at the back of magazines like *Digital Producer*, *Computer Video Editing*, and *Film & Video*. Hang around Internet forums and bulletin boards devoted to digital and analog video production; ask the regulars who they like for replication services. While you're at it, read up on preferred DVD formats and which the pros prefer for projects similar to yours.

Package and Assembly Considerations

After you've chosen your media, you need to decide how to package it and which replication service will do the work before designing anything.

Though there are many DVD packaging options, fortunately for everyone concerned, they're much more stable and predictable than DVD data formats. You have plenty of choices, including, but not limited to: a standard movie DVD-style Amaray case, slimline Amaray, CD-style jewel case, slimline jewel case, paper or vinyl sleeve, brochure wallet, DigiPack, tall DigiPack, and clamshell—among others. Choose the one that compliments the message communicated by your DVD product.

Each has its own style, and many have benefits and drawbacks—chipboard DigiPacks, for example, are environmentally friendly, light, and inexpensive, but they don't hold up to moisture.

Each has its own level of possible decoration as well. For instance, clamshells, hinged plastic holders the size and shape of a CD or DVD disc, are not made to be decorated. Amaray and jewel cases (and slimline versions of either) may have offset printed inserts and even tray cards that appear beneath a transparent disc tray; often they include booklets too. Made out of chipboard or heavy paper, brochure wallets and DigiPacks effectively wrap a sleeve- or tray-held disc in artwork of virtually unlimited size and content.

What does your package need to communicate? If the requirements are light, limited to replicating what will be printed on the disc label, consider a package without decoration of its own. If you choose a sleeve or clamshell, the disc itself can provide the identifying artwork. On the other end of the spectrum, some DVD projects require the inclusion of booklets and lots of information—video games, for example, are often accompanied by printed books. In such cases, consider something with more room, such as Amaray, jewel, or DigiPack cases.

Each package option carries its own price tag, as does assembly.

How much work are you willing to pay the replication service to perform, and how much are you willing to do yourself? Do you want a one-stop shop that assembles everything before sending it to you, or will you have the replication service ship you DVDs on a spindle that you will insert into their containers? Do you require the packages shrink-wrapped? Must any special materials such as RFID tags or security seals be added to the package? Is your DVD for sale? Will it need a barcode? If so, will you obtain the barcode on your own, or will the production plant do it for you?

 TIP

Look in Appendix B, "Resources," for pointers to barcode fonts and generators.

Design Considerations

When burning your own discs, printing your labels on an inkjet or laser printer is definitely the way to go. In such cases, you'll either already know, or quickly learn, the limitations of your own printer. When preparing artwork for delivery to a replication service, however, there are some very important factors to consider.

Most CDs and DVDs are decorated by screen-printing directly onto the disc, which produces richer color and more durable artwork than printing and applying paper or vinyl labels. It also allows the metallic surface of the disc to shine through, if desired. Screen-printing is a lower-resolution process than offset printing, with a dramatically diminished range of color tints.

Type smaller than 6 points doesn't always print. Avoid fine detail, and add extra weight to strokes and type if printed reversed (light objects on a dark background). *Bleeds* can be problematic for many production houses—consult your replication service about bleeds.

Tint or *screen* refers to the density of an ink color—0% tint is no ink (white or *substrate* color), 100% is full coverage. These percentages do not refer to transparency, however. In screen printing, many screens plug up higher tonal values, meaning that as little as an 85% tint may render the same as 100%, printing with full coverage. Similarly, they often blow out the bottom 15% of highlights, rendering up to 15% color as no color at all.

Ever notice how most music CDs are printed with only a few colors and often include only text and maybe basic line art on the disc itself? There's a reason for that. Screen printing is usually done in *spot colors*—premixed inks—rather than four-color *process*, which mixes some combination of cyan, magenta, yellow, and black to concoct all the printable colors. Each color in a screen-printed job is laid down separately (tints are percentages of the same color, so all tints of one color apply at the same time). Every color requires its own reusable screen that must be cleaned and burned, the ink changed out, and the media allowed to dry between colors. Each new ink also increases the likelihood of *misregistration*, which increases the number of throwaway copies and the overall cost of the job. When you're talking about printing onto a disc surface, every color is an additional cost.

So, you might (should) ask, if it's so expensive, why are DVD movies and games typically labeled with high-color imagery? Two reasons: First, movies and games are visual experiences, so they have to maintain a more visual identity to be marketable. And, second, the profit margins in film and game industry DVDs and CDs are higher than the profit margins for music CDs. Music industry record labels rely on CD sales as their primary revenue stream (the film industry relies first on box office revenue), so they need to cut costs on production.

Limit the colors in your disc label to save money. In this chapter we'll make a nice-looking two-color disc label backed by a full-color Amaray case—offset printing is not as dependent on costs per ink, so the cost differences between a two-color and four-color Amaray insert are negligible.

Project: DVD Label

In eight easy steps we'll convert our source artwork into monotone and duotone, create from them a two-color DVD label, and lay out the DVD disk label:

1. Creating the Knockout
2. Choosing and Applying Spot Fills
3. Converting Gradients
4. Preparing a Grayscale Image in Photoshop
5. Building the Template
6. Creating the Print Mask
7. Coloring with Opacity Masks
8. Typing Text on a Path

Creating a DVD Label

Because the DVD itself will be screen-printed with spot colors, we're going to save some dough by using only two colors. Technically, it's three colors as we'll be employing white too, but white would be applied to the DVD surface as a base coat for other inks regardless.

Books like this always start projects at the beginning. Every now and then someone mixes it up by working backward from the end. Let's really mix it up—start in the middle and spiral our way outward.

STEP 1 ▼
Creating the Knockout

The point of a knockout is to prevent the background imagery or disc mirror surface from bleeding through any areas with transparency or less than 100% ink tints.

1. Open the grayscale version of your logo in Illustrator. If you don't have one, Chapter 2, "Designing a Logo (From Scratch or From a Scan)," will help you create a grayscale version from your color logo. If you're following along with this chapter's resource files, open the **Chap10\Assets\Logo - Grayscale.ai** file. To guard against catastrophic (well, somewhat inconvenient at least) accidents, immediately save a copy of the logo file as **Logo Duotone.ai**.

2. Because the logo was created in a document with an RGB color space, which is useless to printing, the very first step is to convert it by using File > Document Color Mode > CMYK Color.

3. If your document has any hidden or other layers you don't want to find their way onto your DVD label, delete them. Got all the layers you want to keep showing and unlocked? Good. Choose Object > Unlock All to make sure we don't miss anything tucked away on a sublayer, and then choose Select > All, which will select all objects on all layers. Copy these with (Cmd-C) [Ctrl+C].

4. Create a new layer entitled **Knockout**, and drag it to the bottom of the Layers palette. Hide all other layers by Opt-clicking (Alt-clicking) on the **Knockout** layer's visibility eyeball (neat trick, huh?). Now press (Cmd-F) [Ctrl+F] to paste everything in exactly the same place on the new layer.

5. Delete the needle sweep (the blurry cone above the *E*'s needle) and any drop shadows, glows, feathering, or other appearance attributes that affect the outside edges of your logo.

6. Select all again, and then, on the Pathfinder palette, click the Add to Shape Area button. Click the Expand button and inspect your new amalgamated shape (see Figure 10.2). Double-check the Appearance palette to ensure that the last appearance attribute is Default Transparency. If it's anything else, drag the attribute onto the Delete Selected Item button, which will revert the object transparency to default.

FIGURE 10.2 My knockout shape created from the objects in REV's logo (shown in gray to be visible on white paper).

7. Fill the merged shape with white and no stroke, and lock the layer. Save your document.

STEP 2 ▼
Choosing and Applying Spot Fills

In order to convert a full-color logo into only two spot colors, we'll need to do some quick and unusual creative problem-solving. Anyone who has ever had his parents drop by the dorm unexpectedly will find this type of thinking familiar.

1. Step outside your Logo Duotone document for just a moment to examine your color logo for its two predominant colors. Whip out your handy-dandy Pantone Solid Coated swatch book and find the two colors you want to use for the logo as it will appear on the DVD label. These would probably be the nearest match to the logo's signature colors—or they could be your high school colors. What do I care? It's *your* project.

Write down the swatch numbers of the colors you've chosen. In the case of the REV logo, I chose Pantone 354 C and Pantone Process Black C (because my high school colors were ugly).

⊘ CAUTION

Never choose for-print colors based on what your monitor shows you. Color display between the monitor and press will differ—sometimes horrifically—and you could wind up making an unsavory choice between distributing DVDs with the wrong colors or paying for a second print run with the correct colors. Choose colors from specially made swatch books by *Pantone*, Inc., the company that defines the worldwide standard in ink colors.

2. *Now*, go back to your `Logo Duotone` document. Leaving the **Knockout** layer locked, view all other layers.

3. Open the PANTONE Solid Coated library from the Window > Swatch Libraries menu. It should appear in a new floating palette. Locating numbered Pantone colors on this palette in the default small thumbnail view is like rummaging through a drawer of black socks in the dark looking for the mate to a blue sock. Choose List View from the palette's flyout menu to turn on the light. The list is in numbered order, so scroll down until you find your first color, and then drag it from the PANTONE Solid Coated library palette to your document's Swatches palette.

   Drag your second color to the Swatches palette as well. Even if you're using one or more standard process colors at 100%, screen-printing DVDs typically requires colors defined as spot. At the top of the PANTONE Solid Coated palette you'll find spot versions of process cyan, magenta, yellow, and black. Use those swatches in place of actual process inks. Don't use Hexachrome swatches from the PANTONE Solid Coated library without your vendor's prior approval; they're a different ink system not every printer carries.

   After adding the swatches, close the PANTONE Solid Coated library palette.

4. Now decide which elements of the logo to color with each of the two colors. Keep in mind that you cannot mix the two in a gradient—gradients are possible, but only of different tints of the same color. Select all the elements to receive the first spot color as a *solid fill*—use the Layers palette to help in selection, and to ungroup objects as necessary.

Check each object in the Appearance palette for multiple fills and/or strokes—all of them must be colored with your spots.

5. Apply the necessary spot fill from the Swatches palette. Will any of these selected objects get a stroke (not if they eat well and don't smoke! Ba-da-dum-bump)? If so, color their strokes—again, only one spot swatch or the other. Then lock the objects with (Cmd-2) [Ctrl+2], which gets them out of your way while keeping them visible.

6. Repeat this process until you've colored and locked all solid-filled or solid-stroked elements with either color. Apply the spot color fills to tinted objects as needed—for example, the needle in the REV logo is 46% process black, so it must be filled with 46% Pantone Process Black C. Do not fill any gradients for the moment.

7. Got all solid elements filled or stroked with the spot colors? Good. That means the only objects left unlocked on the artboard are those that include gradients or blending or transparency effects, right? Excellent! Of your blended or transparent objects, are any going to blend with objects of the other spot color? If so, well, they can't. Either delete them or make them solid—feel free to use tints or percentages of one of the spot colors.

8. It's safe to leave the transparent effects if the transparency will blend only with objects of the same color. Merely fill or stroke them just like the previous objects; doing so shouldn't affect their other appearance attributes. Lock 'em when you're done, leaving only gradient objects on the artboard.

CHAPTER 10: Designing a DVD Package

STEP 3 ▼
Converting Gradients

The REV logo has various gradients and even an opacity mask (the star bursts radiating through the logo). They're all built in process black, and they need to be Pantone Process Black C—a spot color.

1. 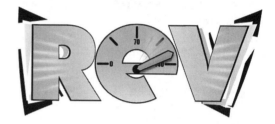 Expand all layers and groups in the Layers palette. Any unlocked objects or sublayers should be gradients. Select one by clicking the target circle to the right of the layer or object name. When it's selected, a ring will appear around the target circle and a colored square will cozy up to the target circle.

2. With the gradient object selected, check the Appearance palette. Is the gradient fill the currently selected appearance attribute? Open the Gradient palette. Each of the gradient stops—the arrows at the bottom—must be in the same spot color. Even if the gradient stop is white, it must be assigned to a spot color with a 0% tint. Why? Because white is really process black with a 0% tint, and process black cannot be *defined* as being in the document—whether it's actually visible is immaterial.

   Click once on a gradient stop and note its tint percentage in the Colors palette. Now, from the Swatches palette, drag the desired spot color and drop it directly only the gradient stop. If you miss, creating a new stop, undo with (Cmd-Z) [Ctrl+Z]. Click on the gradient stop again, which loads it into the Colors palette, and change the tint percentage there to match the original setting. Repeat to convert any other stops in the same gradient.

3. Move through the remaining objects in the document, converting their gradients one at a time, changing all gradient stops to spot colors. Be careful not to mix both spot colors in the same gradient! As you convert each object, lock it. When all objects are done, save and close your Logo Duotone document. Figure 10.3 shows my now duotone logo.

FIGURE 10.3   The REV logo in duotone (not that you can really tell in grayscale print).

How will you know if you got all objects? Print separations. Choose File > Print, and, on the Output panel, change Mode to Separations (Host Based) and print to your printer or Adobe PDF (if you have Acrobat installed). A separate page will print for each ink in use—you should have only two. If you wind up with more than two, examine the extra pages to determine which object(s) weren't converted to spot colors.

STEP 4 ▼
Preparing a Grayscale Image in Photoshop

To convert our full-color background image to grayscale, we must employ Photoshop.

If you don't have Photoshop, skip this Step. In this chapter's resource files I've provided both the RGB image to use in this Step as well as the same image already converted to grayscale to use in later steps.

1. Open **Chap10\Assets\cantop.psd** in Photoshop. If you look closely, you should notice that the aluminum shows off not only shades of gray but also pinks and blues. We need to get rid of that and make this a one-color image.

2. Select Image > Mode > Grayscale. Answer OK to the warning about discarding color information. The image will convert to grayscale, as evident on the Channels palette (Window > Channels).

3. Select File > Save As. In the Save As dialog box rename the file to **cantop gray.psd** and set its file type as Photoshop (*.PSD; *.PDD). Quit Photoshop.

> ### ⊠ NOTE
> Illustrator cannot place *TIFF* images with transparency, nor can it place monotone, duotone, tri-tone, or quad-tone Photoshop PSD or Photoshop PDF files. When creating a monotone (and so on) image, save it from Photoshop as an *EPS*. If transparency is required, first create a clipping path in Photoshop.

Laying Out the Label

Now that all the assets are prepared, we'll define and design the label.

STEP 5 ▼
Building the Template

Before assembly, let's set up our template, so we know where we can put things.

1. Begin a new document entitled **DVD Label**, and set it to **8.5 × 11** inches and CMYK. You'll probably want Units set to Pica or Inches, but use whatever you prefer.

2. Set your swatches to their default by pressing D. In the Toolbox, click and hold on the Rectangle tool to reveal (and select) the Ellipse tool behind it.

3. Instead of clicking and dragging to draw an ellipse, click the Ellipse tool once on the artboard and release. In the resulting Ellipse dialog set both Width and Height to **4.5669** inches. This is the outer diameter of your DVD's printable surface. Don't worry about where the circle winds up on the artboard.

4. Click again with the Ellipse tool and set the measurement of this circle to **4.4419** inches. This, your live area guide, is 0.125 inches smaller than the outer ring. Keep any critical elements such as logos and text inside the live area ring, but do decorate out to the full diameter of the label.

5. Make two more circles measuring **1.8504** and **0.7874** inches in diameter. Respectively, these are your mirror ring and hole.

> ### ⊘ CAUTION
> Although CD and DVD physical dimensions are fixed standards, the measurements used in this section are not necessarily universal. The media and printing processes employed by some CD and DVD replication services require different specifications. Consult your vendor for her label specs or to obtain her template.

6. Got all four circles? Good. Select them all with the Selection tool, and open the Align palette from the Window menu.

7. From the flyout menu on the Align palette, check Align to Artboard. Now click Horizontal Align Center and Vertical Align Center from the top row of buttons. All four circles should center relative to each other and to the artboard itself (see Figure 10.4).

FIGURE 10.4   **Your document should have four circles, each performing a specific function. From the outside in: outer diameter, live area, mirror ring, and hole.**

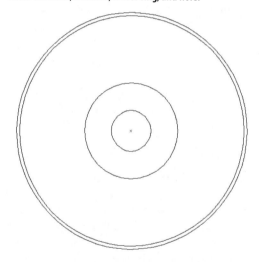

8. In the Layers palette, double-click the layer and rename it to **Guides**.

9. Duplicate the **Guides** layer, rename the duplicate to **Print Mask**, and hide it.

10. Select all the circles of your **Guides** layer again and choose View > Guides > Make Guides. This converts the shapes to non-printing guides. Save your document.

STEP 6 ▼
Creating the Print Mask

Although we could add clipping masks on objects that hang outside the live area—or within the hole—let's do this thing the easy (and still right) way.

1. Lock the **Guides** layer and show the **Print Mask** layer again.

2. On the **Print Mask** layer, delete the live area and mirror ring circles, leaving only the outer diameter and hole.

3. Grab the Rectangle tool and, just as you would when creating an ellipse, click and define its size as **8.5 × 11** inches. Align it to the center of the page as you did the circles; then send the rectangle to the back with the Object > Arrange > Send to Back command.

4. Select both the rectangle and the outer ring. On the Pathfinder palette (Window > Pathfinder), Opt-click (Alt-click) the Subtract from Shape Area button, which will knock the circle out of the rectangle. Make sure both the page-sized rectangle and the hole circle are filled with white but devoid of strokes, then lock the **Print Mask** layer. What it accomplishes is simple: Come print time, it masks any artwork that overhangs the DVD or its hole—with less work than making clipping masks.

5. Create one more layer called **Artwork**, which should be positioned between the **Guides** and **Print Mask** layers in the Layers palette.

6. Let's place the monotone **cantop gray.psd** we created earlier (or from the Chap10\Assets folder) via File > Place. Use the Align palette to center it on the artboard horizontally and vertically.

Size as necessary. When the image is in place, lock it. Notice how the **Print Mask** layer creates the disc hole without the extra steps of creating clipping masks on the image (see Figure 10.5)? Not too shabby.

FIGURE 10.5 The Print Mask layer limits objects on the Artwork layer to the printable disc surface. Notice how it masks the rectangle.

> **NOTE**
>
> Avoid using white objects as masks for offset or other forms of printing. They work in this scenario because this is the standard workflow for DVD replication services.

7. Now bring in the duotone logo in the same way. Position and size it however you like, and save your document.

STEP 7 ▼
Coloring with Opacity Masks

Before moving on to adding text, let's give this project a professional touch by adding the DVD Video logo.

1. Place the **DVD-Video 1.tif** file from the Assets folder. It's black and white, which may work for you, but even if it

does not, humor me. Let's say you want to fill the DVD-Video 1.tif with one of your spot colors. You *could* convert it to a monotone image in Photoshop, but only a masochist would choose that route because getting monotone (and duotone, tri-tone, and so on) images from Photoshop into Illustrator is like debating psychiatry with Tom Cruise—it can be done, but really the only way to win is simply not do it.

2. Note the dimensions of the DVD Video logo in the Transform palette and create a rectangle with the same dimensions. After unchecking Align to Artboard from the Align palette flyout menu, line up the DVD Video logo and the rectangle.

3. In which of your spot colors would you like the DVD Video logo to appear? Remember, it doesn't have to be full ink; you can use any tint percentage of either color, or even make it white simply by setting the tint to 0%. Fill the rectangle with the color and tint of choice.

4. Send the colored rectangle backward with the Object > Arrange menu so that it appears behind the DVD Video logo. With the rectangle still selected, Shift-click on the DVD Video logo to select it as well.

5. Open the Transparency palette from the Window menu, and, on the Transparency palette's flyout menu, choose Make Opacity Mask. Instant colored DVD Video logo! But wait; something's amiss. The logo itself is knocked out, and the *background* is colored. D'oh! Don't have a cow, man; check the Invert Mask box (see Figure 10.6).

6. Now size and place the logo as you like. If you decide to change the tint or color of the DVD Video logo, do it as you would any other object—via the Color, Swatches, or Gradient palettes—just make sure you've selected the colored box thumbnail and not the mask thumbnail in the Transparency palette. The selected thumbnail is denoted by a bold outline.

7. Lock the position of the DVD Video logo and save your document. Figure 10.7 shows how I placed the logo and where my DVD design is so far.

FIGURE 10.7 My DVD label so far.

STEP 8 ▼
Typing Text on a Path

With all of our graphic elements in place, let's insert the title, copyright notice, and other requisite text in a circle around the label.

1. For organization's sake, let's lock the **Artwork** layer and create a new layer called **Text**.

2. Remember how to create a circle with the Ellipse tool? Well, let's make another one around 2.5 inches in diameter. We're going to set text on the outside of this circle, so adjust the diameter to suit your design—but don't be too fanatical; it can always be resized.

⊠ NOTE

Resizing a path type object resizes the type as well. Before resizing, note the point size of the type on the Character palette, and then restore that point size after resizing the path type object.

3. In the Toolbox click and hold on the Type tool to reveal the Type on a Path tool. Click directly on the circle where you would like the text to begin. The circle will convert to an unfilled, unstroked path, and an I-beam cursor will be waiting for you to type the DVD title. Give it a title; I began with **REV Up Your Creativity** (naturally).

4. Style the text to taste using the Character palette, and remember to highlight the type and fill it with one of your spot colors (or a tint thereof). If the text isn't aligned to where you want it, first try the paragraph alignment buttons on the Paragraph palette. Did

they do the trick? If not, grab the Selection tool; in doing so, you will select the path type object rather than the characters of the text (see Figure 10.8).

See the three vertical lines along the path? Those are brackets—yes, I know what brackets really look like—hey, *I* didn't name these things! So, anyway, they're called brackets. At the beginning of the type (most easily visible when the text is left aligned) is the start bracket and its in port. (Good assumption! Yes, type on a path *may* be threaded just like area type.) On the other end (which, at this point, is most likely directly to the left of the start bracket) is the end bracket and its out port. Midway between them is the center bracket.

Positioning the Selection tool directly over any of the brackets causes the cursor to change to a different black arrow with an inverted T shape. Clicking and dragging either of the end brackets is like adding indents to area type—it adjusts how far from the beginning or end of a path type is indented. Dragging the center bracket adjusts the midline of the text, altering its center point. And, if the center bracket is dragged across the path—to the inside of the circle, say—it flips the text inside the circle. Hold (Cmd) [Ctrl] while dragging the center bracket around to avoid accidental flips.

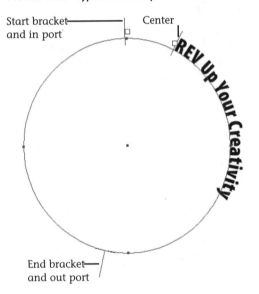

FIGURE 10.8   Type on a circular path.

Start bracket and in port

Center

End bracket and out port

REV Up Your Creativity

◎ **TIP**

Various path type options, including flip, are available by double-clicking the Type on a Path tool in the Toolbox or by choosing Type > Type on a Path > Type on a Path Options.

---

5. Got your type set up the way you want it? Good. With the path type object still selected, open the Attributes palette from the Windows menu. On that palette, check Overprint Fill, which tells Illustrator to print the text on top of any ink beneath it rather than the default behavior of knocking out other inks in the shape of the text.

Just what the heck does this accomplish? Well, I'll tell you. As a limitation of the process, screen-printing introduces a higher probability of ink misregistration. In a situation with inks knocking out of other inks, misregistration will cause white gaps where the misregistration occurs. By overprinting, however, knockout doesn't occur—the overprinting ink prints on top of other ink instead of holes—and slight misregistration produces no white gaps (see Figure 10.9).

FIGURE 10.9 In the example on the left, the text knocks out of ink below it. On the right, however, the text overprints.

 TIP

Black, the only truly opaque of the four process inks, overprints by default in standard offset printing. Setting any other ink—cyan, magenta, or yellow—to overprint will cause it to combine with inks below it, creating mixed colors. Screen printing ink, however, is thicker and more opaque than printing press ink; in most cases even lighter shades will overprint without mixing. Before setting overprint on light colors, talk to your vendor.

Overprinting is especially important with smaller type or typefaces with delicate, thin strokes to prevent the type from being swallowed up by other inks. Don't overprint white objects, though, as white is by definition in this context, a knockout.

6. Create and style any additional text you need—either path, area, or point type—and set its attributes to overprint as well. Don't forget your copyright notice and to insert any trademark or registered trademark symbols beside logos (including the DVD Video logo), taglines, and other proprietary intellectual property.

7. Save and close your document; the DVD label is finished. My finished design is shown in Figure 10.10.

FIGURE 10.10 My finished DVD label.

Project: DVD Amaray Insert

We'll now design the Amaray insert in three easy steps:

1. **Creating the Template**
2. **Setting the Spine Title**
3. **Placing and Using Photoshop Documents with Layer Comps**

Designing the DVD Amaray Insert

What we think of as a standard DVD case—the off-black, hinged plastic case that snaps closed and opens like a book to hold one or more DVDs—is called an Amaray case. So are the green cases of XBox games. Despite the hypocrisy of the marketplace decrying the environmental impact of chipboard CD long boxes in the early nineties (man, those were fun to design!) while embracing the proliferation of over-sized, non-biodegradable polypropylene DVD cases, the Amaray is far and away the most common container for DVDs. It is even increasingly used to house software, game, audio, and other non-DVD discs.

There are other types of DVD cases, from clamshells to paper sleeves, as well as chipboard containers called DigiPacks, which are the size and shape of CD jewel cases or Amarays. No other container, however, has penetrated the market as thoroughly as Amaray. Unlike DigiPacks, it won't warp with humidity or disintegrate if it gets wet, and the standard plastic container can be mass-produced for millions of titles simultaneously. DigiPacks, by contrast, are constructed almost entirely of custom-printed material, requiring each lot to be manufactured for a specific title.

Amarays are decorated by inserting a single sheet of printed artwork into the clear plastic outer sleeve and wrapping around the folding case like a book cover. Being a single, continuous sheet, of course, makes them a breeze to design.

STEP 1 ▼
Creating the Template

Again, most DVD replication services have their own specific template to which you should adhere. Because dimensions and artwork area of Amarays are industry standards, though, they're easy to design in advance of a vendor's template. Standards also work for your wallet: If your local printer can offer you a better price than the DVD replication service for printing your cover art—and you're willing to insert the printed pieces—you can certainly divide the production tasks among multiple vendors.

So, let's build the template from which you'll need to work.

1. Begin a new Illustrator document in the CMYK color space titled **Amaray**. Set the dimensions to **11.25** inches wide × **7.75** inches tall.

2. Employing the same technique as with the circles on the DVD label, click and release on the artboard with the Rectangle tool to create rectangles of a prespecified size. We'll need three unfilled rectangles with 1-pt strokes measuring

   ▶ **10.875 × 7.325** inches with a blue stroke (the bleed guide)

   ▶ **10.750 × 7.200** inches with a red stroke (the trim guide)

   ▶ **10.625 × 7.075** inches with a green stroke (the live area guide)

3. Using the Align palette with Align to Artboard checked, center all three boxes horizontally and vertically. Now lock them.

4. Make another rectangle, but this time with the Rounded Rectangle tool (behind the Rectangle tool). This will be an alternate trim guide placed atop the first one. Set its measurements to **10.75 × 7.2** inches, with a **0.25 inch** corner radius. Notice the rounded corners? Make sure this trim guide matches the first one—no fill and a red stroke—then align it to the center of the artboard and lock it.

5. Just one more rectangle (honest). Make this one with square edges, sized at **0.5512 × 7.2** inches, and a red stroke. From the flyout menu on the Stroke palette, choose Show Options; then turn on Dashed Line. The default dash setting will work, but feel free to customize it to suit. None of these boxes will print.

6. Align the new rectangle to the artboard's center. This box is the spine of your Amaray insert. To the right is the front cover of your DVD case, the back cover ("bacover" as we say in the biz) to the left. Your document should look like Figure 10.11.

7. Double-click the layer you've been working to access the Layer Options. Rename the layer to **Guides**, and uncheck the Print option. Now these lines can't print. Check the Lock option and click OK. Save your document.

STEP 2 ▼
Setting the Spine Title

Now that you we can see where to design, let's set a quick spine title.

1. Create a new layer entitled **Spine**—make sure this *is* set to print.

2.  Under the Type and Type on a Path tools is the Vertical Type tool. Select it, and click once near the top of the spine.

3. Type the title of your project; it will set vertically rather than horizontally as it usually would. Options on the Character palette affect vertical type differently. For example, vertical spacing is not handled by leading, which adjusts the horizontal space between multiple vertical text lines; rather, spacing between letters is controlled by the Tracking field—which makes perfect sense (unless you're reading this at 3 a.m., at which point you should probably just tune in to "Family Guy").

4. To convert vertical type to horizontal— or vice versa—select the type object and choose Type Orientation from the Type menu. Save your document.

STEP 3 ▼
Placing and Using Photoshop Documents with Layer Comps

I'm going to leave you to design your Amaray artwork on your own. Design within one of the trim guides (whether you want

FIGURE 10.11   **The Amaray template.**

your insert to have square edges or rounded), but keep your important elements inside the live area guide in case of misregistration. Also in case of misregistration, extend out to the bleed guide any artwork or backgrounds you want to print to the edge.

Before letting loose your imagination, there's just one other thing I'd like to show you.

Introduced in Photoshop CS, layer comps are snapshots of the state of the Photoshop Layers palette—which layers are on, which off; the position of, and styles active upon, layers. As layers are modified, new layer comps may be created for instant recall to previous Layer palette states. Creating and activating layer comps is accomplished through the Layer Comps palette (in the palette well by default). Layer comps are highly useful as an added stratum of security when experimenting with different layouts. They also have practical uses outside of Photoshop—specifically, within Illustrator.

1. 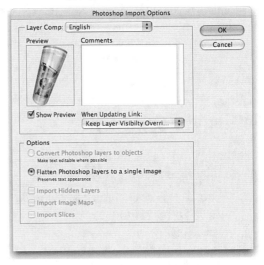 Let's say we want to release our DVD in both English and Spanish. Create a new layer entitled **English**. Then, within that layer, create a new sublayer entitled **Front Cover**. Create the sublayer by highlighting the **English** layer in the Layers palette, then clicking the Create New Sublayer button at the bottom of the Layers palette.

2. Go to File > Place, and navigate to **Chap10\Assets\Drink Can - Multilingual.psd**. After you click the Place button another dialog box will come up—the Photoshop Import Options dialog (see Figure 10.12).

   In Photoshop Import Options you'll see the Layer Comp menu, containing entries for Last Document State (the state in which the file was last saved in

Photoshop) and two other layer comps that I created and named, English and Spanish. If Show Preview is checked, you can see the differences between the image states when changing layer comps, and any comments written into the layer comps at creation time.

FIGURE 10.12 **Photoshop Import Options for the Drink Can - Multilingual.psd file.**

In case you haven't surmised by now (if you're reading this at 3 a.m. the night before a deadline, for instance), the one Photoshop document contains two images of the REV drink can—one with an English-language label, and one with a Spanish-language label. Both versions were, of course, created in Illustrator, and then the Illustrator AI file opened into Photoshop just for light and shadow touchup. (OK, I have to be honest: Everything could have been done in Illustrator—and was in Chapter 7, "Creating 3D Product Packaging Mockups"—but I needed a demonstration file to show you Illustrator CS2's support for layer comps. So, there you have it.)

For now, select the **English** layer comp and set When Updating Link to Keep Layer Visibility Overrides, which preserves your chosen settings regardless of whether a different layer comp is active next time the asset is saved in Photoshop.

3. Position, size, rotate, style (and so on) the image to your heart's content on the **English** / **Front Cover** layer. If you made a **Spine** layer, drop that into the **English** top-level layer.

4. Ready? Drag the **English** layer and drop it on the New Layer button, which will duplicate it and its **Front Cover** and **Spine** sublayers. Rename the duplicate to **Spanish** (or **Español** if you want to be precise). Hide **English**. Everything should still look the same, with the REV can in the same place.

5. Click on the REV can image, and open the Links palette from the Window menu. The `Drink Can - Multilingual.psd` should already be highlighted. Click the Relink button, but don't exchange the image for another. Instead, link to the same file— `Chap10\Assets\Drink Can - Multilingual.psd`—which will bring up Photoshop Import Options again.

◎ TIP

If you decide a placed image needs to be edited, highlight it in the Links palette and just click the Edit Original button button, which will launch the application that created the image *and* open the file in that application. Upon saving the file in its originating application, Illustrator will automatically update the placed instance in your document.

---

6. Select the **Spanish** layer comp and click OK. Notice how your REV can is now in Spanish? One image asset to manage, but multiple versions of that asset— that's what support for Photoshop layer comps is about.

What we just did is a very simple demonstration (I've created seven-language documents, all utilizing single, seven-language PSDs with layer comps), but it can be used for other things besides multilingual documents. For example, consider using adjustment layers in Photoshop to colorize or otherwise alter image layers. As long as layer comps are created in Photoshop from the various states of the Photoshop layers, Illustrator can turn off certain adjustment layers and on others, allowing multiple versions of the same image to be placed side by side and used however you can imagine. Try to think beyond my examples, too; the potential for using this feature is quite vast.

7. Now, go forth and design the rest of your Amaray—setting your copy in English and Spanish (if needed)! My Amaray design (see Figure 10.13) is in this chapter's resource files, and was designed using techniques from other projects in this book. Feel free to examine what I've done if there's something you don't quite get.

FIGURE 10.13 My finished
Amaray insert.

Final Thoughts

For a project like this I would normally recommend adding crop and registration marks, but each DVD replication service has its own template to use. In it, they have created crop, registration, and other marks that conform to their workflow's requirements. And, if you're printing labels on an inkjet or laser printer, you have no use for registration marks.

Included in the Extras folder of this chapter's downloadable resource files are several TIF images of standard CD and DVD logos I found around the Web. It's always a good idea, prior to using any logo, to check with the company or standards body issuing the logo and governing the CD or DVD technology in your project. Your DVD replication service will know who to talk to and how to go about it and, most often, they will offer to place the appropriate logo into your artwork for you.

Why didn't I include audio track format logos like Dolby, DTS, and THX? Use of those trademarks is strictly managed by, and must be licensed from, their respective trademark holders. Until you sign a (usually no-fee) licensing agreement and certification that your film meets certain technical standards, companies like Dolby prohibit the use of their logos on CDs and DVDs. If you want to include such a mark on your disc, contact the trademark holder. In most cases, your DVD replication service can help you make contact; many will even handle the process for you when they have your master disc.

For a truly unique package, consider having custom containers made. Even the polypropylene of Amaray cases can be customized during manufacture—witness Nintendo's special Amarays to hold its GameCube mini-discs or the mouse-ears Disney logo embedded in the spine of Disney DVD cases. Companies like AGI Amaray (**www.Amaray.com**) offer interesting branding opportunities through custom manufactured cases. Naturally, this is only an option for larger-budget projects.

On the other end of the spectrum, empty and standard Amaray and other containers are often sold in bulk at electronics, computer, office supply, and even warehouse stores, making it easy to package your one-off or short-run DVD project. In fact, when inserted into an Amaray's clear plastic outer sleeve or inside the clear lid of a CD jewel case, even (decent) inkjet-printed artwork can look (almost) offset printed. Thus putting forth a professional look on even home-grown DVDs is not difficult.

Whether to print artwork inside the mirror ring is a question you should discuss with your vendor. Most replication services *do* offer printing on the mirror ring, but there may be an additional cost. Also, the mirror ring has different reflective properties than the rest of the metallic disc surface, and it may show deviations in ink color and density.

As with any other project involving an outside vendor, communication is critical. Most DVD replication services provide an FAQ (frequently asked questions) or other material to help you develop your designs and plan your project. All of them are ready to answer your questions. The only stupid question is the one unasked.

CHAPTER 11: Designing a Website and Flash Animation

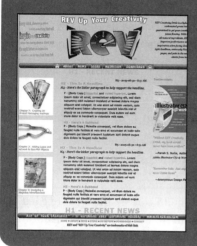

About the Projects

In this project we will design a graphically rich web page—a job for which Illustrator is ideally suited—to use as either a single page or as a template for an entire site. In the process, we will learn to create both static raster and animated vector Flash graphics for online use.

Prerequisites

It would be helpful if you had a basic understanding of drawing basic shapes, setting and styling type with the Character and Paragraph palettes, creating guides, positioning and resizing objects using either the Selection tool or Transform palette, applying fills and strokes, placing external text and graphic files, and working with layers.

You will also need a web browser and a working knowledge of using the web.

@work resources

Please visit the publisher's website to access the following Chapter 11 project files:

- ▶ **Chap11** (Website Layout.ai, Website Layout.html, bg.ai, bg.gif, Logo - Animated.ai, Logo - Animated.html, and Logo - Animated.swf)
- ▶ **Chap11\Assets** (Logo.ai, Tagline.ai, Deck.ai, cover-IllustratorAtWork.gif, illo - ad.psd, illo -cans.psd, illo -lanyard.psd, illo -mug.psd, Copy - Guts.txt, Copy - Premise.txt)
- ▶ **Chap11\Extras** (Web Safe Fonts List.pdf, iawlinklogo.gif)
- ▶ **Chap11\Web Output** (Website-Layout.html, Logo – Animated.html, Logo – Animated.swf, bg.gif) and **Chap11\Web Output\Images** (sliced graphics used by Website-Layout.html)
- ▶ **Chap11\Finished Project** (where you place your finished projects)

Planning the Projects

You are about to enter a world not only of sites and links, but of mindless clicking, a journey into a nebulous and confusing design field limited only by the discordance of a million imaginations. That's a signpost up ahead—your next stop: The Web Design Zone.

The Right Tool for the Job

Is Illustrator the right tool for this job? Actually, it's ideally suited for this job, though few web designers realize it.

Many accomplished web designers sketch sites in Illustrator because the nature of the program affords endless experimentation without data destruction (unlike Photoshop, where resizing, rotating, or adjusting an element forever alters it). Sketches can be created and proofed to the client or other departments rapidly either as a PDF or JPG. With Illustrator's built-in paragraph and character styles, graphic styles, and symbols, major revisions are easily and adroitly accomplished in little time. After approval of a sketch, the site may remain in Illustrator for finishing work and then be *sliced* and saved out as standard web graphics.

Can Illustrator do the whole job by itself? Rarely. If the site is a one-pager, the world's greatest vector drawing program will do it. Usually, though, even if the site can be designed and coded entirely in Illustrator, you will still want an *HTML* editor or at least a text editor to add and edit copy. Most often, Illustrator is employed to create a template from which some or all of the site's pages will be derived.

Appendix B, "Resources," lists some of my websites. Each was designed in, and templated from, Illustrator, and then the code was heavily massaged in an external *CSS* and *XHTML* editor.

Organization and Hierarchy

Organization—the difference between every successful website and every failure is organization.

Allow me to convey the least-heeded piece of advice in all of amateur and semipro design—especially web design: Like any other form of visual communication, web design is about *communication*. The web designer's job is to *convey* and *support* the textual information of the site as clearly and effectively as possible. It is not about showing off the latest coding trick or everything you've learned in this book. Design what the message wants; don't try to fit the content to match a preconceived design. The distinction between these is what separates a professional designer from an amateur.

Plan your content *first*. Determine the site's macro structure—how many *domain names* will it span? Will the site employ *subdomains*? Will it have multiple sections with each requiring its own variation on a related visual identity?

Build a site hierarchy chart—a flow chart mapping the sections of a website, the pages in a section, and which page(s) link off from which other page(s). Then write the content for each section and each page, spell-checking and proofing it to the client. Make sure the copy is broken up into logical chunks that aren't too long or too short. Though web pages are theoretically unlimited in length, rarely will someone actually read the entirety of a page that would print out to more than two paper pages. The same amount of copy on multiple pages *seems* like less to the reader. A hierarchy is a script from which the scenes are set.

Plan your reader's navigation. Using the site hierarchy chart as your map, how many levels of content do you have? With the home page at the top, how many pages/sections need to be linked from the home page? How many pages/subsections will need to be linked from each page beneath the home page? Follow the chart down until you've accounted for all levels. When building a site navigation system, you must account for and provide space to accommodate all of these levels in a way that clearly denotes that they are not equal levels of information.

Include in your site hierarchy the common required elements. These typically include the navigation system (twice), the logo, a tagline, a heading to identify the page should the user enter the site directly through that page (which is more often than not), copyright and other required notices, and so on. Have these written and ready before beginning your design, to avoid forgetting them.

Additional Questions

The next phase of planning is the physical structure of the site. Will you put each section of the site into its own folder, or will all the pages reside in a single folder with images and other assets in other folders? Will your site be built on HTML, XHTML, PHP, or another language? Do you want CSS formatting? Which version of CSS will you use, recognizing that each has a compatibility tradeoff with browsers? Do you want the site to be compliant with web standards? If the content calls for animation, will you employ *Flash*, *SVG*, or *GIF*?

The web, though a public medium for more than 10 years now, is still young and largely undefined. There are many, many questions to consider about the physical and code structure of a website, and no one book can answer them all—none can answer them definitively. Every web professional has a different opinion about what structural considerations and conventions make good site development. If you ask the questions in the preceding paragraph to a hundred different designers, all of whom are paid, professional web designers or developers, you will get a hundred different answers—some fanatical. It's up to *you* to decide what *you* believe, and what works best for *your* websites.

In this project, the concentration is on the mechanics of building a website in Illustrator. The focus is decidedly on the *hows*, but for the hows to make sense, some of the *whys* must be explored. I've been careful to present the logics of the whys, as much as possible removing my professional beliefs and any biases I may carry.

Finally, ask yourself *who* will build the site's parts. Can you do it all? Do you want to? Will you be working within a team? Do you need to hire subcontractors for programming or coding? Does the client plan to bring in other personnel?

Project:
Grid and Background

We'll set up the page grid and draw its tiled background image in two easy steps.

1. **Building a fluid grid**
2. **Drawing the tiled background**

Creating the Grid and Background

In for-press or even for-PDF projects, Illustrator allows you to control the placement and size of objects to within a hundred-thousandth of an inch. That functionality is still there, of course, when working on a for-web project, but it's useless. Even with absolute positioning techniques in CSS (which are beyond the scope of this project), the viewer of your website has ultimate control over the look of your design. She can override all of your work, and, even if she doesn't, her browser, computer, and monitor resolution combination may render your website differently for her than for the next reader. Design within a flexible grid and work in whole pixel sizes and positions to minimize the carnage.

STEP 1 ▼
Building a Fluid Grid

Every page layout—for web or print—is only as effective as its grid. Given the way people read online, the dynamic nature of online content, and the limited typographic control, online layout grids must fluidly adapt to whatever content they're tasked to contain. Planning and organization are the first step to effective web design, and building a flexible grid is the second.

1. Begin a new document (File > New). Set its Units to Pixels, the standard unit of measure on a computer screen (and thus, online), and the Color Mode to RGB. Although the New Document dialog contains an 800 × 600 preset, that's more useful for creating PDFs or slides that can be displayed full-screen. When building a website that might be viewed on an 800 × 600 pixel monitor, we need to account for the space occupied by fixed elements of the browser—things like scrollbars and window borders horizontally, and title and toolbars vertically. Set the dimensions to **730 × 900 px**. Title the document **Website Layout**.

> ⊘ **CAUTION**
>
> More than all other terrible annoyances, people hate scrolling horizontally to read a web page. Unless you *know* the majority of your audience uses a screen resolution higher than 800 × 600 (as with a closed *intranet*), limit your site designs to 760-px wide or less.
>
> If you try to justify a wide page layout with the notion that these days everyone has at least a 17-inch monitor, consider when you last stopped by the coffee shop, public park, or airport. Say, just how big *were* all those laptop monitors?

2. Show your rulers by pressing (Cmd-R) [Ctrl+R]. Drag a horizontal guide off the horizontal ruler and drop it at the vertical 480-px mark. If you can't get it lined up perfectly, select View > Guides > Lock Guides to toggle the lock off. Then use the Transform palette to align the Y-axis to **480 px**.

Because Illustrator begins the vertical ruler at the bottom of the artboard, at the 480-px position, your guide is 420 px from the top of the 900-px-tall artboard. After subtracting the space taken up by the title bar, status bar, and default toolbars in the average web browser on an 800 × 600 monitor, the vertical space remaining is 420 px. So the guide you just set is your *fold*; it's a safe bet that the average visitor will see everything above it before needing to scroll.

3. We're going to create a symmetrical three-column layout, which provides a great deal of flexibility and, for that reason, is very common. Drag four vertical guides into the layout and set their X coordinates to **150**, **180**, **550**, and **580** px. Now we have our basic grid, with sidebar columns 150-px wide each, a main content column 370-px wide, and 30-px gutters between them (see Figure 11.1).

TIP

Thirty pixels is the widest you should make gutters. Any wider, and the sidebars would become disconnected from the main copy column—but keep your main content column to no more than 10–14 words wide.

Each column is independent of the others and will grow downward with its content. Their bottoms will likely not balance. This is unavoidable online, and is what makes the layout fluid.

FIGURE 11.1   **A flexible three-column grid.**

4. Because we need to work in pixels—whole pixels, and nothing but pixels—this is a good opportunity to turn on Pixel Preview from the View menu. Everything you do from this point forward will preview exactly as it will export.

5. Lock the guides again with View > Guides > Lock Guides, and save your document.

STEP 2 ▼
Drawing the Tiled Background

If your page has a background, it can be anything you want—a solid color, a repeating pattern, a single image, or a gradient. In this step we'll create a simple gradient for subtle style.

1. With the Rectangle tool, draw a box that fills the entire artboard (730 × 900 px) from corner to corner.

2. On the Swatches palette, click the flyout menu and choose Open Swatch Library > Other Library. Navigate to where you saved this chapter's resource files and open **Logo.ai** from the Assets folder. A new Swatches palette will appear. These are the REV corporate colors, and we'll build all elements from these colors.

3. With your rectangle still selected, open the Gradient palette (Window > Gradient) and activate a Linear gradient from the Type drop-down (you may need to select Show Options from the flyout). It will probably start out as a horizontal white-to-black gradient (see Figure 11.2).

FIGURE 11.2   **Default options for a new gradient. Note the color indicators beneath the gradient preview—white on the left, black on the right.**

4. First, set the angle to **90°**, which will place black at the top, gradually transitioning to white at the bottom. On the Logo swatches palette, drag the Pantone DS 298-4 C swatch and drop it directly onto the black color indicator in the Gradient palette. The preview and your rectangle should instantly shift to a light green-to-white gradient. If you wind up with a tri-tone gradient, you missed the target when you dropped the green swatch. Undo with (Cmd-Z) [Ctrl+Z] and try it again.

> ◎ **TIP**
>
> To see the name of a color swatch, either hover over it with your mouse cursor, or choose List View from the Swatch palette's flyout menu.

5. In the Layers palette (Window > Layers), double-click **Layer 1** and rename it to **Background**. Copy the contents of the background layer with (Cmd-C) [Ctrl+C], lock the layer, and save the document (but don't close it).

6. Begin a new Illustrator document the width of the copied artwork and at least as tall. Name it **Website Background** or simply **BG** as I did.

7. Paste the background gradient (or image) you created by pressing (Cmd-V) [Ctrl+V]. If your background is a solid color or a gradient, select File > Document Setup. Change the document width to 1 pixel (that's not a typo, trust me).

8. Back in the document, reduce the width of the objects to match the document width and line them up again.

9. Choose File > Save for Web. In the Save for Web dialog, choose the GIF 128 Dithered preset. Then increase the number of colors to **256** (see Figure 11.3).

10. Click Save and save the image as **bg.gif** to a convenient location. Save your Illustrator document and close it.

FIGURE 11.3   The Save for
Web options for the background.

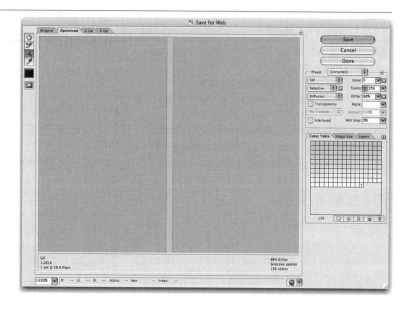

Project:
Static Page Elements

In three easy steps we'll design the layout of the page:

1. Populating the header
2. Designing the guts of the page
3. Carrying through to the user-friendly footer

Creating the Static Page Elements

So you want to create an amazing, Flash-animated website, huh? As George Morrow wrote: "Ambition is a very pretty thing; but, sir, we must walk before we run." And before we walk, we must crawl.

STEP 1 ▼
Populating the Header

Most web pages are divided into at least the basic three sections of header, footer, and guts. Within the header should be the

nameplate (typically a logo and/or tagline) and, usually, the top-level navigation system, though the *nav system* may be included toward the top of the guts in some layouts.

1. On a new layer entitled **Header**, place the prepared `Logo.ai`, `Tagline.ai`, and `Deck.ai` files. Arrange and size them to your tastes, but keep them squarely within the three columns. You *can* span columns, but if this is your first web project, I advise you to keep it simple.

2. Grab the Type tool and drag out a text area somewhere in the header area—I created one to fit within the upper 175 px of the right column. Place (File > Place) the **Copy - Premise.txt** file here. Style the type to your tastes, but make sure you use *web-safe fonts*. After you've styled the type, make a paragraph style from the copy.

3. With the Rectangle tool, draw out a shallow rectangle that spans all three columns. A bit later this will become our navigation button bar. For now, we need it as an *FPO* to get a sense of where elements will lay.

4. If you need to reposition elements, do it now. Be very careful about the height of the header area. It will appear on all pages of the site, and after the first exposure, it won't pique anyone's interest. Moreover, if you make the header too tall, there won't be as much room left above the fold for the guts. Take a gander at Figure 11.4 to see where my layout is so far. When your header sketch is set, save the document.

STEP 2 ▼
Designing the Guts of the Page

Why is this area called the *guts*? Think about it: A website is a hollow, non-functioning shell without content—like a human being without viscera. This is the most important part of any website. (Incidentally, I don't personally know any other web designer who calls this section the guts. They usually just say "content area" or something equally lame. The term guts comes from the print publishing world, on which web publishing is based, much to the mortification and choler of many a too-hip-for-print web designer.)

1. Lock the **Header** layer and create a new layer called **Guts**.

2. In your center column, create a text area from just below the nav bar FPO, and almost to the bottom of the page. From the File menu choose Place, and select the **Copy - Guts.txt** file in the `Chap11/Assets` folder. When the Text Import Options dialog appears, specify the Encoding Platform as Windows, but leave all other options at their defaults.

FIGURE 11.4 With the FPO nav bar, deck block, logo, and other elements in place, I can begin working on the guts.

Copy · `Guts.txt` is a proxy, or FPO, for real copy and includes codes similar to HTML entities common to most websites. Each of the odd codes—the *Hx* codes and the *P*—corresponds to your information hierarchy. The H1 is your top-level headline, usually the page title; H2 is the second most important piece of information in the hierarchy, the headline of a particular story; H3 is a subhead, which ranks in importance just below a headline; and so on through H4 and H5 (up to H6). Body copy is denoted with a *P* to signify the *HTML/CSS* code designator for Paragraph tagged (body) copy. HTML and related languages all have hierarchical conventions built in, and they correspond to the H (headline level) codes used herein. Working with them here will make coding HTML and CSS more familiar when you reach that point.

 NOTE

The hierarchical codes just described are very important to your Search Engine Ranking (SEO). Search engines like Google, Yahoo, and MSN depend on Hx and P codes to properly interpret the content of your site pages. Failing to use them will almost certainly lead to lower rankings, miscategorization, and possibly even exclusion of your site from search engines.

3. Style the first instance of each code (and its corresponding line or paragraph) to create a visual hierarchy so that your site's visitors will immediately understand the relative importance of each element. In Figure 11.5 you can see my styling presenting a clear hierarchy to readers—the page title (H1) is the most important piece of information, followed by the story headline (H2), subheads (H3), *kicker* (H4), date and time (H5), and finally the body copy (P)

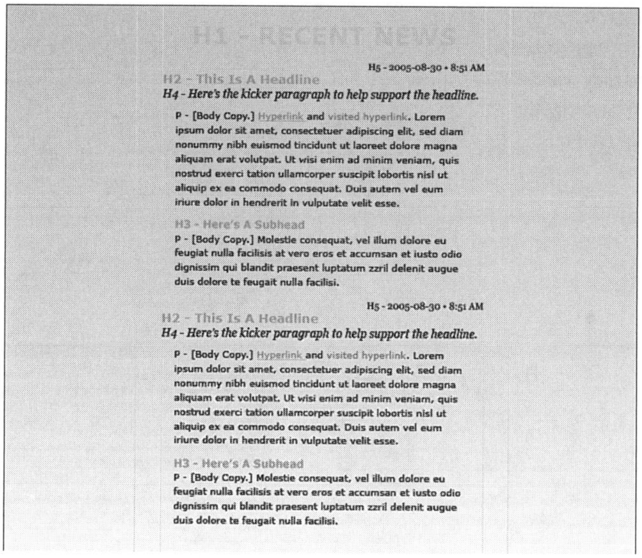

FIGURE 11.5 Typeface, type size, color, and alignment establish a clear hierarchy for readers.

4. Look closely at the first body copy paragraph. The first word after the brackets is "Hyperlink," followed shortly by "visited hyperlink." These are your proxies to use for styling, respectively, unvisited and previously visited links—to other locations within the site or to external resources. It's important that website visitors be able to quickly identify and differentiate both hyperlinks for places they haven't yet been, as well for places they have. Highlight "Hyperlink" with the Type tool and, using the Character, Swatches, and/or Color palettes, style it as you would like to see links on your site.

5. **T** Highlight "visited hyperlink" and style it as well, but slightly different from "hyperlink." If you would like to add an underline to either or both, choose Show Options from the Character palette's flyout menu and click the Underline button.

6. Finish the guts section by filling the sidebars with your expected content—your own styled text (FPO or genuine) and/or images (see Figure 11.6). If you're at a loss, I've provided some FPO *illos* in the `Assets` folder.

FIGURE 11.6 With a few FPO illos and all my copy styled in a clearly defined hierarchy, the website is taking form.

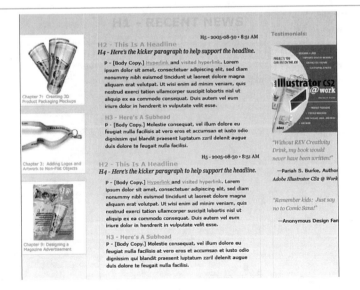

STEP 3 ▼
Carrying Through to the User-Friendly Footer

The site footer is often the last thing novice designers think to create, typically omitting it from their design sketches and only creating it later during coding. As such, it frequently fails to carry through on the overall page design, looking more often than not like the afterthought it was. If the design doesn't follow through all parts of the site, it breaks down. Without a strong footer, the design doesn't have a leg to stand on. (Go ahead and groan, I understand.)

1. Lock the **Guts** layer and create a new layer called—you guessed it—**Footer**.

2. Common and important elements of a footer include: a reiteration of the navigation system, copyright and/or trademark notices, and, of course, the designer's credit. Decide whether your bottom nav system will be graphical like the top (we're getting there) or textual. The latter makes the site accessible to visitors who can't or won't display graphics (for example, visually impaired persons using screen readers or Braille keyboards, mobile visitors browsing on PDAs or cell phones, and those who surf with graphics display turned off).

   Create your footer nav section now, either as a plain text area or as a placeholder shape you will replace with a copy of your nav buttons after we make them. If you use straight text, do your visitors a favor and style it to match the hyperlinks in the guts main content column.

3. Create a text area to hold your copyright notice, designer's credit (for example, "designed by Moi"), and, if applicable, a trademark, service mark, or registered trademark notice. Style the type however you like.

4. If you want any other elements in your footer, build them now. Just make sure they match and complement the design of the rest of the page (see Figure 11.7), and that they adhere to the grid.

REV UP YOUR CREATIVITY™ • © COPYRIGHT 2005 (COPYRIGHT HOLDER) • WWW.REVDRINK.COM
HOME • ABOUT • NEWS • STORE • NUTRITION • DOWNLOADS • CONTACT
REV and "REV Up Your Creativity" are trademarks of blah blah

Project:
Navigation Buttons

We'll build an intuitive navigation bar and
buttons in four easy steps:

1. **Drawing the navigation bar**
2. **Drawing the navigation buttons**
3. **Adding button labels**
4. **Carrying the navigation scheme to the footer**

Creating Navigation Buttons

Now that you can crawl, let's try walking.

STEP 1 ▼
Drawing the Navigation Bar

Most navigation systems are based on graphical buttons—even if, in their CSS wizardry,
the site designers have merely styled lists of
textual items.

1. Create a new layer called **NAV Top** and
   lock the rest of the layers.

2. Unlock the Header layer, delete the
   placeholder, and draw what will
   become the real nav bar. If you're

making a rounded-end bar like the one
on the REV site (see Figure 11.8), draw
a standard rectangle with the Rectangle
tool (trust me).

3. Style the bar however you like. I filled it
   with the green-to-black gradient swatch
   from the Logo swatch palette (imported
   from the `Logo.ai` file, remember?). Then
   I gave it a **2-pt** black stroke, and a
   second fill with the **DS 286-2 C** green and
   offset by **2 pt**.

4. With the bar still selected, go to Effects
   > Convert to Shape > Rounded
   Rectangle. In the Absolute section set
   the width in pixels as 730 minus twice
   the number of points taken up by any
   strokes and offsets (twice because you
   must account for both ends). Set the
   height desired and click OK. Your
   rectangle should now have rounded
   ends like the one in Figure 11.8. Unlike
   a rectangle drawn with rounded edges,
   this one, by virtue of its live effect, will
   remain perfectly rounded at the prede-
   termined corner radius no matter how
   you may resize or distort it.

5. Finished styling your bar? Then create
   a **NAV Bar** graphic style from it and lock
   the nav bar path.

ABOUT   NEWS   STORE   NUTRITION   DOWNLOADS

Drawing the Navigation Buttons

With the bar finished, it's time to turn our attention to the buttons themselves. Depending on the particular style of buttons your site will employ, it might be helpful to create the labels first (in the following step sequence).

1. Though buttons can be any shape and size you like, the nature of the web forces their exported graphics to be rectangular in shape (even if the rectangle is invisible). To keep things simple, let's draw a simple rectangle somewhere in the bar. This will be our first button.

2. Apply the NAV Bar graphic style.

3. Because we specified a width for the rounded rectangle effect, the button will suddenly become the same width as the bar, which we definitely do not want. If you would like to keep the rounded edges, thus making a pill-shaped button, double-click Rounded Rectangle in the Appearance palette; edit the width to be appropriate. If you want right-angled corners, delete the Rounded Rectangle attribute on the Appearance palette.

4. Apply any other styling you like to the button, and then create a **NAV Button** graphic style from it. Duplicate and position all the other buttons you need (see Figure 11.9). If all your buttons will be the same shape and size, create a symbol called **NAV Button**, and use instances of that symbol for the other buttons.

Adding Button Labels

The form your button labels take—textual or iconic—depends on your preference and where the buttons lead. Your site visitors can read (obviously), so textual labels are always safe. Using icons to represent different areas is possible, but, unless you also include text labels, you must only use icons that are universally identifiable; otherwise your visitors will be lost. For example, icons of envelopes and telephones implicitly stand for either a direct means of contact or a page containing a direct means of contact; houses equate to the home page. You must also be careful not to use an icon with an existing meaning inappropriately—don't use a magnifying glass, the symbol for search, as the link to your puzzles page.

1. 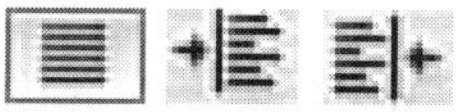 If you will be using strictly iconic buttons, skip down to step 3. If you are creating textual labels, make either one text area or multiple text areas. In Figure 11.10 I created a single text area the width of the main guts column and set the single-word labels to (force) Justify All Lines on the Paragraph palette. This impels the space-separated words to distribute across the horizontal area evenly without making me work with multiple text areas and the Align palette. To prevent crowding the borders, I used the Paragraph palette's left and right indents to give the labels 10 pixels of padding on either end.

FIGURE 11.9 Because all my nav buttons will be different widths, I can't make use of symbols without introducing distortion when I resize to fit.

FIGURE 11.10 For evenly spaced button labels, try a single text area with force-justified, space-separated type.

2. Style the text of your labels as needed and, to make editing and potential reuse easier, build any needed graphic styles—but not paragraph or character styles!—from the type.

3.  If you are using icons or graphically labeled buttons (with or without text), select Window > Symbol Libraries > Web Icons. A new palette will appear with many of the most common icons your visitors will recognize (see Figure 11.11). To make use of any of these, drag them into your layout and click the Break Link to Symbol button on the bottom of the Symbols palette. Now style to your tastes.

FIGURE 11.11 Included with Illustrator CS2, the Web Icons symbol library contains many universally recognized navigation icons.

4. If you have your own icons or images to use on the buttons, place or draw them now.

5. Position all labels—text or imagery—to fit within the button shapes (group them if it makes things easier), and finish your navigation bar. My finished bar is shown in Figure 11.12.

> **⊗ NOTE**
>
> If your labels appear outside the buttons (for example, you may have round buttons with text encircling them), draw shapes to encompass all parts of the buttons. Set both the fill and stroke on the shapes to none, and then send them to the back and group with their respective button contents.

STEP 4 ▼
Carrying the Navigation Scheme to the Footer

Let's apply some finishing touches before we slice and export the website template.

1. If your design mirrors the header navigation into the footer, duplicate the NAV Top layer by clicking Duplicate NAV Top in the Layers palette's flyout menu.

FIGURE 11.12 Using familiar icons to represent buttons leading to the home page and the contact page, and textual links for other pages or sections of the site, I'm able to achieve a balanced and intuitive navigation system.

2. If you went the route of text navigation on the bottom, apply the NAV Bar graphic style to the necessary footer elements (see Figure 11.13).

3. This is the last phase of sketching or design before we launch into the mechanical operations needed to generate an HTML document and sliced graphics, so finish up any design work now. When ready, save the document and let's dive into slicing.

Project: Slice and Export

We'll slice our website layout in five easy steps:

1. **Defining auto slices**
2. **Defining manual slices**
3. **Setting slice options**
4. **Saving for web HTML and graphics**
5. **Setting output options**

FIGURE 11.13 The final site design, including the footer, which picked up my nav bar's graphic style as well as the text formatting and graphic style of the button labels.

Slice and Export the Page

Unlike a for-print or even a PDF piece, graphically rich web designs are not solid documents. Instead, they're made up of pieces and assembled in real time by the user's web browser software. Graphics download as separate files, assembled by references within the code of the HTML container. And, because they must download to the user's computer before being displayed in the browser, the larger the images' dimensions, the longer they take to download before the user can see and begin interacting with them. As every web user knows, there is only so long people will wait for a page and its images to download before exiting the site.

As a compromise between imagery and download times, larger images should be broken up or sliced into several smaller images. Although the reality is that the sum of the parts' file sizes (on disk and on modem) is almost always larger than the file size of the whole, the users' perception is that the site loads faster because the pieces download and begin to display sooner than would the whole.

Slices also determine the structure of the page code when exporting.

STEP 1 ▼
Defining Auto Slices

Auto slices are a wonder in Illustrator CS2. They allow you to define an object as a slice—and dynamically update the slice to reflect changes in the object—rather than forcing you to make adjustments manually.

1. Unlock all layers but the **Background** and select the main column text box on the **Guts** layer. Ensure that guides are showing.

2. Select Object > Slice > Make. Immediately numbered outlines will appear around various areas of the artboard (see Figure 11.14). These are slices. The moment you define a single slice by any means, Illustrator slices up the rest of your artwork.

FIGURE 11.14 Close-up of auto-slice identifier.

> **NOTE**
>
> **The color of your slice lines and numbers may be different—perhaps even difficult to see. Fortunately, you can change their color. From the Edit menu (on Windows) or the Illustrator menu (on Mac), choose Preferences > Smart Guides & Slices. In the bottom of the Smart Guides & Slices panel of the Preferences dialog, change the Line Color to whatever you prefer.**

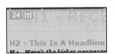

3. With the text area still selected, go to Object > Slice > Slice Options. Change Slice Type from the default of Image to HTML Text. In the Text Displayed in Cell area should be the main content column copy, probably littered with HTML code (see Figure 11.15). The box is inaccessible because with an auto slice, the text must be edited on the artboard, which will automatically update the slice content.

4. Set the alignment of your text in the Cell Alignment area, and, if the text area will have a background color or image unique to it (and separate from the rest of the page), choose it in the Background drop-down. Click OK. The indicator in the top-left corner of the slice will change from a crossed box to a T referring to its HTML text content.

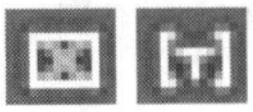

FIGURE 11.15 **Slice options for my main content column in the Guts area.**

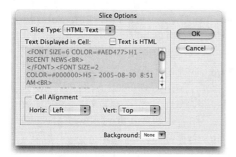

5. Back on the artboard, check the size and positioning of your slice. Does it fill up the area required? Note that the slice is relative to the *contents* of the text area, not its bounding box. Ensure that the text box slice runs the full height of the column—from the base of the header

area to the cap of the footer area. If you need to fill more space, fill in more text. This is a template for multiple pages, so our goal is to build a clean layout with only one slice per section, per column (excluding the navigation bars); extraneous text is nearly irrelevant.

6. Now select your top navigation buttons and make auto slices of them the same way. Repeat for your bottom navigation buttons (or text area as you should not make individual slices from textual links), the nav bar(s) itself, and any objects that span the entire width of a column or the page. If you're following along with the REV website design, make an auto slice from the tagline as well. Your document should look something like mine at this point (see Figure 11.16).

FIGURE 11.16 **The dimmed areas are not auto-sliced.**

7. If any of your auto slices break out of the grid's columns (again, except the navigation bars), adjust the size and/or shapes of the objects; Illustrator will update the auto slices to match.

Defining Manual Slices

Auto slicing is fabulous for objects that completely fill their intended areas. Sometimes, however, you need control over slicing.

If your sidebars look like mine, they have multiple paths, objects, and text areas in them. We can't turn them into auto slices because doing so would break the fluidity of continuous columns. We need to slice them manually.

1. Just above the Hand tool on the Toolbox is the Slice tool. Choose it, and, in the left sidebar column, draw a rectangle from top (the bottom edge of the header area) to bottom (the top edge of the footer area). You've just made a manual slice, as indicated by the change in slice numbering rolling throughout your display.

2. Create another manual slice encompassing the right column.

Ultimately you should have only five slices in the guts area—the main column's auto slice, a manual slice for each of the sidebars, and Illustrator will have filled in the slices for gutters between the columns.

3. Move into the header area and draw manual slices above the nav bar to divide it like the guts. Remember: If you used a separate tagline object like REV's website, the tagline and logo should divide the center column vertically into two stacked slices.

4. Do it again for the footer area (if necessary). When you're finished, each area of the page should have a slice in each of the three columns (except the nav bars, which should have a slice per button). Each of the rows in the grid of slices will become a row in your HTML table (or CSS-arranged layout), while each column of slices will create a column within the row. Check your sliced document against Figure 11.17. If you have trouble getting manual slices of exactly the right size and position, select the slices with the Slice Select tool (see the next Step) and use the Transform and/or Align palettes to whip them into shape.

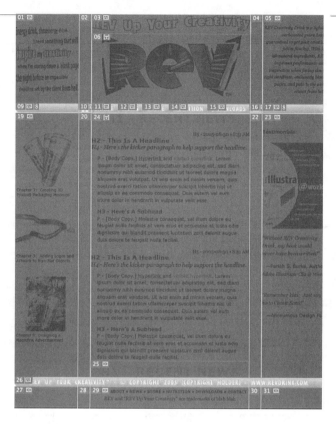

FIGURE 11.17 **We should wind up with clean, aligned rows (shown in alternating color) and columns.**

STEP 3 ▼
Setting Slice Options

With all the planning and organization that went into designing our page, it behooves us to continue that organization with the exported graphics and content.

1. In the Toolbox, click and hold on the Slice tool to access the Slice Select tool hidden behind it. With this very handy tool you may *select* slices without *creating* them.

2. Click on the left column slice and choose Object > Slice > Slice Options. The familiar dialog will appear.

3. This time, instead of setting the type to HTML Text, set it to No Image, which looks very much like the HTML Text setting. The difference is that now nothing created within that slice area on the artboard will find its way into the exported HTML document. Instead, it will be replaced by an area the size of the slice, and containing only what you enter in the Text Displayed in Cell area. Type in anything you may want—I usually enter some kind of identifier such as **Left Sidebar** to help me figure out where I am when filling in the content of the page in my HTML editor. Set any other options you want and click OK.

4. Repeat for the right column. If you're thinking that traveling up through the Object menu to set the options on all these slices is tedious and there must be a better way—well, you deserve a gold star. There *should* be a better and faster way of setting slice options—and there *is*.

5. We'll get to that way in just one moment. (I know: I'm a tease.) For now, save your document.

STEP 4 ▼
Saving for Web HTML and Graphics

All sliced up? It's time to go.

1. Hide the background layer. From the File menu choose Save for Web.

2. In the Save for Web box make sure you're looking at the Optimized tab, and that the Toggle Slice Visibility button is depressed (top left of the window). Now choose the Slice Select tool.

3. Double-click on one of the column gutter slices. Voilà! A faster, better way to access the Slice Options! Set this to No Image as well. In fact, set all the slices that will contain text, voids, or objects not created in the design to no image (don't change the auto slices to no image).

4. Choose one of the nav buttons and double-click on it. This one we do want to be an image, so make sure that's its type. Then fill in the URL (for example, **http://www.REVdrink.com**), the Target (if desired), status bar Message, and, in the Alt field, the alternate text for people who can't (or don't) see the button graphic (for example, **Home**).

Set the background to none, and make the Name—that will be the filename of the exported image—one that will be meaningful in a well-organized website like ours—for example, **nav_home** (see Figure 11.18).

FIGURE 11.18   The Slice Options for my Home button.

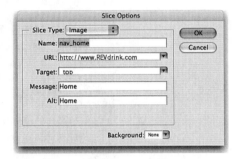

5. Run through setting the slice options for all the nav buttons and for all image slices (exclude URL and Target on non-button images).

6. In the right column of the Save for Web window, click on the Image Size tab. If the Original Size says anything other than the measurement we intended—730 × 900 px in this case—something, possibly some effect or auto-slice option, is pushing out the borders. Check the Clip to Artboard option, then Apply to affix the clipping the slices to the artboard.

7. With the Slice Select tool, select one of your image slices. In the upper section of the right panel are the graphic format options. Start with a preset like GIF 128 Dithered (meaning GIF format, 128 colors, with some colors dithered to create the illusion of additional colors outside the specified 128) and customize it until you're happy with the result.

8. Set the options you want for all image slices either one or several at a time by holding Shift while clicking in the preview window on multiple slices. When you're ready, click the Save button (but stop just after that).

STEP 5 ▼
Setting Output Options

Now that we've set the options for the individual slices, we still have to tell Illustrator how we want our HTML document built.

1. After you click Save in the Save for Web dialog, the Save Optimized As dialog appears. It has the typical save-inspired options—File Name, Save as Type—but it has two other crucial options: Settings and Slices. Choose All Slices from the Slices drop-down and Other from the Settings drop-down. Up pops the Output Settings dialog.

2. There are four tabs here, each containing various options you should consider. There are volumes of books on the subject of these options (not specific to Illustrator, of course), so I'm afraid I haven't the space to be able to tell you what they all mean and when you may want one over another. For now, let's leave the HTML tab set at its default. Click Next.

3. On the Slices tab choose whether you want to generate your page as a table or CSS. Tables are older and in the process of being phased out of web design—"deprecated" is what fancy-pants, college-edumacated web-boys say—, but they have the distinct advantage of appearing almost exactly the same in all major web browsers. CSS, by contrast, is more versatile and standards-compliant, but its implementation varies wildly between browsers.

4. Change the options in the Default Slice Naming section for any slices you haven't specifically named in the Slice Options steps. Click Next.

5. Background is important. As you may recall, years ago when we began this project we created a background image and saved it as a GIF. Here is where you tie it to your design. Click on the Choose button and navigate to where you saved the bg.gif file. If you prefer not to use a background image in your design, set the color beneath the Background Image area. Click Next.

6. On this last tab set image file-naming options, the folder into which your sliced images will be placed (a subfolder called images is the default), and the additional options there. Click OK.

7. Back in the Save Optimized As dialog, verify the filename you want for your HTML file and click Save. If this is not your first time outputting, you'll be prompted to replace the prior set of files—say yes.

8. Save your Illustrator document so that the optimization and slice settings you just created embed in the AI file.

9. Now open your favorite web browser to see your handiwork! Most browsers have an Open command on the File menu that will enable you to navigate through your hard drive to /Chap11/ Finished Project/Website Layout.html (or whatever you named your HTML

file). See Figure 11.19 to compare what my design looks like in Illustrator versus my web browser. My next step would be to take it into my HTML editor and insert the sidebar copy and illos. If I had fewer objects in my sidebars, I could have made them HTML Text or Image slices and used the page straight out of Illustrator.

FIGURE 11.19   My artwork in Illustrator (top) and the exported page in my web browser (bottom).

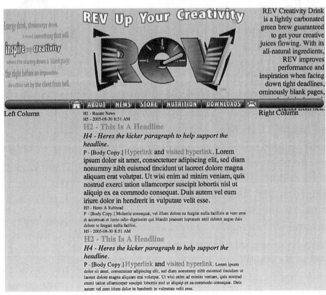

Project: Flash Logo Animation

We'll animate the REV logo and save it as a Flash animation in three easy steps:

1. Setting up the space
2. Animating the logo
3. Exporting to Flash SWF

Animating the Flash Logo

Ok. Enough walking. Get into your Nikes.

Animation and action should be used sparingly and where the design warrants it. In the following steps you will be given power. As Uncle Ben said, "With great power comes great responsibility." Superman's pop—and I—agree with him; use your power wisely, Kal-El.

STEP 1 ▼
Setting Up the Space

In our website layout, we dropped in a static logo. That was just an FPO. The finished website will actually use our nifty animated logo. First, we need to set the scene.

1. In your `Website Layout.ai` file, draw a rectangle that matches the dimensions of the logo slice and fill it with the color (or artwork) that appears behind the logo FPO.

2. Select the rectangle you drew and copy it to the clipboard.

3. Open **Logo.ai** from the Assets folder and save a copy of it (via File > Save As) as **Logo - Animated.ai** in the Finished Project folder.

4. Paste the rectangle onto a new layer titled **Background**. Note the dimensions of the background rectangle and lock its layer. In the Layers palette, drag the **Background** layer beneath any other layers.

5. Select all the logo paths and objects and size them proportionally (by holding Shift while you scale) to fit within the background rectangle just as the FPO did.

6. Select File > Document Setup and change its dimensions to match those of the background. Set the Units to Pixels while you're there.

7. Reposition the background and logo if necessary to fit the new document dimensions (see Figure 11.20). Save the file.

FIGURE 11.20 The REV logo on a solid color background matching the background gradient in the header area of my website Layout.

STEP 2 ▼
Animating the Logo

Flash (the format) is the standard in online vector artwork and animation. But if you thought Macromedia Flash (the application) is the only program capable of making Flash *SWF* files, you're mistaken. Illustrator can too. (Duh! Otherwise why would I mention it in an Illustrator project book, right?). To give our website some life, let's animate the logo.

1. Except for the background layer we just added, the logo file is exactly as it was created in Chapter 2, "Designing a Logo (From Scratch or From a Scan)"— it has three layers, REV, Star and Mask, and Speedometer. Although this is good organization for a drawing, it won't work for our Flash animation. So create a new layer titled **Frame 1**.

◎ TIP

Flash isn't the only online vector format. *SVG*, or Scalable Vector Graphics, a newer, open-source, XML-based challenger, is quickly gaining momentum on the web and in mobile content publishing—rich graphical content delivered to cellular phones and PDAs. Unfortunately, until the average user's web browser supports SVG, it can't be widely used; *you* can see SVG files in your browser, but that's only because the Adobe SVG Viewer browser plug-in is installed automatically with Illustrator (and all other recent Adobe applications). Your visitors would have to manually download the viewer plug-in, which most are loathe to do.

2. With the Selection tool, Shift-click on the needle and the needle's motion sweep in the *e*. Shift-drag the selected objects to the Symbols palette (Window > Symbols), which will create a new symbol while simultaneously converting the artwork to an instance of that symbol. In the Symbols palette double-click the new symbol and rename it to **Needle**.

◎ TIP

When you're making a Flash animation from Illustrator, symbols are especially important. The contents of symbols are only stored within the file once, with each instance becoming a pointer to the original data. The end result is a much smaller SWF file, which downloads faster with no discernable quality difference.

3. Using the same symbol creation procedure, select the green jitter outside the *R* and make it a logically named symbol instance. Repeat for the black jitter path, then for the green and black paths outside the *V*. When each of those has been converted to a symbol, select all the remaining paths and objects and collect them as a new symbol titled **Static Face**. Check your symbols against Figure 11.21.

FIGURE 11.21 The animation should contain only symbol instances—these six symbols in this case.

CHAPTER 11: Designing a Website and Flash Animation

4. Select all the symbols and cut them (Edit > Cut). In the Layers palette click on the **Frame 1** layer, and Paste in Front with (Cmd-F) [Ctrl+F]. That should place all six symbols onto the **Frame 1** layer, leaving the initial three layers empty. Go ahead and delete the empty layers.

5. As the name implies, the Static Face symbol will not move throughout the animation. So, with just it selected, press (Cmd-2) [Ctrl+2] to lock it. As we duplicate layers, the locked property of this symbol will persist through the geminations.

6. Duplicate the **Frame 1** layer by dragging it onto the Create New Layer button at the bottom of the Layers palette. Double-click the resulting **Frame 1 copy** and rename it to **Frame 2**. Are you seeing the progression? When you're exporting to SWF, the layers will be in reverse order—the bottom layer is the first frame, then progressing upward—so we'll keep naming and working with them in that order.

7. On the **Frame 2** layer, subtly reposition each of the symbols that must move. With the REV logo, that would be the five symbols that remain selectable. Try moving both green jitters up one or two presses of the Up Arrow key on your keyboard, the black jitters down the same amount. The idea with the jitter objects is to create the sense of the REV logo shuddering, like an engine revving up.

8. To animate the needle, don't use the Selection tool. Instead, select the needle symbol and grab the Rotate tool. Click once at the bottom-left tip of the needle to set the rotation axis, and then drag any other place on the needle to rotate it. We want to create

the illusion of a revving engine, so the needle should bounce a few degrees either way—try to avoid drastic changes unless your design calls for dramatic jumps.

> **◎ TIP**
>
> The animation will loop, going from the end straight back to the beginning frame. To create a smooth range of motion and avoid an abrupt jump from the end state back to the initial state, duplicate all but **Frame 1** and reverse their order.

9. When you're satisfied with this frame, repeat the last three steps to make frames 3, 4, and so on until you have the full range of motion you want (see Figure 11.22).

FIGURE 11.22   My animation for the REV logo is subtle, requiring 11 frames to achieve the full range of subtle motion.

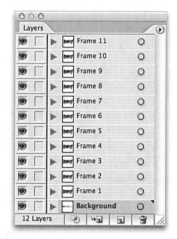

STEP 3 ▼
Exporting to Flash SWF

Now all that animation work pays off—
opening up a new world of online motion
power—and responsibility. (Thanks, Uncle
Ben. Have some rice.)

1. Go to File > Export. When the Export
   dialog comes up, name your file **Logo**,
   and save it to the `Finished Project`
   folder. In the Save As Type (or Format)
   drop-down, choose Macromedia Flash
   (*.SWF). Click Save. Up will pop the
   Macromedia® Flash™ (SWF) Format
   Options dialog. (Whew! Shall we save
   your eyes and my fingers by just referring to it as the SWF Options dialog?
   Let's.)

2. In the SWF Options dialog, set Export As
   to All Layers to SWF Frames. Turn on
   Generate HTML, so Illustrator will make
   an HTML page to contain the animation, Protect from Import (no one can
   edit your resulting SWF), Clip to Artboard

Size, Compress File, and Looping (auto-
rewind and play). Check Use as
Background and select the Background
layer from the list beneath. Leave all
other options at their defaults (see Figure
11.23). Click OK. It will look as if nothing
happens—unless you foolishly didn't use
symbols, in which case the screen may
appear to freeze while Illustrator churns
through your document.

> **TIP**
>
> Adjust the Frames Per Second (FPS) to speed up or slow
> down the playback of your animation.

3. Open your favorite web browser and
   load up `Chap11/Finished
   Project/Logo.html`. When you open it,
   the `Logo.swf` embedded in the HTML
   will begin playing (in perpetuity
   because we checked the Looping option
   in the SWF Options dialog).

FIGURE 11.23 **The SWF
Options dialog, ready for export.**

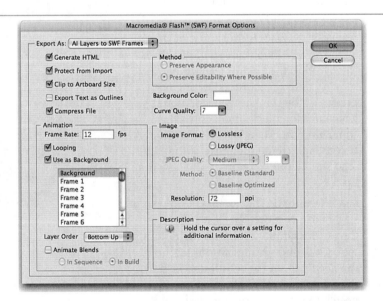

4. How does it look? If you need to make changes, make them in Illustrator and repeat the export process—answering Yes to the prompts about replacing the SWF and HTML files.

5. To integrate the animation into your website template, open **Logo.html** into your HTML or text editor (for example, Notepad on Windows or Text Edit on Mac). *You must be able to see the page code.* Copy the code beginning with <OBJECT... all the way through </OBJECT>, and paste it into your Website Template.html in place of the logo image.

Final Thoughts

What's next? Open your HTML template in an HTML or text editor and go to work inserting hyperlinks and content, tweaking the code, and adding any code or features Illustrator can't. Ultimately you will want to upload the page(s) and its sliced graphics to your web server.

Rather than exporting to HTML from Illustrator, you could simply save the sliced AI file and, if you have GoLive CS2, bring it in as a Smart Illustrator object. GoLive would then generate the HTML and images—and enable more advanced features like inserting

textual hyperlinks and creating rollover effects on the buttons so that they change appearance when the user's mouse hovers over them. See the GoLive topics in the Adobe Help Center.

Illustrator's Flash export creates a very simple SWF file. The Flash technology is capable of much more than Illustrator can export—animation is not, after all, Illustrator's primary function. For more advanced Flash work like creating buttons that trigger events, layered animations, adding sound and video into your SWF, creating user-fillable forms, and much more, look into Macromedia Flash (the application), which can pick up Illustrator's SWF files and run with them.

Should you get stuck on any part of this project, examine my sample files in the Chap11 folder. Incidentally, this was *not* introductory website design; this was intermediate—and you did just fine. Congratulations!

Some web designers uphold the pseudo-tradition of declaring how or with what tools they created their websites. You may have seen "Made with Mac" or "Made with GoLive!" buttons in the footers or sidebars of some pages. If you would like to take part in this tradition, showing your enthusiasm for Illustrator as your web design tool and this book for lighting the way, I've included a "Made with Illustrator @work" button graphic you are more than welcome to include anywhere on your site. You'll find it in the Extras folder of this chapter's resource files under the name iawlinklogo.gif. If you use it, please share the knowledge by linking it to **http://www.REVdrink.com**.

If you do include the "Made with Illustrator @work" button graphic linked to the site, stop by **http://www.REVdrink.com** and send me an email. I would sincerely love to see how you've used this book to help you with your Illustrator CS2 projects (web or otherwise). And, just to show how much I appreciate *you*, I'll include a link on **REVdrink.com** to any family-friendly website you create with the help of this chapter!

CHAPTER 12: Creating Graphs for a Report

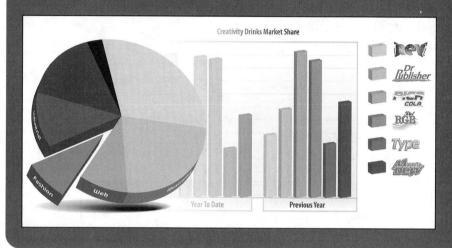

About the Projects

In these projects we will create visually compelling graphs from raw data and explore several techniques for enriching graph designs and presentation.

Prerequisites

It would be helpful if you had a basic understanding of applying fills and strokes, setting and styling type, and working with the Layers, Character, Paragraph, Appearance, Color, and Swatches palettes.

One section of this chapter uses Microsoft Excel. Though completing that section is optional, working hands-on in Excel will allow you to experience and understand the graph creation workflow more thoroughly and effectively than by simply reading about it.

@work resources

Please visit the publisher's website to access the following Chapter 12 project files:

- ▶ **Chap12** (complete projects to use as a reference while you work: **Pie Graph.ai, Column Graph.ai**)
- ▶ **Chap12\Assets** (**Column Design Elements.ai, data Market Share.xls, data Market Share.txt**)
- ▶ **Chap12\Finished Project**

Planning the Projects

Is Illustrator CS2 the best tool for this job? Sometimes.

If you only create the occasional graph or you need to build highly creative graphs, Illustrator is absolutely the *best* tool for the job.

If, however, you need to create and update graphs often, or your creative needs don't extend much further than flat charts or rudimentary 3D-style graphs, consider using a dedicated graphing application or Microsoft Excel.

In Excel, graphs are updated in real time to reflect changes to their dataset. In a comparison of annual sales, for example, it's easy to add another year's data by inserting a column; the graph will update to match. Adding a column or row of data anywhere but to the end of the dataset in Illustrator, however, can be a two-step process at best, and a pain in the neck of total retyping at worst. If your graph is based on external data, you'll need to change the data in its original file (which may be a two file operation), then re-import it for Illustrator to reflect the changes. Copying and pasting data between cells can be even more aggravating.

If the *dataset* changes frequently or if the graph requires modification by non-creative personnel, Illustrator is probably not your best choice. I've taught Illustrator to some extraordinarily unlikely users, but even I wouldn't try to convince an overworked comptroller to use Illustrator when her only need is to generate or update graphs.

Those are the reasons you *shouldn't* use Illustrator for graphing. The reasons you should... Well, they're just too numerous to list! Anything you can do in Illustrator CS2, you can do in, to, or with a graph. Brushes, live effects, multiple fills, gradients, 3D Extrude & Bevel...

Column and row graphs may be constructed of repeating, stacked objects, of sliding objects, or of anything you can imagine. Every piece of a graph—from the columns or radar points to the legend, from the value axis to the tick marks—is completely under your control for style and customization with the full breadth of Illustrator's tools.

Illustrator enables levels of freedom, control, and presentation enhancement for graphs that Excel cannot even approach.

As always, prepare your data in advance. Although graphs, more so than any other type of project, typically require changes throughout the workflow, try to hold off on graph creation until the figures and dataset are as close to final as possible.

Project: 3D Pie Graph

In four easy steps we'll enter data, build a 3D pie graph, and export it for placement into presentation and print applications:

1. Manually entering data
2. Coloring a pie graph
3. Making the pie graph 3D
4. Exporting graphs for other applications

Creating a Pie Graph

REV is revving up for its annual stockholders' meeting, and they need clearly stated, high-impact, and creatively enticing graphs to communicate their report data. The graphs will appear in both a printed annual report and a slideshow presentation before the shareholders. As usual, they've given us carte blanche to create what we think they really need.

REV conducted an online survey (they gave away a couple of iPods as incentive) and, among other things, asked REV drinkers what type of creative they were. We've been provided with the collected responses from that question and asked to create a pie chart so that REV shareholders understand who is buying.

Pie graphs are used to present percentages of a whole as slices of a pie (or wheel of cheese, as my cat and I would prefer). These types of graphs are invaluable for communicating how different pieces of a whole relate. For example, you could use a pie graph to better understand how your 8- (14?) hour work day is broken down between your various tasks and responsibilities. We're going to use a pie graph to help our client understand who is buying REV Creativity Drink.

STEP 1 ▼
Manually Entering Data

Before making it look pretty, let's get the data into Illustrator.

1. Begin a new RGB document entitled **Pie Graph**. Unless you have a specific size in mind, set the size to Letter landscape (11 × 8.5 inches).

2. On the Toolbox, click and hold on the Column Graph Tool to reveal the other graph tools behind it. We want the Pie Graph tool. With the Pie Graph tool, click and drag out a rectangular area to contain the graph and its legend. When you release, the Graph Data window will appear (see Figure 12.1).

The Graph Data window looks (pretty much) like any spreadsheet application. This is the brain of your charts, where all data, labels, and categories are entered and modified. The cells may hold values (numbers) or labels and categories (text and numbers). Data may be entered many levels deep to create fiendishly complex graphs, but we're going to keep it simple with just one row of labels and one row of data.

FIGURE 12.1 The Graph Dat window.

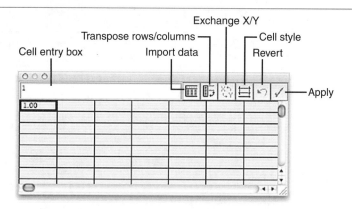

Exchange X/Y
Transpose rows/columns —
— Cell style
Cell entry box
Import data
Revert
Apply

TIP

If you know the exact size for your graph, don't draw the rectangle. Instead, select the correct graph tool then click once on the artboard. When the Graph dialog—not the Graph Data window—appears, specify the height and width. Note that the area you specify will include only the graph itself, not its legend and labeling, which will appear beyond the area of the graph.

3. Click in the top-left cell, which will load that cell into the cell entry box above, and type **Graphic Designers**, our first data label. Press the Tab key after typing to commit the change and advance to the next cell along the top row. Enter the remaining labels the same way: **Illustrators**, **Web Designers**, **Fashion Designers**, **Industrial Designers**, **Writers**, and **Others**. In the end, you should have seven labeled columns along the top row (see Figure 12.2).

Naturally, if you're working on your own graph project at work, replace my labels (and later data) with your own.

4. Now that the labels are done, let's enter the actual data from which our pie and its pieces will be drawn. Click in the cell just below the **Graphic Designers** label, and enter **758**, the number of survey respondents who identified their industry as graphic design. Then, under each of the other labels, enter their numbers: **625**, **242**, **212**, **301**, **419**, and **76**.

 TIP

Even though a pie graph is based on percentages, you needn't convert your data to percent values prior to entering them in the Graph Data window. Illustrator will interpret the sum of all your values as a relative 100%, and draw slices proportionally dividing by 100%.

5. Got the data entered? Good. Now click the Apply button. Behind the Graph Data window you should see something akin to Figure 12.3. Go ahead and close the Graph Data window and save your document.

FIGURE 12.2 Labels in place along the top row of cells.

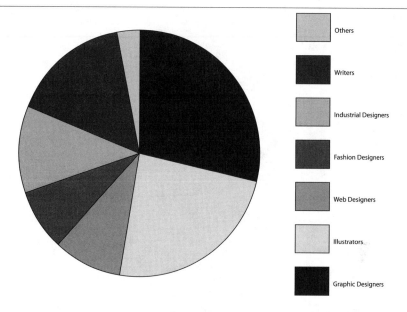

FIGURE 12.3 **The initial grayscale pie chart.**

Others

Writers

Industrial Designers

Fashion Designers

Web Designers

Illustrators

Graphic Designers

STEP 2 ▼
Coloring a Pie Graph

If you're content with a graph as boring as Abe Vigoda's roast, go ahead and stop working now. In this Step we'll add some color before giving the graph some depth in the next Step ("Making the Pie Graph 3D").

1. Grab the Group Selection tool from behind the Direct Selection tool. Click *twice* on one of the pie sections to select both the slice *and* its legend. Cool, huh?

2. Now, using the Swatches or Color palette, give it a fill—a solid color, gradient, or pattern—and/or a stroke. If you plan to make your pie three-dimensional in the next Step, don't give it a stroke. Because of the blessed Group Selection tool, both the slice and the legend can be styled at once without breaking the graph's link to its data—you can go back and change the dataset at any time.

🚫 **CAUTION**

Do not ungroup your graph unless you are absolutely sure its dataset will not change. Ungrouping breaks the association to the data, preventing that graph from ever being updated with new values.

3. Using the same technique, move around the pie coloring each slice and its legend to your tastes. My colored pie is in Figure 12.4.

STEP 3 ▼
Making the Pie Graph 3D

Colors are great, but a little dimensionality can often (not always!) give a pie chart more impact, making the data easier to stare at going into that third hour of a 20-minute meeting.

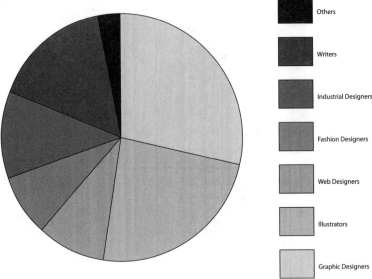

FIGURE 12.4 My colored pie. (Yes, I know it looks very much like Figure 12.3. It's a black-and-white book! Cut me some slack, will ya?)

Others

Writers

Industrial Designers

Fashion Designers

Web Designers

Illustrators

Graphic Designers

1. The very first thing we need to do is *86* the legend—otherwise it too will become 3D (no, it's not as cool as you're thinking). So, grab the Direct Selection tool and drag a selection rectangle around just the legend (labels and colored boxes). Copy them with (Cmd-C) [Ctrl+C].

2. Make a new layer, and paste (in front) the copied legend to it with (Cmd-F) [Ctrl+F]. Rename the layer to **Legend**. This legend is totally disconnected from the graph, so if you intend to make changes to the number of slices in your graph or even to the colors, stop now and come back when your data or colors are finalized. Hide the **Legend** layer.

3. Back on your first layer, select the graph with the Selection tool, and choose Object > Graph > Data, which will get you back to the Graph Data window.

4. In the Graph Data window, click the first cell in the top row and press Delete on your keyboard to wipe it out. Repeat until you've emptied the top row.

5. Select your second row by clicking in the first cell and dragging to the last. Instead of deleting, however, press (Cmd-X) [Ctrl+X] to cut the information. Click once in the leftmost cell of the top row and paste the data in with (Cmd-V) [Ctrl+V].

🚫 **CAUTION**

As of this writing, pasting data into the Graph Data window on Windows does not work. The data goes in, but so do codes so funky they should be part of a George Clinton groove. If you are using Illustrator CS2 on Windows, you're better off retyping the data into the top row.

Click the Apply button and close the Graph Data window. If your graph gets significantly smaller, it's because there's still something—maybe just a space—in the second row. Highlight the cells and delete again.

6. Select the graph with the Selection tool. If your graph has a stroke, remove it. Now, choose Effect > 3D > Extrude & Bevel.

7. In the 3D Extrude & Bevel Options dialog (see Figure 12.5), turn on Preview and begin by choosing a Position preset from the drop-down menu at the top. For most graphs, I would suggest beginning with Off-Axis Bottom and working from there.

Click and drag any face, side, or corner of the track cube to change the graph's rotation in three-dimensional space, or adjust the values in the X-, Y-, and Z-axis measurement fields. The measurement fields accept angles from negative 180° through positive 180°. Changing either the track cube or the axis fields will update the other. The blue face of the track cube is the front surface of your graph.

Changing the Perspective measurement field will distort your graph to create the impression of distance—use this sparingly as it will introduce distortion of your pie that may render the relative size of the pieces difficult to ascertain.

FIGURE 12.5   3D Extrude & Bevel Options dialog.

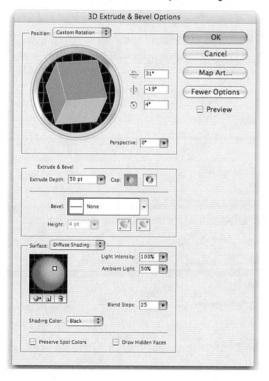

◎ **TIP**

Using patterns for slice fills creates some very intriguing effects because 3D Extrude & Bevel sees them as more than flat colors. It will actually add dimensionality to the paths contained in the pattern! (Of course, this will increase your rendering time, but it's often worth the wait.)

If you're happy with the thickness of your graph and its lighting, just click OK (see Figure 12.6). Otherwise, play with the Extrude Depth to get the thickness you'd like. Changing the Bevel can give you rounded, beveled, or scalloped edges.

Clicking the More Options button will reveal advanced lighting options where you may choose a shading type and modify the light(s) and shadows created from the extrusion and rotation. When you've finished setting the options for 3D Extrude & Bevel, click OK (for a more detailed look at the 3D Extrude & Bevel options, see Chapter 7, "Creating 3D Product Packaging Mockups").

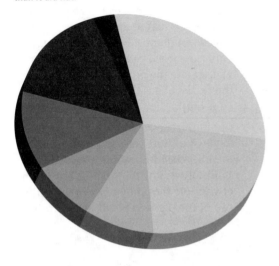

> ◎ **TIP**
>
> 3D Extrude & Bevel is a live effect, and will automatically adapt to changes in objects. If the dataset of your graph changes, the effect will instantly redraw to reflect the changes.

8. Turn on your **Legend** layer. Look at those color key swatches. Are they too big? They were for mine (see Figure 12.7), so I resized them in one swift motion. Unless you're making a pie chart for the elderly, you may want to do the same. With the Selection tool, select all the colored rectangles. Then choose Object > Transform > Transform Each.

9. In the Transform Each dialog, turn on Preview in the bottom right, then change the Horizontal and/or Vertical scale to suit your graph. Unlike scaling via the Transform palette, Transform Each will scale each object within its own space rather than treating the individual paths as a group and transforming them relative to one another—which would force you to manually realign each block to its text label after scaling.

10. Style the type of your labels (if desired), and save your document. It's now ready for export. Figure 12.8 shows my final pie graph after adding a few details. How did I get the labels on the side? Keep reading; it's all here, pal.

FIGURE 12.7 The original legend (left) as generated by Illustrator was a little on the large side. So I resized them (right).

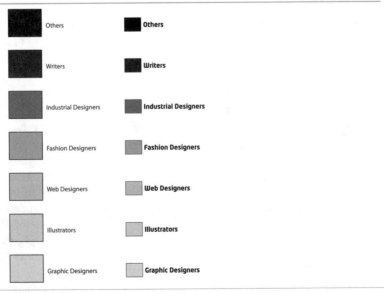

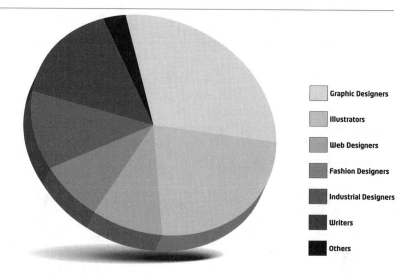

FIGURE 12.8 My final Pie Graph; incidentally, the shadow is a blend, not the Drop Shadow live effect.

- Graphic Designers
- Illustrators
- Web Designers
- Fashion Designers
- Industrial Designers
- Writers
- Others

Exporting Graphs for Other Applications

Now that you have this spiffy new pie graph, what are you going to do with it? Although in rare circumstances a graph might never need to leave Illustrator, most of the time you'll need to insert it into a report layout or slide presentation. Let's run through the exceedingly facile ways to do that.

Saving for Placement into Adobe InDesign

InDesign can place native Adobe Illustrator files of the same or earlier versions. In other words, if you have InDesign CS2, it will place Illustrator CS2 .AI files as well as AI files created in Illustrator versions CS, 10, 9, and so on. If you're using InDesign 2, however, you might have some difficulty placing your Illustrator CS2 file. Follow the instructions for saving for placement into QuarkXPress if you have earlier versions of InDesign.

1. Save your document—which you've already done, right?

2. In InDesign, with a document open, choose File > Place, and navigate to your `Pie Graph.ai`. Select that file and click the Place button.

3. InDesign will prompt you to choose how to crop the placed document. Select to crop to Artwork, which will remove any extraneous empty space if the graph was smaller than the full artboard; it will also extend the selection to include any parts that extend beyond the scope of the artboard if you drew large.

There's no need to flatten your transparency or expand your 3D or other effects (if used) ahead of time in Illustrator. Even though InDesign doesn't do 3D itself, it will respect *anything* you draw in Illustrator. The relationship between Prince InDesign and Queen Illustrator is based upon a tremendous mutual respect (and late night rendezvous, but who am I to spread gossip).

Because you're placing Illustrator's native file format, any changes you later have to make to the dataset or visual aspects of the graph will cause InDesign to want to update the graph in its layout—there are no intermediary formats to encourage discrepancies between the version of the original graph and what appears in your InDesign layout.

Saving for Placement into QuarkXPress

As of this writing, QuarkXPress supports native Photoshop .PSD documents, but not native Illustrator .AI files (there's a new version of QuarkXPress on the horizon, so that may change). Still, this limitation is not a major impediment because recent versions (within the last 10 years) of QuarkXPress support placement of PDF files, and Illustrator's .AI files *are* PDF.

1. From File > Document Color Mode, select CMYK color.

2. From the File menu, choose Save a Copy.

3. In the Save a Copy dialog, set the Save As Type to Adobe PDF (*.PDF), give the file a name, and click Save.

4. Up will pop the Save Adobe PDF dialog. Here, just choose the [Illustrator Default] Adobe PDF Preset at the top, and then click the Save PDF button.

> ## ✖ NOTE
> If you don't care to see your new PDF opened in Acrobat immediately after clicking Save PDF, uncheck the View PDF After Saving option.

5. In your QuarkXPress layout, draw a picture box and then choose File > Get Picture. Navigate to your `Pie Graph.pdf`. Select that file and click the Open button. Done. There's no need to use the PDF Import options at the bottom of Quark's Get Picture dialog because your graph will be a single-page PDF.

6. Right-click or Ctrl+click (Mac) and choose Fit Box to Picture to resize the containing box to the dimensions of the graph.

Saving for Placement into Other Print Applications

If you need to get your graph into PageMaker, FrameMaker, or another application for print, your best bet will be EPS format.

1. Draw a rectangle atop the artwork that encompasses the graph and its legend without extending beyond.

2. Choose Object > Crop Area > Make. You now have a crop area that will cut away any extraneous white space.

3. Unlock all layers.

4. From File > Document Color Mode, select CMYK color.

5. Select your graph and choose Object > Flatten Transparency.

6. In the Flatten Transparency dialog (see Figure 12.9), pick the [High Resolution] preset, and then turn on Convert All Text to Outlines, which will cause the preset menu to change to Custom. Leave everything else as set.

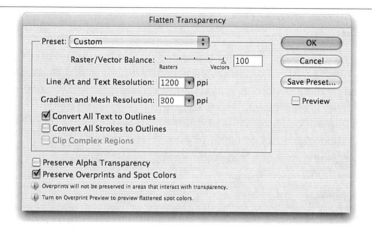

7. Go to File > Save A Copy. In the dialog choose Illustrator EPS (*.EPS) from the Save as Type drop-down. Name the file and click Save.

8. In the EPS Options dialog our goal is to maximize compatibility, so set the Version to be Illustrator 8 EPS.

9. Set the Preview to TIFF (8-bit Color) and Transparent. Turn off Embed Fonts and leave the rest of the options as they are. Click OK.

> ◎ **TIP**
>
> The TIFF (8-bit Color) preview in EPS files is a low-resolution, low-color proxy or thumbnail embedded in the EPS to make it viewable in applications without a built-in PostScript interpreter.

Saving for Placement into PowerPoint or Keynote

The odds are quite good that you may want to get your graphs into a slide-show presentation application like Microsoft PowerPoint or Apple's Keynote. Getting graphs—or any artwork—from Illustrator into either of these applications (as well as into Microsoft Word or Excel) is so simple that I feel guilty even writing about it.

1. Make your crop area as in the previous set of steps.

2. Choose File > Save for Microsoft Office. Give it a name and click the Save button.

3. Go refill your coffee cup.

Project: Column Graph

In eight quick steps, we'll create a column graph from an external dataset and style it several ways:

1. Saving datasets from Excel
2. Importing datasets from Excel
3. Changing graph type options
4. Formatting text
5. Basic column formatting
6. Monotone 3D columns
7. Multi-color 3D columns
8. Repeating columns

Creating a Column Graph from External Datasets

If the only way to get data into Illustrator was to hand-type it, you'd find yourself desperately avoiding graph projects. Fortunately, it's not the only way. You can copy and paste (when paste works) tab-delimited data from a text editor or even Microsoft Word, and, the most common method, import data from Excel.

STEP 1 ▼
Saving Datasets from Excel

Microsoft Excel is the world standard in spreadsheet software. There are competitors, but collectively the market share of all Excel competitors is counted in the single digits. If you're going to be building graphs in Illustrator, you really should have Excel installed. People will send you Excel spreadsheets because that's what the world uses.

For this particular activity you will need Excel. If you don't have Excel (we all have budgets), a viable and *free* alternative is OpenOffice, an open-source office suite for Mac, Windows, and various flavors of UNIX. (Did I mention it's free?) If you're too lazy to go get it from **http://www.openoffice.org**, or if IT has blocked you from installing anything on your computer, at least read through this section so that you can explain to the client, boss, or office administrator how to prepare datasets for you.

1. In Excel, open the data Market Share.xls file from this chapter's Assets folder. You should see a very simple market share spreadsheet (see Figure 12.10), although Illustrator can handle much more complicated datasets. Note that the top left cell (A1) is empty. This is necessary for Illustrator to use the left column as categories. Putting anything in the top left cell will cause Illustrator to interpret column A as part of the data rather than as categories of the data.

> ### ⊘ CAUTION
> Another Illustrator limitation to watch out for in Excel is comma usage. You cannot use commas in dataset numbers imported into Illustrator. Make sure large numbers do not include commas—either hand-typed or inserted automatically via Excel's cell formatting.

2. It would be great if Illustrator could use native Excel files. Alas, it cannot, so we must create a tab-delimited text file. From Excel's File menu choose Save As. In the Save As dialog, change the Save As Type to Text (Tab Delimited) (*.txt). If the filename doesn't automatically update with the new file extension, update it yourself.

3. Save the new data Market Share.txt file to the Chap12/Finished Projects folder. Answer Excel's obligatory warnings about formatting not being saved in this file format and blah blah blah, and then close Excel.

FIGURE 12.10 **The data** Market Share.xls **spreadsheet in Microsoft Excel.**

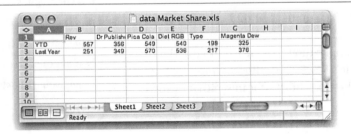

STEP 2 ▼
Importing Datasets from Excel

Now that we have our dataset in a compatible format, let's get it into Illustrator.

1. Begin a new RGB document entitled **Column Graph**. Unless you have a specific size in mind, set the dimensions to Letter landscape (11 × 8.5 inches).

2. Drag out the area for the graph with the Column Graph tool. Remember, the graph legend, labels, and categories will appear *outside* the area you specify.

3. When the Graph Data window appears, click the Import Data button and locate the data `Market Share.txt` file.

4. When you're in the Graph Data window, click the Apply button to have Illustrator generate a graph from the REV market share data (see Figure 12.11).

   There are several things going on here that are worth noting. Along the top row in the Graph Data window are listed REV and its competing creativity drink brands. They translated to graphical columns with a matching legend.

In the first column, **YTD** (year to date) and **Last Year** became categories that split the graph into two sections; the data from the rows corresponding to the categories became the graphical columns in that category. And, finally, Illustrator automatically created a scale on the left side of the chart.

Clicking the Transpose button will counterchange rows for columns, columns for rows. With this particular graph, the effect of the Transpose button would be that the creativity drink brands become categories, and YTD and Last Year become the data labels (see Figure 12.12). Instead of comparing the various brands against each other on an annual basis as it did previously, now the chart has become a means of comparing each brand's individual growth or recession between the two years. In this case, the type also gets cramped into smaller areas, which would require us to make the type much smaller (if we were going to transpose).

If you transposed the data, transpose it again to return to the way it first imported.

5. Save your **Column Graph** document, and let's get on with customizing the graph.

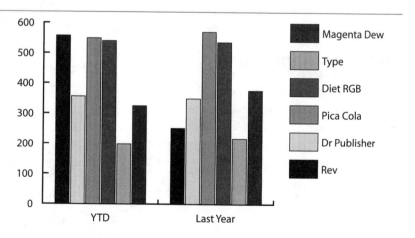

FIGURE 12.11 The default graph resulting from the imported dataset.

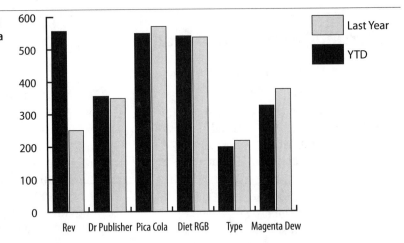

FIGURE 12.12 **Transposing the data creates a graph with a completely different purpose.**

 TIP

To change the number of decimal places or change the width of columns as displayed in the Graph Data window, click the Cell Style button. Neither has any effect on the graph itself.

Customizing the Static Graph Elements

One of the most compelling reasons to use Illustrator for creating graphs is the fact that just about every aspect of the graph is customizable—without breaking the link to the dataset, and thus, your ability to refine the data.

STEP 3 ▼
Changing Graph Type Options

Oh, we can—and most definitely *will*—customize the columns (they're hideous in randomly chosen shades of black). But let's first look at how we can customize the other elements of the graph.

1. Select your column graph with the Selection tool, and choose Object > Graph > Type.

2. In the Graph Type dialog (see Figure 12.13) you may instantly convert your column graph to a scatter graph or any of the other seven types, just by clicking its button. But let's stick with the column graph for now and focus on everything but the type buttons.

Beneath the type buttons the Value Axis drop-down allows us to place the value column on the default left side, the right, or both sides. Wider charts are usually easier to understand if their values mirror on both flanks. I wouldn't do it on this particular chart, but if one or two more years were represented, I would definitely add the value axis to both sides.

In the Style section, Add Drop Shadow creates a solid block drop shadow to columns. It's ugly. Why bother with that when you can use the Drop Shadow filter or live effect to get real drop shadows? First Row in Front and First Column in Front determine the *z-order* of graphical columns. With the flat graph we have now, z-order hasn't much relevance. Style the columns such that they overlap a bit, and these options become important. Add Legend Across Top will convert the legend from a vertical list on the side to a horizontal one above the graph.

FIGURE 12.13   The Graph
Type dialog.

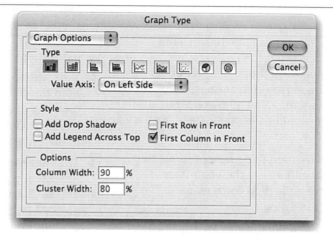

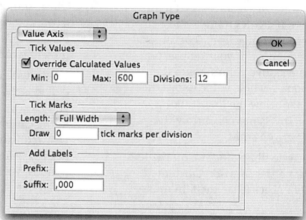

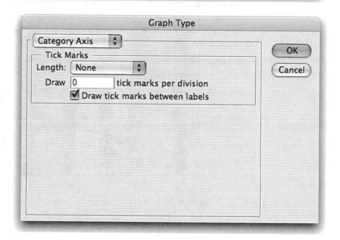

Options set the width of columns and clusters (categories) relative to themselves. Values less than 100% create space between columns or clusters; values above 100% create overlap. Columns exist within clusters, so a cluster width of 90% makes a 90% column width really 90% of 90%, or 81%.

Let's leave everything here at its default values and move to the Value Axis pane from the drop-down menu at the top of the dialog.

3. Illustrator automatically creates a list of values for the value axis based upon your data. It creates round, whole numbers that range from 0 or a round negative number (if your dataset includes negative values) up to the closest round, whole value above the highest (or below the lowest) dataset number. This is not necessarily the breakdown you want.

Let's override Illustrator's default values by checking the Override Calculated Values box. Let's leave the Min and Max fields the way they are, but change Divisions to **12**, which will introduce to our hundreds-increment value axis increments of 50.

4. Next, change the Tick Marks length from the default Short to Full Width to draw the lines all the way across the chart, making the column values easier to understand.

5. The values in the market share data are actually per thousand units—REV's YTD of 557, for example, is actually 557,000 units. Therefore, we could give the value axis values the suffix of **k**, which stands for thousands. After trying it, however, it looks awkward. Instead, let's enter **,000** in the suffix field (note the comma before the zeroes).

The last section of the Graph Type dialog is the Category Axis pane, where you may set options for the tick marks in the clusters created by the YTD and Last Year categories. I'm leaving mine at their default. After setting the options, your graph should look something like mine (see Figure 12.14).

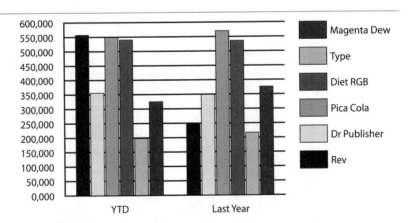

FIGURE 12.14 **My graph so far.**

CHAPTER 12: Creating Graphs for a Report

STEP 4 ▼
Formatting Text

When Illustrator creates a graph it will use the default character format settings to style autogenerated text like the legend labels, categories, and value axis labels. Sooner or later, you'll want to override the defaults or even edit the text.

1. With the Group Selection tool, click twice on the top value along the value axis. That will select every value.

2. Now change the type styling on the Character, Paragraph, and/or OpenType palettes. There's nothing special about these—they're just plain old point type objects. I'm choosing to format mine as Myriad Semibold Condensed at about half the point size Illustrator drew them. After that, I tapped my keyboard up arrow a few times to realign the text's baselines with the tick marks (see Figure 12.15). You can even change the color or apply graphic styles if you like.

FIGURE 12.15   Value axis labels are standard point type objects that may be selected, styled, and moved like any other object.

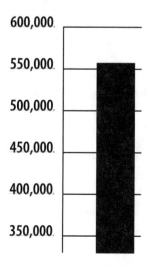

3. Using the same method of selecting them with the Group Selection tool, go ahead and style your category and legend labels. Just make sure you click on the text of your legend not on the swatches. Selecting the latter with the Group Selection tool also selects the columns.

 TIP

To make your work even easier—especially if you intend to create several similarly styled graphs—make paragraph and/or character styles for your labels, values, and other point type objects.

4. Aw, *nuts*! If you look at the bottom of the value axis you'll see that appending **,000** to all our values in the previous step also changed the bottom entry from 0 to 0,000. That's just plain stupid, like a rap star outside without a gun. Grab the Type tool and take out the **,000**. No big deal; you won't break the graph's link to its dataset—just plain ol' text, remember?

 TIP

If your graph presents monetary values, insert a dollar sign ($), Euro ( ), or any other symbol before (or after, as may be appropriate) the value at the top of the value axis.

5. Finish up any text edits and save your document.

STEP 5 ▼
Basic Column Formatting

Why would I call this "Basic Column Formatting"? Well, because it is. There's nothing wrong with basic—especially not when your goal is turning numbers into easily understood graphics. But there's so much more that can be done with column graphs... Make a quick run through this section, then check out the next Project for the seriously cool stuff. (I'm such a tease.)

1. Duplicate your column graph's layer. Rename the original layer to **Basic** and the duplicate layer to **Monotone 3D**. Hide the **Monotone 3D** layer.

2. Click once, twice, three times (a lady) on any of your columns with the Group Selection tool. Notice anything different? Right: Not only are the one column and its legend swatch selected (two clicks), but so is the matching column in the other category (third click). They're all objects nested in groups. Every time you click with the Group Selection tool, it selects the next group up in the nest of containing groups; in this case, one column is its own group, but it and the other column are grouped, and both column groups are grouped together with the legend swatch. If you had three categories you'd need four clicks to select all matching objects; four categories would require five clicks, and so on. This makes it easy to select and style the same set of data across multiple categories.

Run through the columns with the Group Selection tool and give them each color fills to enliven your graph. I'll wait right here.

3. Ready? Now, again with the Group Selection tool, click *four* times on one of the columns. That should select the entire group of columns and legend swatches without getting any of the labels or tick marks.

> ## ◎ TIP
> Want your tick marks in front of your columns so that values are easier to interpret? With the Group Selection tool, click on a column until all columns are selected, then choose Object > Arrange > Send to Back. Voilà!

4. In the Colors palette, bring the Stroke swatch to the front and set it to none.

5. If you went through the Pie Chart project, you know you can colorize the bars and legend swatches simultaneously. You also know you can extrude and bevel the entire graph in 3D. I wouldn't recommend that for a column graph because, although you *can* do it, 3D revolution also revolves on the Z-axis. Because the columns have a z-order, they will shift forward or back in relation to one another, throwing off their relative heights and defeating the whole purpose of presenting data in this format. (If you don't understand what I mean, apply a 3D Extrude & Bevel effect, then compare the bottoms of the columns.)

In the next section I'll show you how to get 3D columns. For now, feel free to play with other things on the Effects menu. Figure 12.16 shows what my columns look like after applying Inner Glow and Convert to Shape > Rounded Rectangle.

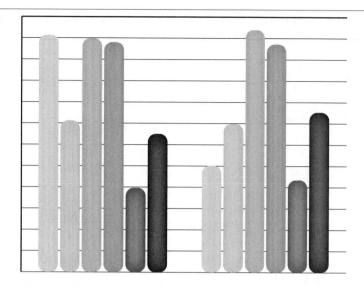

Column Graph Design

Here's where graph design gets really fun—and where you're given the potential to commit offenses on par with anything you might have seen Courtney Love do on CourtTV.

There are four kinds of column designs:

- **Vertically Scaled**—A design element is scaled vertically to fill the column area, even if that element distorts horrifically.

- **Uniformly Scaled**—The design element scales both vertically and horizontally until it fills the vertical area of the column.

- **Repeating**—Instead of scaling, the design element repeats vertically until it fills the column.

- **Sliding**—Portions of the design element remain fixed as either top, bottom, or both top and bottom of the column, while the middle section of the element stretches to fill in the remaining space.

Let's have some fun with the lower two.

STEP 6 ▼
Monotone 3D Columns

Here's how to make 3D columns without distorting your data.

1. You should have already created a **Monotone 3D** layer, so turn it on and hide the **Basic** layer.

2. Leaving the **Column Graph** document open, create a new document named **Column Design Elements**. Make it RGB, 11 × 8.5 inches.

3. With the Rectangle Tool, make a rectangle around 1.5 × 1 inches. Set a stroke of none, and fill it with the color you'd like to use for all your columns.

4. Select the rectangle and give it a 3D Extrude & Bevel effect that pleases you. Make sure there's some area in the middle of the block unaffected by the extrusion or beveling visible along the top and bottom of all sides of the block (see Figure 12.17).

FIGURE 12.17   My 3D block so far.

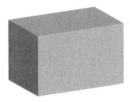

5. After closing the 3D Extrude & Bevel Options dialog, keep the block selected and choose Object > Expand Appearance. The 3D effect is now committed as a set of grouped paths instead of a live effect.

6. 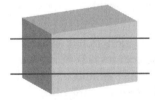Zoom in close on the block and grab the Line tool. Starting outside the block, and while holding the Shift key to constrain the angle, draw a line that completely bisects the block, ending just beyond the opposite side. Position the line just above the bottom of the block's 3D effects (see Figure 12.18). Give it a stroke color.

FIGURE 12.18   With both the top and bottom horizontal lines in places, the blocks' top and bottom with 3D effects are divided from the relatively unremarkable middle.

7. Repeat the previous step to create a line just below the top of the block.

NOTE

Make your lines just *slightly* wider than the block. Their length will determine the column width, and lines that are too wide will result in pencil-thin columns.

8. Select the block and both lines, and group them. Deselect the group.

9. With the Direct Selection tool, click on one of the lines and Shift-click to also select the other. Choose View > Guides > Make Guides.

CAUTION

Although steps 8 and 9 might seem out of order and even illogical given what you know about guides, trust me; they must be in this order. If you convert the lines to guides prior to grouping, you won't be able to group them in with the block. It's critical that they are part of the group as guides.

10. Select the group again, and choose Object > Graph > Design. In that dialog, click New Design. A New Design entry will appear in the list, and your 3D block will show up in the Preview. Rename New Design to **3D Bar 1**.

11. Save the **Common Design Elements** file. Leaving that file open, switch back to the **Column Graph** document by choosing it from the bottom of the Window menu.

12. With the black arrow Selection tool, select the graph. Go to Object > Graph > Column.

13. See the **3D Bar 1** entry in the Graph Column dialog? Select it, then set the Column Type to Sliding. After clicking OK, you should see something like Figure 12.19.

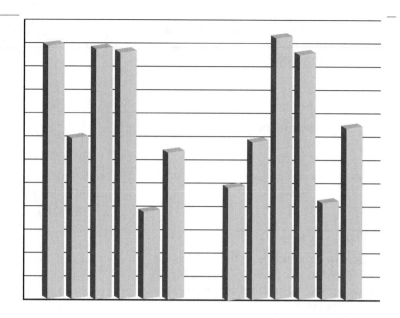

FIGURE 12.19 My sliding
monotone 3D column graph.

14. Use the Graph Type dialog to adjust the width of columns if they wind up too narrow or if they overlap. If you see the horizontal lines (sliding lines, they're called), simply hide guides from the View > Guides > Hide Guides menu item. Save your document.

STEP 7 ▼
Multi-Color 3D Columns

Although many graphs work better if all columns (or rows, for that matter) are the same color and design, the REV market share graph really needs color to differentiate the various columns. So, let's make everything a different color again.

1. Hide the **Monotone 3D** layer, and make another duplicate of the **Basic** layer. Name this new one **Multi-Color 3D**. You know why we're doing this, right? Exactly: We're leaving an easy breadcrumb trail for ourselves in case we

don't like the final result and want to return to some stop along the way—even after closing the document.

2. With the Direct Selection tool, drag a selection rectangle that encompasses only the swatches in your legend and copy them.

3. Switch over to the **Common Design Elements** document and create a new layer, hiding the existing one.

4. Paste the legend swatches and keep them all selected. At this point, they should be separate paths rather than a group. Remove any stroke they may hold.

5. Press (Cmd-Shift-E) [Ctrl+Shift+E] to reapply the same 3D Extrude & Bevel settings from the first round. If you want different 3D settings, skip that and go directly into Effects > 3D > Extrude & Bevel. You'll have 3D boxes now (see Figure 12.20).

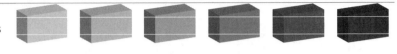

FIGURE 12.20 Six colored boxes representing the six colors from the market share graph legend.

6. Expand the appearance of these blocks.

7. Draw horizontal lines on each block just as you did in the "Monotone 3D Columns" section, group the lines with their corresponding blocks, and convert the lines to guides.

 TIP

The fastest way to create the pair of horizontal lines on all your blocks is to draw them once, select the lines, and drag them atop the next block while holding (Opt+Shift) [Alt+Shift].

 TIP

A fast way to select all the lines, even grouped, is to select one with the Direct Selection tool, then go to Select > Same > Stroke Color. Then convert them all to guides in one fell swoop.

8. Make each set of block and guide lines into a new graph design with Object > Graph > Design, and name each instance.

9. Save the **Common Design Elements** file and jump back to **Column Graph.**

10. This time, instead of selecting the entire table, grab the Group Selection tool and click on a column until you've selected it, its counterpart in the next category, and their related legend entry.

11. Now choose Object > Graph > Column. Set your first design—don't forget to change the type to Sliding—and click OK. Move on to the next column set, and repeat. Your end result shouldn't be too far off from mine (see Figure 12.21).

FIGURE 12.21 My sliding monotone 3D column graph.

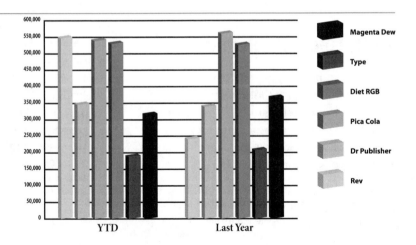

STEP 8 ▼
Repeating Columns

Another type of column graph that, when used sensibly, can really drive home the meaning of a dataset, is the repeating column. Instead of a single object stretched or sliding to fill a column, this style repeats or stacks an object to fill the column (or row) area.

1. On a new layer in the **Common Design Elements** file, draw a relatively uncomplicated object that represents the data communicated by your graph. If you'd rather just try this technique before drawing, open up my Common Design Elements.ai file from this chapter's Assets folder. You'll find a layer entitled **Repeating**, containing a simple drink can drawing (see Figure 12.22).

FIGURE 12.22   A simple drawing to be used for a repeating graph design.

2. When you have your drawing, group its paths and objects (if you haven't already), and make a new graph design from it. With repeating elements there's no need for sliding lines—there's no harm, though, either; if you want to leave yourself the option of using the drawing as any type of column fill, add your sliding lines. If you're using my Common Design Elements.ai file, copy the can drawing to your own file before making a design, then close my Common Design Elements.

3. Save **Common Design Elements** and flip to **Column Graph**.

4. Once again select the whole graph and go to Object > Graph > Column. There, highlight your new design.

5. This time, for options, choose a column type of Repeating, and decide how many units each instance of the object should represent. With the REV market share chart, each value tick mark represents 50,000 units sold, but (and this is a big but), remember that the actual dataset didn't include the trailing ,000. The dataset used a scale in hundreds. Therefore, set the Each Design Represents measurement field to **50** not 50,000.

6. In the For Fractions drop-down, decide whether you'd like to chop the can design off or squish it (vertically only) when a unit less than 50 must be drawn. In other words, if your chart must use this design to represent 25 (thousand) units, chopping the design will create a full can with a half can above it. The half can will be cut through the middle. Choosing to scale the design in the same situation will create an intact but half-sized can atop the full-sized can. The column design may always be changed, so you can afford to experiment. Click OK when ready, and you should be looking at columns of stacked drink cans (see Figure 12.23).

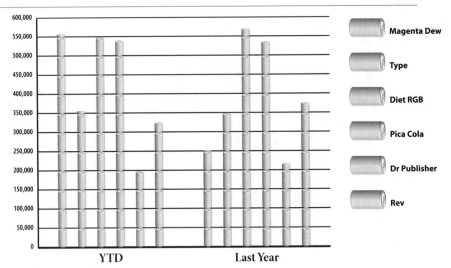

FIGURE 12.23
Because this graph is presenting data on the number of drink cans sold, using a drink can to represent every 50,000 units sold can make the numbers much easier to interpret and digest.

Killer Techniques for Expert Presentations

In this section you'll learn six killer techniques for building expert presentations in Illustrator CS2:

- Pie piece highlighting
- Tearing out pie pieces
- Tearing out pie pieces (the alternate live method)
- Glowing columns and rows
- Emphasis through transparency
- Labeling 3D graph slices

This section isn't called Expert because I feel you should come back to this when you feel like an Illustrator expert—I don't draw distinctions between novice, intermediate, and expert skills when I'm teaching, remember? Rather, the reason for the title is that the following techniques will help you (or your client) look like an expert *presenter*. These are what we call in the design instruction biz "killer techniques." (Rarely does anyone die.)

Pie Piece Highlighting

Want to call attention to one slice of a pie graph? Add a new fill! This is a killer technique for slideshow presentations where each slice of a pie will be discussed individually.

1. Style your pie graph as you want—colored, 3D extruded, whatever—then copy its layer. Make as many duplicates of the layer as there are pieces in your pie. Hide all but the first one.

 NOTE

If your graph data may change, don't copy the layer. Instead, just move around the pie performing the technique described in the following steps and exporting one slice at a time.

2. Grab the Group Selection tool again and click *twice* on a pie piece to select it and its legend as well. If the legend is no longer attached, just click once.

3. In the Appearance palette, click on the Path entry below Graph. From the Appearance palette flyout menu choose

Add New Fill. A new fill attribute, identical to the existing one, will appear.

4. Select the lower fill appearance attribute and give it a contrasting fill color via the Swatches and/or Color palette. You should see no visible change in your graph.

5. With the new fill still highlighted in the Appearance palette, go to Effect > Path > Offset Path. In the Offset Path dialog, turn on Preview and try different Offset measurements until you get the result you like. Notice how, if you used 3D effects, the offset fill also adopts the 3D effects and lighting? Figure 12.24 shows the way I set up mine.

6. 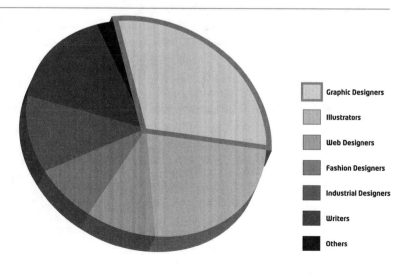 With the pie piece still selected, open the Graphic Styles palette and create a new graphic style with the New Graphic Style button at the bottom. Rename the new graphic style swatch to **Piece Highlight**.

7. Hide the current layer and turn on the next one. Select the pie piece and its legend. Make note of the fill color in the Color palette—or, better yet, take the opportunity to make a color swatch.

8. Click on the Piece Highlight graphic style. The offset fill will apply, creating an outlined piece identical to your first.

9. Select the upper, plain fill in the Appearance palette and reset its color using the values you noted from the Color palette or the fill swatch you made.

10. Keep moving around the pie, one layer—one piece—at a time, repeating the preceding three steps, until you have all slices highlighted individually. If your legend was disconnected from the graph earlier, follow the entire procedure to make separate layers of highlighted legend swatches corresponding with your highlighted pie pieces.

11. To export your highlighted pie pieces for a digital presentation, turn on one highlighted pie piece layer (or one set of highlighted pie piece and matching legend layers) and go to File > Save for Microsoft Office. Then turn off the first layer (or set), activate the next, and Save for Microsoft Office again. Repeat until you have separate PNG files for all pieces to be called out and discussed during the presentation. Use the same basic technique to export separate files for print layouts.

FIGURE 12.24 **Highlighting a single piece is easy with a second, offset fill.**

Graphic Designers

Illustrators

Web Designers

Fashion Designers

Industrial Designers

Writers

Others

Tearing Out Pie Pieces

Instead of outlining via an offset fill, another way to emphasize a slice of a pie graph is to physically tear it out.

 CAUTION

This technique will break the graph's association to a dataset, rendering it just a normal object. Employ this technique only after the dataset has been finalized.

For a flat pie graph:

1. Select the flat pie graph and choose Object > Expand Appearance. Then, ungroup.

2. Make a copy of the pie graph layer. Make as many duplicates of the layer as there are pieces in your pie. Hide all but the first one.

3. Deselect the graph and select just one slice. It can be moved, rotated, skewed, and styled all by itself like any other object.

For a 3D pie graph:

1. Double-click the 3D Extrude & Bevel attribute on the Appearance palette. In the 3D Extrude & Bevel Options dialog, click More Options. Then, at the bottom, check Draw Hidden Faces. Click OK.

2. Select the 3D pie graph and choose Object > Expand Appearance. Then, ungroup and deselect the graph.

3. Make a copy of the pie graph layer. Make as many duplicates of the layer as there are pieces in your pie. Hide all but the first one.

4. Because we've just expanded the 3D— including faces that are currently not visible—each slice is now made up of at least five independent paths. Find the slice closest to you, preferably one whose top, extruded back, and angled sides are visible (see Figure 12.25), and, with the Selection tool, select and Shift-select the visible faces.

FIGURE 12.25 **With two surfaces of this pie piece moved, the remaining three are easier to access.**

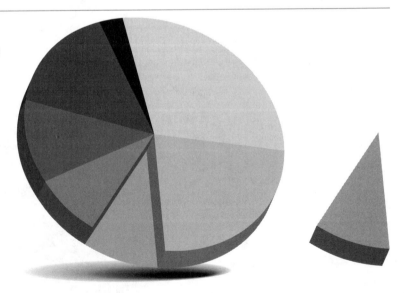

CHAPTER 12: Creating Graphs for a Report

5. In the Transform palette, click once in the X measurement box and move your cursor to the end of whatever is there. Type **+3 in**. and press the Enter or Return key . The selected faces should jump away from your graph, revealing what's below. If the pieces didn't jump completely clear of the pie and all other objects, undo the move and do it again with a measurement that would leave the faces alone in the whiteness of space.

 TIP

If your document units are already set to inches, you can omit the "in." shorthand from your X coordinate modifier and simply enter +3.

6. Look at the opening you just created in your pie graph. What do you see? Right: You see the bottom of the pie piece. When you checked the Draw Hidden Faces option in the 3D Extrude & Bevel Options, you told Illustrator to draw *all* sides of your pie pieces, thus creating truly three-dimensional objects with volume. There are sides there as well. If you used a beveled edge of some type, you'll have even more surfaces. Select the bottom face, then Shift-click on the two sides of the pie piece and any additional surfaces to select them as well.

TIP

Selecting surface paths here can be extremely difficult. Choose View > Smart Guides to allow Smart Guides to help you identify and select various surfaces.

7. In the Transform palette, repeat the move operation by entering **+3 in**. (or whatever you used the first time) in the X coordinate again. The bottom and sides (and so forth) should jump over to rejoin the other faces of this first piece.

8. Select all of these surface paths and group via Object > Group.

9. Now position the hollow pie piece where you'd like it (see Figure 12.26).

FIGURE 12.26 **Serving out a piece of the pie.**

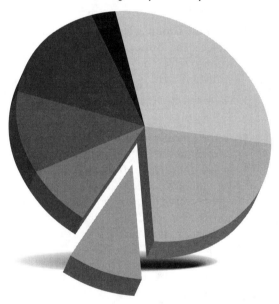

10. Working one slice at a time—on one layer at a time—repeat the procedure you just learned until you've torn out, grouped, and positioned all of the pie pieces you will discuss during your presentation.

Tearing Out Pie Pieces (The Alternate Live Method)

This is an alternative method of tearing out pie pieces. It has one drawback when compared to the previous method—not quite as much control; but it also has two distinct advantages: It's faster and easier, and you won't break the link between the graph and its dataset.

1. Copy your graph's layer as many times as there are pie pieces. Hide all but the first one.

2. With the Group Selection tool, click on a piece. For this technique, you don't want to select the corresponding legend swatch as well.

3. Go to Effect > Distort & Transform > Transform.

4. In the Transform dialog, turn on Preview in the bottom-right corner. Now adjust the Horizontal and/or Vertical Move sliders until your pie piece is offset the way you like. Of course, you could also adjust its scaling or rotation, if that strikes your fancy. Click OK when you're done.

Transform is a live effect, so if you decide to edit it later, simply reselect the pie piece and, in the Appearance palette, double-click the Transform attribute.

5. Working one slice at a time—on one layer at a time—repeat the application of the Transform effect until you've torn out all of the pie pieces you will discuss during your presentation. Figure 12.27 shows my live-effect torn-out pie piece.

Glowing Columns and Rows

If you use graph designs like sliding or repeating objects with columns or rows, you can't just add a new fill to highlight one column for a presentation slide. However, you can add strokes—or better yet, call out the column with a glow.

1. Copy your graph's layer as many times as there are columns or rows. Hide all but the first one.

2. In your column, stacked column, row, stacked row, or any other type of graph, click with the Group Selection tool until you have the entire column selected.

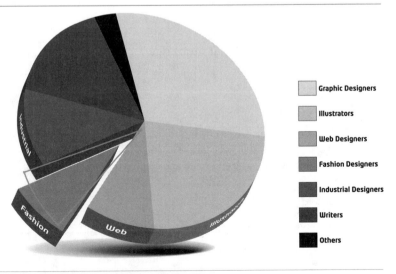

FIGURE 12.27 This torn-out pie-piece is a live effect, so the graph is still linked to its dataset and may be changed easily at any time.

3. From the Effects menu, choose Stylize > Outer Glow. Change the mode to Normal, and click on the swatch to access the color picker. Choose a contrasting, attention-getting warm color like orange or red.

4. Set the opacity to 100%, and adjust the blur to your tastes. Click OK. You now have a nice highlight to call out the column in this slide (see Figure 12.28).

5. Create a graphic style, then, one layer at a time, move through your columns sequentially, highlighting them with the new graphic style.

6. When they're all done, isolate each layer and export it using File > Save for Microsoft Office.

Emphasis Through Transparency

Another killer technique of expert graph presentation is to add emphasis through transparency. This technique can be used to de-emphasize all pieces but the current focus,

or it can be used to render one piece semi-transparent or completely transparent to dramatize the effect of removing one set of numbers has on the whole model.

1. Follow the steps in either the "Tearing Out Pie Pieces" or "Tearing Out Pie Pieces (Alternate Live Method)" technique as far as needed (in other words, if you don't need to emphasize every piece, don't tear out every piece).

2. When you have all necessary pieces segmented, select the piece or pieces to de-emphasize or hide.

3. On the Transparency palette, change their opacity to the desired amount via the Opacity measurement box or slider (click the down arrow beside the measurement box to access the slider). In Figure 12.29 I used this technique of tearing out the Writers slice and rendering it almost invisible as a means of communicating the effect that a proposed new advertising campaign targeting only visual creatives would have on REV's overall customer base.

FIGURE 12.28 **Outer glow focuses audience attention on one column, facilitating presentation relevant to the column.**

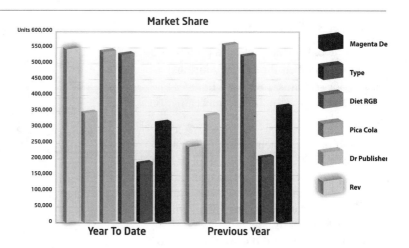

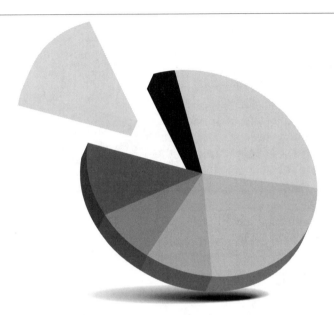

FIGURE 12.29 **If the new REV advertising campaign launches as proposed, it would ignore the Writers segment of REV's customer base, potentially taking this slice out of the pie.**

4. If you're working one piece at a time, one layer at a time, you might find it easier to set the opacity once and create a reusable graphic style to quickly reapply the changes to subsequent pieces.

Labeling 3D Graph Slices

For a little extra clarity of data presentation, try applying labels directly to your pie pieces—or columns, rows, or whatever in other chart types—in addition to your legend.

1. Off on the pasteboard or on a new layer, click with the Type tool to create a point type object. Now type in your first legend label. With the pie graph we built for REV the first item would be **Graphic Designers**. Style the type as you like, but make it a color that contrasts with the color of the pie pieces.

2. Hold the Cmd/Ctrl key and click away from the point type object to deselect it. Now click again with the Type tool and make your second label. Repeat this until you have separate point type objects for each of your pie pieces.

3. One at a time, drag your type labels into the Symbols palette to create new symbols from each of them. I heartily recommend you rename the new symbols to something meaningful like **Label — Graphic Designers**, **Label — Illustrators**, and so on. After creating symbols, delete the original path type objects.

4. Select the 3D graph with the Selection tool, and, on the Appearance palette, double-click the 3D Extrude & Bevel attribute to reopen the 3D Extrude & Bevel Options.

5. Turn Preview back on (annoying, isn't it, that Preview turns off every time you come back?), then click on the Map Art button. In the Map Art dialog, the Symbol drop-down contains the label

symbols we just made. Top right is the surface to which they will be applied. The arrows allow you to navigate between all the faces created by 3D Extrude & Bevel. Dominating the dialog is a preview of the object's surface. A light surface in the current view indicates a face that is visible with the current rotation of the graph; a dark rectangle denotes a surface that is not currently visible.

6. If you peer around the Map Art dialog, you will see on the 3D graph a red outline revealing which surface is currently shown in the Map Art dialog. Using the arrows, move through the surfaces of your graph until you reach a visible side (see Figure 12.30).

7. From the Symbol drop-down, choose the correct label for that slice. It will instantly appear in the main part of the Map Art dialog, and, if you remembered to check Preview in the 3D Extrude & Bevel Options prior to entering Map Art, your graph should update as well to show the placement of the label.

8. Is the label where and how you want it? Note that the symbol instance in the Map Art dialog has a bounding box. Use the bounding box to move, resize, and/or rotate the label until it fits your graph where and how you'd like. To rotate, hover your cursor just beyond a corner control point. When the cursor becomes a curved, double-headed arrow, click and drag to rotate (Shift-drag to constrain to increments of 45°).

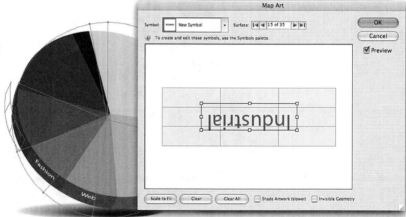

FIGURE 12.30 Note the outline (left side) showing which face of the graph corresponds to the surface in the Map Art dialog, and the bounding box (right) that reveals the actual shape of the path.

9. Again using the arrows, move through the 3D graph's surfaces, applying the labels where needed. If you may at some point rotate your graph, go ahead and apply the labels to surfaces hidden now that may become exposed during a rotation. Doing it now will save on accidental omissions later. Just before you click OK, turn on Shade Artwork—or don't, as you prefer. Labels add an extra touch to my pie chart, as you can see in Figure 12.31.

Final Thoughts

The entire point of graphs is to communicate numerical data more intuitively. When you create graphs you are tasked with communicating effectively and *clearly*. A little bit of creativity goes a *long* way with graphs, and a little more creativity easily crosses into the realm of too much, defeating the function of graphically representing data. Don't get carried away.

Although your graph may be used in a presentation wherein the presenter will discuss the data and have the opportunity to clarify audience questions, it will also likely wind up in a printed report the audience will take away from the meeting. If they step out

FIGURE 12.31 The final REV customer base breakdown chart.

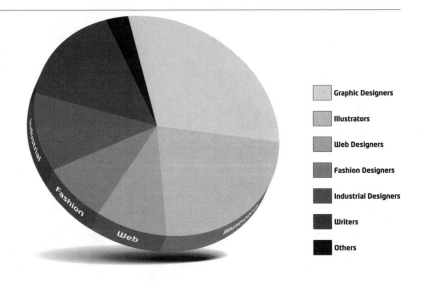

Graphic Designers

Illustrators

Web Designers

Fashion Designers

Industrial Designers

Writers

Others

(physically or mentally) during the presentation, they need to be able to understand this graph on its own, with no one around to explain it. Look for areas and elements that don't instantly make sense, and fix them. As you can see in Figure 12.32, I added a title and several other finishing touches to help make the graph clearer.

Want to change the graph type without starting all over? Let's say you build a column graph, but later decide the data is easier to understand as an area graph. Changing graph types is as easy as pie graph (you knew that had to be coming sooner or later). Just select your graph, then choose Object > Graph > Type. In the middle is a row of buttons corresponding to the various graph tools and types. Just click one, set whatever options you may want, and click OK. Instant graph change!

Do you need two or more related pie graphs? Well, friend, let me enlighten you to another cool technique. Instead of making separate

graphs, just enter the data for subsequent pie graphs on new rows in the Graph Data window. Each new row will create an additional pie graph sharing styling and a legend with the first.

 NOTE

Some types of graphs have certain limitations. A column graph, for example, may contain both positive and negative values in its dataset; however, pie graphs may contain only positive *or* negative values. Thus Illustrator will not allow conversion into a pie graph if both types of values are present in the dataset.

Looking for more graph designs, including several sliding and repeating column designs? Look no further than your own computer. Just open one of the design files from the Cool Extras > Sample Files > Graph Designs, and each of the graph designs will instantly become available in your main documents' Graph > Column dialog.

FIGURE 12.32 The final REV market share graph, ready for export and delivery to the client.

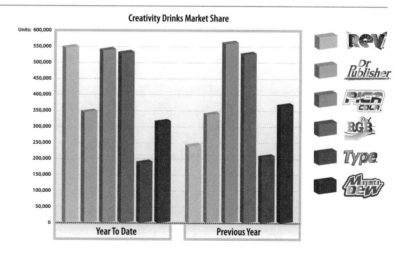

PART III: Appendixes

86.— American slang meaning to omit, do away with, stop attending, or pretend never existed (as the author fervently attempts to do with Paris Hilton). 86 is a term widely used in the food service industry to concisely communicate that the kitchen is out of a particular food item, thus servers should 86 the item from the menu. Most restaurant kitchens have an 86 board on which out-of-stock items and dishes are written for the benefit of servers. The term allegedly first achieved popularity in American greasy-spoon diners in the 1920s because it rhymed with "nix," a colloquialism of the day meaning the same thing, and because, as a code, 86 could be spoken (or shouted) within earshot of customers without their under-standing. This particular theory of the term's origin is the most plausible because 86 not only means discontinue serving this food item, but also discontinue serving this dead-beat customer. It is because of this latter vari-ation that the term 86 gained popularity in bars and drinking establishments where it was often necessary to stop serving an inebri-ated patron or to have him bounced from the premises.

8-bit—A *color depth* that has sufficient spaces to hold 256 different hues and shades.

24-bit—A *color depth* that has sufficient spaces to hold the full human range of discernible colors—approximately 16.8 million different hues and shades. *RGB* is a 24-bit *color space*.

Acrobat—Adobe Systems, Inc.'s flagship application for creating, editing, and viewing Portable Document Format (PDF) files.

Ambient Light Controls—In the 3D Effects dialogs (Extrude & Bevel, Revolve, and Rotate), ambient light is illumination that does not shine directly on an object. The controls change the indirect light illuminating all surfaces of all objects uniformly.

artboard—The visible page in the Illustrator document window.

artifacts—Slight imperfections that mar a design. Screen artifacts, such as those that result from using the 3D Effects on some paths, are temporary or ethereal bits of color or jagged edges that appear only onscreen; they neither print nor export for web. Artifacts in scans, digital photographs, or printouts, however, do exist in the document. In such cases they are created by some failing or glitch in either the software, hardware, or combination of the two. Depending on the devices in question, artifacts may be minimized by changing color or resolution settings. Consult the manufacturer's technical support department for specifics.

ascender—The portion of a character or *glyph* that extends above the x-height or main body height of lowercase glyphs in a typeface. For example, the vertical bar rising above the body of the lowercase *h* is the ascender.

asymmetrical—Not balanced. An asymmetrical design is one in which the two sides are not mirrored if folded at its center point.

auto slices—*Slices* defined by the shape of an object or group of objects and that change size and/or shape automatically to reflect changes in their contained object or group.

baseline—The invisible line on which the base of type aligns. Typically, the baseline is aligned to the bottom of lowercase characters such as *x*, with *descenders* extending down below the baseline. The baseline may be shifted up or down via controls on the Character palette, and within the Area Type Options and Type on a Path Options dialogs.

bleed—When an image prints all the way to the edge of the trimmed page, the ink is said to bleed. Also refers to the area past the *trim size* into which image and objects extend to account for paper shifting during printing and cutting.

blend—In Illustrator a blend is the result and action of morphing one object into another, and the steps between. QuarkXPress uses the term blend to mean *gradient*.

blend steps—The number of steps or intermediate versions of a transformation between one object, color, or light intensity and another in a *blend*.

bold—The variation of a *typeface* in which some or all of the strokes of the *glyphs* have been thickened.

bounding box—An imaginary border surrounding all portions of a selected object or objects. In Illustrator, the bounding box appears when an object (or objects) is selected, and includes control corners for resizing, rotating, and distorting the object.

brand—The holistic image and persona of a product, company, or individual as experienced by others. Although logos and visual identity material are the most tangible elements of a brand, every way in which an individual may experience or interact with a product, company, individual, or any representative thereof, is part of the brand. Also a form of self-mutilation wherein decorative symbols or other artwork is branded into the skin with a hot metal implement by individuals too masochistic for tattoos.

callout—An explanatory label on an illustration; can be graphical, textual, or both. For example, an automobile illustration may have a callout that magnifies the headlights and provides additional relevant visual and verbal detail.

character styles—A reusable, recorded set of character-level formatting attributes such as the *font* family, font size, and *OpenType* options. Character styles work in conjunction with paragraph styles, and are created in, applied by, and managed through the Character Styles palette. Both character and paragraph styles are often referred to as style sheets, owing to their origins as paper-based definitions of type formatting.

CMYK—Cyan, Magenta, Yellow, and Black, which are the four inks of *process* printing. CMY is a subtractive color model, meaning that the more pigment is added, the closer to black the composite color becomes (as opposed to the additive model of *RGB*). Theoretically, 100% of C, M, and Y should produce pure black. It doesn't. Because color and density vary between different applications of Cyan, Magenta, and Yellow inks, the result is usually a yucky brown. Black ink is added to these subtractive colors to compensate, creating a four-color process.

color—Color of type refers to the density of type-solid areas (ink) to negative areas (*substrate*). Also called grayness.

color bars—Standardized strips of ink-filled blocks that allow accurate evaluation of the quality of printed material, with particular focus on *registration*, dot gain, and ink density. Color bars are printed outside the trim size of a document, in the "wasted space." Each document includes one color bar per ink color used in the document (for example, a standard *process color* print job has four strips, one each for cyan, magenta, yellow, and black); each strip is a graduated scale of tints of the color, beginning at 100% (full, solid ink coverage) and fading down toward 5% or 0% tint of a given ink.

color depth—In an image, color depth is the potential number of hues and shades of color—for example: *8-bit* color depth only allows for 256 colors, whereas *24-bit* color depth includes spaces for 16.8 million color values.

color management—The process by which variances in color interpretation and rendering ability among different devices are learned and compensated for to produce consistent color on all devices. See *ICC*.

color separation—See *separation*.

color space—See *color depth*.

Comic Sans—A friendly, free *font* with a style similar to handwriting, provided by Monotype+Agfa type foundry and Microsoft Corp. Distributed by Microsoft since the late 1990s along with several other high-quality free *typefaces*, Comic Sans offered web designers an alternative to the three typefaces common on all computers of the time— Helvetica/Arial, Courier, and Times/Times New Roman. Sadly, although Comic Sans is a well-designed typeface, rampant overuse has rendered it the poster child for sophomoric design.

copy—Text. When used formally, copy refers to text specifically used in marketing or advertising materials. One who writes such commercial text is called a copywriter.

copy proof—The text (*copy*) of a project sent to a client for review, revision, or approval.

crop marks—Lines that define the *trim size* of a document. After printing and during finishing, a cutting machine operator will align the machine's guillotine blade to the intersection of right-angled crop marks.

cross section—A portion of a drawing, diagram, or model that has been removed or rendered invisible along a plane to omit the section or reveal the interior of the object.

CSS—Cascading Style Sheets. On the Web, style sheets are reusable definitions of the visual appearance of content, specifying *fonts*, colors, positioning, and layout attributes of text and code. The "cascading" property of CSS refers to the manner in which style sheets inherit properties from one another in a parent-child relationship. Changing common attributes in the parent style sheet, for example, "cascades" the same change down through the children unless individual attributes have been specifically overridden in the child styles. Although this concept has been used in print design for decades, CSS only recently came to the web. Some web designers who have never known the world of print think the idea of style sheets is revolutionary and hope it will someday be available to lowly print designers.

dataset—A table of numbers from which a *graph* or chart is generated.

descender—The portion of a character or *glyph* that extends below the *baseline* or main body height of glyphs in a typeface. For example, the tail of the lowercase *q* is the descender.

Desktop Publishing Revolution—In 1985 Adobe Systems, Inc., then solely a printer language systems company, teamed up with Apple Computer Corp. to release the Apple LaserWriter desktop printer running Adobe's graphically rich *PostScript* printer language. The LaserWriter included and produced high-quality, Adobe-created digital *fonts* licensed from venerable print and type manufacturer Linotype. The combination took the power of typography out of the domain of proprietary typesetting stations and put it into the hands of the people. It sparked a revolution that put the cost of producing quality printed work under $8,000 when comparable systems of the day were in excess of $75,000. Thus, Adobe put the power to publish onto the desktop where it was previously a lofty power held only by the typesetting shop.

die-cutting—The process of creating non-rectangular *trim sizes* or special holes by cutting with steel dies.

digital printing—A *plate*-less (and thus *film*-less) means of printing in which the *RIP* is part of the printing press, enabling customization of every piece—a feature not possible with plate-dependent systems like *offset lithography*.

domain name—The identifying human-readable address of a server or website. Top-level domains (TLDs) are the parts that come after the owner-chosen portion, such as .com, .net, and .ca, and are unique to individual countries and roles. For example, .gov is a TLD available for registration and use only by United States' government agencies, whereas .com is a generic TLD that may be registered and used by any organization or individual throughout the world. Domain names are managed and registered by government agencies or appointees within various countries.

DPI—Dots Per Inch, a resolution measurement defining the number of *halftone* dots that will be printed within an inch.

embossing—In print production, the process of creating relief by impressing a page under high pressure into a mold to create raised or recessed areas.

EPS—Encapsulated PostScript. Containing either (or both) embedded *vector* and *raster* image data, as well as potentially the fonts used in their designs, EPS is the precursor file format to *PDF*. EPS files contain all the *PostScript* code necessary to render a document on a PostScript-compatible output device, as well as an optional low-resolution raster preview image of the high-resolution PostScript content.

exploded—Having displayed a violent emotional reaction, the severity of which is usually determined by the number of times a client has said: "I don't how to describe the design I want, but I'll know it when I see it." Also, the expanded and flattened view of layouts designed to fold, as in packaging design.

film—A photosensitive sheet of plastic printed by an *imagesetter* and then exposed to form full-sized, high-resolution positive or negative color *separations* of a design. Where ink will print (positive space), the film is imaged black; where ink will not print (negative space), the film is clear. Print-making *plates* are aligned with sheets of film and exposed to special lights to burn the printable image into the plate. Film is often referred to colloquially as plates (see *plates*).

Flash—(as a file format): A vector illustration format that is capable of animation, multimedia, and scripting. Used primarily on the web and, increasingly, in mobile devices (cellular phones, PDAs, and so on), as well as in other electronic media. As an application, originally created as Splash in 1995 by FutureSplash Corp., it was purchased by

Macromedia soon after its creation and redubbed Flash.

flattening—The process of removing transparency by creating solid areas of opaque color and texture resembling the original transparent results. Also, in print production, the process of breaking curves into many tiny straight line segments.

foil stamping—Stamping thin metallic foil onto a printed piece either flat, embossed (bulging outward), or impressed (indenting the page).

fold—In print publications, the place where a piece (for example, a newspaper) will be folded in half. In web design, the bottom of the browser window. In both, everything above the fold is available as the initial view a reader has on the layout, whereas everything below the fold is only visible with reader interaction (flipping or opening the paper or scrolling down in a browser).

font—In modern terminology, the electronic file containing the *glyphs* of a *typeface*. Originally a font was the set of lead type sold with a typeface.

FPO—For Position Only, the process and product of replacing an image or block of text with a temporary surrogate.

gamut—The *color depth* producible by a particular device.

gang printing—Printing multiple pages or jobs concurrently on the same sheet of paper to save time, cost, or materials.

ganged—See *gang printing*.

GIF—Graphical Interchange Format. (Pronounced with a hard G, as in gift or goat; not with a soft G like Jif brand peanut butter). GIF files, which were originally developed in 1987 (pre-World Wide Web) by the online network service CompuServe, are, along with *JPEG*, Web standards, which is their only practical use. GIF files are smaller in file size than JPEGs, owing to their limitation of containing as few as two colors and no more than 256 colors (black, white, and a variable palette up to 254). Used online for non-photographic images to preserve large areas of solid color, fine detail (for example, type), or to simulate transparency through their ability to replace all pixels of one, user-definable color with emptiness. The GIF format supports animation by storing individual frames as separate images inside the same file. GIFs are 72 *dpi* only and not usable for printing.

glyphs—The characters, symbols, and pictograms that make up a printed language or font.

gradient—Two or more colors blended smoothly into one another. Desktop layout application QuarkXPress uses the term blend to mean gradient.

gradient mesh—See *mesh.*

graph—A visual representation of a set of numbers or *dataset* as precisely sized objects on a grid. Pie, column, bar, radar, line, area, and scatter are all types of graphs used to present different types of data.

greeking—Any instance of text or imagery replaced by nonsensical data or cross-hatching. Used most often to describe the replacement of text with nonsensical Latin called "Lorem Ipsum."

grid—Structural organization of a page.

guts—Content of a publication, book, or website as opposed to supporting devices such as covers, tables of contents, indexes,

and, in the case of websites, the header, footer, and other non-content areas.

gutter—The space between columns. Often used to also describe the gap between pages on the *spine*. Also, where you've fallen if you find yourself using the *Comic Sans typeface* in anything but a cartoon or kid's birthday party invitation.

halftone—An area composed of dots, or the dots themselves, making up printable images on *film* and *plates.*

hard-proofing—Simulating final output conditions of print work by printing to the final output or a surrogate device such as a desktop printer or dedicated proof-printing system.

highlight intensity—The amount of light reflected by an object; its shininess.

Highlight Intensity Controls—In the 3D Effects dialogs (Extrude & Bevel, Revolve, and Rotate), the amount of light reflected by the object (for example, its shininess).

highlight size—The size of the highlight shining on the object, from a pinpoint at 1% to a floodlight at 100%.

Highlight Size Controls—In the 3D Effects dialogs (Extrude & Bevel, Revolve, and Rotate), the size of the highlight shining on the object.

HTML—HyperText Markup Language, a programming language to define and structure pages and content on the Web.

ICC—International Color Consortium. An independent standards organization whose charter is to develop and promote the use of *color management* systems and practices. Also, the more common file extension for *ICC profiles.*

ICC profile—A file describing the color capabilities and rendering characteristics of a given device in the common *ICC color management* system. ICC profiles are simple ASCII text files with the *.ICC* or *.ICM* file extensions.

ICM—See *ICC profile*.

illo—Industry jargon for illustration.

imagesetter—An ultra high-resolution *PostScript* printer that prints in *halftones* on *film* instead of paper.

in port—In text boxes and text areas in Illustrator, the indicator of where the type it contains originates. If the text box/area is the first in the *thread*, the in port will be empty but it will display an arrow for subsequent boxes into which the same story flows.

inset—The process or result of pushing inward away from the edges, as in text boxes where the text may be inset from its box.

intranet—A private website or collection of websites, often used within a company by that company's employees.

italic—So named for Italy, where it was first popularized, this *type style* is a slanted, often more delicate, script-like variation of a particular *typeface*. Oblique, by contrast, is a simple slanting of the type.

JPEG (also JPG, JFIF, and JPE)—Joint Photographic Experts Group. (Pronounced JAY-peg). Originally created by this group to answer the need for a compressible, long-term archival format for digital photographs, the JPEG format has since become the standard for photographic images on the web and in digital cameras (although it is being phased out in digital cameras in favor of the more robust RAW data format). JPEG images may be compressed for a smaller file size, but

it is a lossy compression; compression is accomplished through destroying image data. Each time a JPEG file is edited and resaved, more data is destroyed, which is why professionals either disable compression or refrain from converting images to JPEG until all potential editing has been finished. JPEG images are *24-bit RGB* only, so they are rarely used in a for-press process, which requires *CMYK*. TIFF files are preferred in press.

Justify—Align (usually text) to a particular edge. Left-justified is text aligned to the left edge, leaving the right edge *ragged*. Full justification (also known as left and right justified or forced justified) spreads text evenly between both the left and right edges, leaving no rag edge.

kicker—In copy writing or typesetting, a paragraph that supports and explains a headline.

knockout—Boxing term referring to rendering (or being rendered) unconscious. In printing, the visible or topmost ink color creates a non-printing area in other colors beneath, as opposed to an *overprint*.

leading—(pronounced leh-ding) The vertical space between lines of text.

ligature—Two or more characters joined together as a single glyph, often to avoid awkwardness created by the proximity of the individual shapes of each.

light intensity—The brightness of the selected light source—0% is off; 100% is the brightest possible setting.

Light Intensity Controls—In the 3D Effects dialogs (Extrude & Bevel, Revolve, and Rotate), the intensity of the light shining on the object.

line screen—See *LPI*.

lines of force—The implied or explicit planes of an illustration or design that direct the viewer's attention.

live area—The area of a document in which elements may be safely placed without fear of being cropped off during trim.

LPI—Lines Per Inch. The number of dots or lines per inch in a *halftone* screen. Print production deals more often in terms of LPI than *DPI*.

mesh—A grid wherein segments called *mesh patches* are defined and connected by *mesh points*. Meshes are used for distortion and coloring.

mesh line—The lines connecting *mesh points* in a *mesh* grid.

mesh patch—A single cell in the grid of a *mesh*, defined by four *mesh points*.

mesh point—Anchor point-like devices that define the boundaries of *mesh patches* in a *mesh* grid and which are joined to one another by *mesh lines*.

misregistration—Misalignment of colors in printed matter; ink colors do not line up to one another.

nameplate—The stylized name of a publication (print or web) appearing on the front page. Also called the flag. Often erroneously referred to as the masthead, which is the area in which publication staff and contact information are listed.

nav—Short for navigation or navigation system, such as on a website.

offset lithography—The leading process of paper printing in which rollers or drums convey ink (and often water) from wells to a *plate* roller, which contains the paper, vinyl, or metal plate onto which the printing image has

been burned or etched. The plate roller transfers ink in the shape of the image to the rubber-coated blanket drum, which in turn transfers ink to the *substrate*.

offset press—See *offset lithography*.

out port—In text areas and other text objects in Illustrator, the indicator of where the type it contains ends. If the text object is the last in the *thread*, the out port will be empty, but it will display an arrow if the same story flows into subsequent text objects.

overprint—One or more ink colors printed on top of other inks, lending to a slight mixing of colors. Black, the most opaque of the four CYMK process inks, is typically printed last and overprinted atop the other three to reduce the effect of slight *misregistration*.

Pantone—Short for Pantone Matching System (PMS), which is a color system for ensuring color consistency from choice at the design phase through prepress and printing. Pantone inks are premixed colors often used as *spot colors* in place of *process colors* and referenced by number within the Pantone library. PMS colors are typically communicated verbally or written as "PMS 941" or "Pantone 941." Pantone is also the name of the company that invented the color Pantone Matching System, and which defines the standards in color through printing, fashion, and other industries.

paragraph styles—Reusable, recorded sets of paragraph-level formatting attributes such as the text alignment, spacing, and hyphenation, and may also contain character-level formatting such as *font* family, font size, and *OpenType* options. Paragraph styles work in conjunction with character styles, and are created in, applied by, and managed through the Paragraph Styles palette. Both character and paragraph styles are often referred to as style sheets, owing to their origins as paper-based definitions of type formatting.

PDF—Portable Document Format. A *PostScript*-based electronic file similar in origin to *EPS*, PDF files are the standard electronic document format for the printing, prepress, graphic communication, and many other industries worldwide. They are self-contained document transportation systems, often including all image assets and *fonts* used by the document. PDF files may be read by, printed from, and modified to varying degrees within most modern creative applications, but are most usable in their home applications, Adobe's *Acrobat* or *Adobe Reader*, and similar dedicated software applications. Since version 10, Illustrator's *.ai* file format has been effectively the same code as a PDF file, allowing Illustrator-native documents to be opened and edited within PDF applications.

perfect bound—A square binding where pages or signatures (pages printed two-up pages per side, per sheet of paper) are glued on the *spine* without staples.

pica—The standard unit of measurement in the press, prepress, and graphic design industries. There are 6 picas in 1 inch, and 12 *points* per pica. Written as Xp, where X is a value.

pixel—The basic unit of measure of a digital display device (for example, computer screen, television, or digital camera CCD, [the light-sensitive component of a camera that converts visual light to digital data]). Display devices break up images into fixed-size grids of rectangular blocks, thus limiting the *resolution* of the viewable image. *Raster* image resolution is measured in pixels per inch or *PPI*.

plane—Flat surface determined by two or more points in space.

plate—Literally, the paper, polyester, or metal (aluminum or copper) sheets onto which an image is burned or etched and from which ink impressions are made on a printing press. Also commonly used in the printing, *prepress*, and graphic design industries as slang to include all forms of color *separations* including digital *film* (from which plates are burned) and even digital color separation proofs.

platesetter—An ultra high-resolution *PostScript* printer that etches directly onto printing press *plates*, bypassing the need for *film*.

PNG—Portable Network Graphics. (Pronounced: ping.) Developed as a patent-free replacement for *GIF* files when, in December 1994, CompuServe, the creator of GIF, and UniSys, which made the compression algorithm in GIF, filed suit against software makers whose products created or imported GIF files and threatened litigation against any website using GIF files made by an unlicensed application. The adoption of PNG online has been slow due to the expiration of the GIF patent, which rendered the threat of litigation moot, and web browser makers' slow support. The PNG format combines the best of GIF and JPEG with animation, high-quality, and lossless compression (image data is not destroyed to make the file smaller). PNGs can be saved into either an *8-bit* 256-color mode like GIF, or a *24-bit* mode like JPEG. Unlike GIF, PNG file supports true transparency through Alpha channel blending, and thus may have not only fully transparent areas but also areas of partial transparency that blend with objects behind the image.

point—The smallest standard unit of measure in the press, prepress, and graphic design industries. There are 12 points in 1 *pica* and 72 points in 1 inch. Written as either X pt or *YpX*, where X is a point value, Y is a pica value, and p stands for pica.

PostScript—The printer description language that enables computers to communicate with printers (including *RIPs, imagesetters, platesetters,* and *digital printing* presses) and render output that matches the screen.

PPD—PostScript Printer Description file, which defines the capabilities and rendering abilities of a printer or other output device (for example, sizes of paper the printer can use, whether it is a color or grayscale printer, and so on).

PPI—Pixels Per Inch. (See *pixel.*)

preflight—Before going to press (flight). Checking a digital file for issues that may affect whether and how well the file will output.

prepress—A set of tasks (and an industry that performs them) that occur, literally, pre–printing press (and post-design). Strictly defined, prepress includes performing the processes of *preflight*, color *separations*, and *film* making, though most modern prepress shops also provide graphic design, printing, and/or photography services.

process—See *process color, CMYK.*

process color—A color that is some formula of one or more of the *CMYK* process inks. Also used interchangeably to describe the system of printing with CMYK inks.

proof—A simulation or sample of some level and depth of the finished product or final output. (See *soft-proofing, hard-proofing, copy proof.*)

prosumer—An amateur, hobbyist, or semiprofessional consumer who uses professional-grade tools. For example, someone adept at Illustrator but uses it only for the occasional personal project is a prosumer, as opposed to a professional who employs Illustrator for a significant portion of her job.

PSD—Photoshop document format. A hybrid file format that may contain both *raster* and *vector* data. PSDs may be read (and often created) by all Adobe Creative Suite applications, as well as other major creative applications like QuarkXPress 6.5 and later and Corel Painter.

pull quote—A passage or quotation extracted from text, emphasized through a size, color, or boxing device, and set outside the main flow of text to generate sufficient interest that the reader will read the main flow of text.

rag—The uneven edge of text opposite the *justified* edge. In fully justified text there is no rag.

ragged—The parent of a two-year old. Also the edge of text opposite the *justification* edge (if there is one). (See *rag.*)

raster—A type of image file that is made up of *pixels* and thus built at a fixed *resolution* and set *color depth*. Typically created by image-editing applications like Photoshop.

rebate—Margin of paper, film, or other substrate imposed by the inability of an output device to print within that area.

reference points—On the Transform palette in Illustrator and other programs, a small grid of points corresponding to corners, planes, and the center point of an object's *bounding box*. Which reference point is selected determines to what quadrant of the object transformations (for example, scaling or rotation changes) will be relative. In InDesign and PageMaker the reference points are called the proxy.

refry—Printing a PDF file to Adobe PDF printer or running it through Acrobat Distiller to make a PDF again. Printing a PDF to become a PDF.

register—How ink plates or impressions line up against one another.

registration color—A special color that appears on all *plates* during *separation*. Special marks and information such as *crop marks*, *registration marks*, and *slugs* are set in registration color to ensure they appear on all pieces of *film* or plates.

registration marks—Small, crosshair-like marks that appear on all color *plates* to provide a reference for aligning the plates to one another.

resolution—The rendering or imaging quality of an output device such as a computer screen or printer. Resolution also refers to the same property of a digital document.

resolution-dependent—Having a fixed resolution. *Raster* images, being made up of a fixed grid of *pixels*, are resolution-dependent.

resolution-independent—Not having a fixed resolution (for example, *vector* drawings). Resolution-independent artwork will always print or render to the resolution of the output device.

RGB—Red Green Blue. Defining the limits of human vision, RGB is the additive color model of light (additive meaning the more pigment added, the closer to pure white the light becomes). Computer monitors and television screens are built to mimic human eyes (because their whole reason for being is to be viewed *by* human eyes—duh!) with red, green, and blue phosphors in each pixel, giving them the theoretical ability to reproduce any of the approximately 16.8 million visible frequencies of the radiation spectrum between ultraviolet and infrared.

RIP—Raster Image Processing or Processor, depending on usage. The process by which digital files are *flattened* and converted to *halftones* for rendering on an *imagesetter*, *platesetter*, or *digital printing* press. When used as a noun, RIP refers to the system (generally software) that performs the RIP process.

rivers—In paragraphs of *copy*, the distracting and ugly alignment of ribbons of empty space between *glyphs*. Rivers occur more often in fully *justified* copy than in flush left or flush right copy because of the increased word and character spacing in fully justified. Rivers: Can we talk?

Roman—In typography, the normal, non-italicized (see *italic*), non-bold (see *bold*) root style of a *typeface*.

Rubylithe—Tinted transparent film cut by hand to create *separations* prior to the *Desktop Publishing Revolution*.

running-down—Similar to *running-up*, running-down a job cleans up after a print run (for example, to clean excess ink off the rollers).

running-up—In *offset lithography* and other commercial printing processes, numerous (up to several hundred) throw-away copies of a job are printed to ensure quality prior to initiating the final printing. Press operators run-up a job to check for ink flow, viscosity, registration, and other concerns, and typically use inexpensive paper before committing to the client's ordered *substrate*.

saddle-stitching—(Also saddle-stapled). A bindery process in which printed matter such as magazines, brochures, and other multi-page documents are printed in signatures (two-up pages per side, per sheet of paper) then folded and stapled in the middle.

screen—Referring to the rendering of printed in *halftone* dots, a screen is a *tint* of a solid color or ink. For example, 100% of an ink is full coverage, although 50%, 25%, and 5% are all screens of that ink.

separation—The process of dividing a full-color design into its constituent ink colors for printing on a press. Often referred to as *seps.*

seps—Slang for *separations.*

service bureau—*Prepress* services provider.

slice—The action and result of dividing a drawing into sections.

slug—Early twentieth-century slang for punch (see *knockout*). In printing, any information placed outside the *trim area*, such as the name of the job or designer.

soft-proofing—Simulating final output conditions on screen.

spine—The area in which pages are bound into a book. Also used to describe the area of the cover that overlays the binding.

spot color—A premixed printing ink that may or may not be a mixture of *CMYK* but is printed as a single impression or ink. Also referred to as spot ink.

style sheet—A reusable set of instructions and settings (usually of type and type styling).

subdomain—The third level, and apportionment, of *domain name. My* is the subdomain of *site.com* in the example http://my.site.com.

subsetting—Relevant to embedding *fonts* in *PDF* files, the process of including only the *glyphs* and other font data in use while omit-ting extraneous glyphs and data not used by the design.

substrate—Paper, plastic, or other material to be printed on.

SVG—File extension for Scaleable Vector Graphics, an XML-based web and mobile content vector graphics format. Supports animation and scripting. SVG is an open-source competitor to *Flash.*

SWF—File extension for Shockwave *Flash* movies, animations, and artwork ready for use on the web; as opposed to FLA, the native Flash application file format that cannot be rendered by a web browser.

symmetrical—Even and balanced. A symmetrical design is one in which the two sides are mirrored if folded at its center point.

threaded—Type that flows into multiple text boxes or areas is threaded between them.

TIFF—Tagged Image File Format. An industry standard *raster* image format (with several subformats) compatible with all modern professional creative applications and systems. TIFF supports both *RGB* and *CMYK color spaces,* as well as high *resolution* and lossless compression (unlike JPEG).

tint—A percentage of ink or color less than 100%. For example, 100% of an ink is full coverage, although 50%, 25%, and 5% are all tints or *screens* of that ink. Tint usually refers to the visual introduction of white—the lower the percentage of color or pigment, the closer to white it becomes. In *process color* printing, a tint reduces the apparent saturation of ink by decreasing the size of, and increasing the space between, *halftone* dots. Tint should not be confused with transparency. Although reducing the percentage of ink may appear to equate to reducing opacity, it is not; as color or ink is lightened, it remains an opaque area *knocked out* of other colors or inks. (See also *screen*.)

trim size—The final, cut dimensions of a printed piece.

type family—A collection of closely related *typefaces*, which may include the *Roman*, *bold*, *italic*, and many other styles and variations on the same basic *typographic* design.

type style—A variation of a *typeface*, which may include *Roman*, *bold*, *italic*, and many other variants.

typeface—The design and form of a set of *glyphs*.

typography—The art and process of styling type, including choosing a *typeface*, setting a *type style*, and choosing size, *leading*, and other formatting options. Also a descriptive noun referring to the appearance and layout of type in a design.

varnish—A thin, usually transparent, often glossy coating applied after printing for appearance or protection.

varnish plate—A *plate* or piece of *film* representing the area for *varnish* application as a color or ink.

vector—A *resolution-independent* image made up of points and curves that join them. These images are understood by a computer as basic geometric plots—each point is positioned relative to the X, Y, and Z axes—and curves—with angles from 0 to 359 degrees. Vector drawings such as those created in Adobe Illustrator may be resized up or down to infinity without loss of quality or detail, and always output to the highest *resolution* of the rendering device (for example, a printer).

Version Cue—Adobe file versioning, management, and collaboration technology included with Adobe Creative Suite and integrated into Illustrator and all Creative Suite point products.

virtual printer—A print driver and *PPD* for an output device not connected to the current computer or network. Used for printing *PostScript* files, *soft-proofing*, and *preflighting* without producing hard-copy output.

web-safe fonts—*Fonts* that may be used in a web design with the reasonable expectation that the vast majority of visitors will have the fonts installed on their computers and thus be able to see the design as intended.

workflow—How a job gets done. Workflow is often used broadly to describe all decisions, acts, actions, and procedures required to complete a task or project, or may be narrowly applied to the systems and tools employed in a given task.

XHTML—Extensible Hypertext Markup Language, a reformation and expansion of the original web programming language HTML to define and structure pages and content on the Web.

Z-order—The stacking order of objects: the X-axis determines the horizontal position; the Y-axis the vertical, and the Z-axis, which is the third dimension, defines the relative distance to target. An object closer to the viewer is higher in the Z-order than one further away.

Accessing the Project Files

All the projects in this book use resource files located on the publisher's website. They are organized by chapter, and each chapter's folder contains both project files as well as finished projects so that you can compare your work with mine. To download the book's project/resource files, go to http://**www.samspublishing.com**. Enter this book's ISBN (0672328011) in the Search box and click Search. When the book's title is displayed, click the title to go to a page where you can download the project Zip files.

Goodies

Some of these goodies are from Adobe, some from me.

▶ Free top-quality OpenType fonts were included with your purchase of Illustrator CS2 or Creative Suite 2. In the downloadable resource files for this section is the file CS2 Fonts List.pdf, a complete list of all the fonts Adobe graciously bundled with Creative Suite 2 and the individual CS2 applications.

▶ Also in this section's resource files is Keyboard Shortcuts.pdf, a complete list of all the default keyboard shortcuts for Illustrator CS2—ready for printing.

▶ Looking for restaurant menu or event-planning templates? Already installed on your computer are dozens of predesigned Illustrator templates. Access them from the Illustrator CS2 Welcome Screen, or by selecting File > New From Template.

▶ Even more goodies wait in anxious silence on your hard drive. There is plenty of sample art, graphs, and SVG graphics to pick apart and learn from hidden in the Cool Extras folder where you installed Illustrator. On Windows, open an Explorer window to C:\Program Files\Adobe\Adobe Illustrator CS2\Cool Extras\. On Mac OS X, open a Finder window to Applications/Adobe Illustrator CS2/Cool Extras.

▶ If you bought Adobe Illustrator CS2 as part of the Creative Suite, check out the Resources and Extras disk (two disks with Creative Suite 2 Premium edition) for a ton of clip art, stock photography, sample scripts, and other great Illustrator resources.

> ⊘ **CAUTION**
>
> Be sure you extract all the files from each Zip file with the Use Folder Names option (for PC users) selected so that you can get the same folders on your computer as included in each Zip file. Mac users can simply double-click the downloaded Zip file and the folder structure should appear intact, as named.

Where to Turn for How-To and Technical Support

When Illustrator isn't working as expected—or at all—who ya gonna call? No, not Ghostbusters.

▶ Included in this appendix's download-able resource files is Known Issues.pdf, which details some of the technical issues (bugs) we encountered while writing and editing the projects in this book, and that you are likely to encounter as well. Also included are any known workarounds for the techni-cal issues. I've included it in a down-loadable PDF because that type of information is fluid, and I can keep a PDF updated much more easily than an ink and pulp list. I'll update the Known Issues.pdf file as new informa-tion (such as patches from Adobe) becomes available. So please check the download from time to time.

▶ Illustrator Help should always be your first stop. If you enjoy spending hours hunting down the smallest scrap of useful information in vague, barely comprehensible software help files, you won't like Illustrator's help. It's concise but detailed, well-written, and organ-ized. It even contains a number of tutorials!

▶ Adobe Technical Support knows their stuff (they should—I trained them).

http://www.adobe.com/support/main.html

Telephone: 206-675-6307

▶ Adobe Expert Support is contract-based how-to support. Technical Support will help you resolve *technical* issues—when something is broken—but when you need help locating, configuring, or using something, that's the domain of Expert Support (whom I also largely trained).

http://www.adobe.com/support/expert_support/main.html

Telephone: 866-692-3623

▶ The Adobe Illustrator Discussion List is a public forum and mailing list on Yahoo! Groups. Moderated by Sterling Ledet & Associates, one of the top Adobe Certified Training Providers, the Adobe Illustrator Discussion List is a first-class place to discuss and ask for help in all things Illustrator- and illus-tration-related. Many of the most active members are published authors (like yours truly) and professional Illustrator instructors (yeah, like me again). Anyone may join, with or without a Yahoo! account.

http://groups.yahoo.com/group/illstrtr/

▶ At more than four years old, the 1,000-member-strong Graphic Design Resource Group is another public Yahoo! Group similar to the Adobe Illustrator Discussion List, though with a broader focus on *everything* design-related (including software like Illustrator). Topics range from how to do something in creative tools like Illustrator, InDesign, Photoshop, Corel, and so on to setting freelance rates and building contracts, copyright law to fonts, and everything else of concern to designers and illustrators. Anyone may join, with or without a Yahoo! account. Both the author and technical editor of this book are highly active members of this group.

http://groups.yahoo.com/group/graphic_design

▶ Adobe's User-to-User Forums are the best company-hosted forums in the software business. In addition to interacting with Illustrator users of all levels, you will find knowledgeable experts and even Adobe product managers and engineers, all gladly helping to answer support, how-to, and other questions. There are separate forums for the Mac and Windows versions of Illustrator.

http://www.adobe.com/support/forums/main.html

▶ On Usenet the Illustrator newsgroup is active and informative.

nntp://alt.graphics.illustrator

Other Projects by the Author

If you've read this whole book and you still want to read more by me—well, then you're probably a friend of my mother. Regardless of who put you up to it, here are some of the other places you will find me writing about Illustrator and related fields and technologies. The following list is not exhaustive—I always have new projects brewing—Google me.

▶ RevDrink.com. What? You didn't think I'd use it over and over in the book—and other places—just to let some other schmuck register it and promote *his* book, did you? Actually, because I use REV in many of my tutorial projects, RevDrink.com has become a reference to them and to additional resources and downloads.

http://www.RevDrink.com

▶ Designorati.com. News, articles, and tutorials on everything from Illustrator to Photoshop, Acrobat to InDesign, illustration to publishing, the graphic design business to creative time wasters.

http://www.designorati.com

▶ Quark VS InDesign.com. "The Authority for News & Opinion on the War of the Desktop Publishing Giants, QuarkXPress and Adobe InDesign."

http://www.QuarkVSInDesign.com

▶ I Am Pariah.com, my personal website, portfolio, and blog. Stop by and say hi.

http://www.iamPariah.com

▶ Need hands-on training customized to *your* specific workflow? Enroll in any of my Illustrator, InDesign, Photoshop, QuarkXPress, Acrobat, or other creative classes at training centers throughout the United States, or bring me on-site to your offices in the U.S. or worldwide. Please contact Sterling Ledet & Associates for my available dates.

http://www.Ledet.com

Telephone: 877-819-COOL (2665)

Book Recommendations

I don't read books on the subject of software, so I'm not the best person to ask for book recommendations (you already bought my book, so *that* recommendation is out). However, there are a few I urge every graphic designer or illustrator to own.

- ▶ *The Elements of Graphic Design*, by Alex W. White. Allworth Press (ISBN 1581152507).

- ▶ *The Mac Is Not A Typewriter*, by Robin Williams. Peachpit Press (ISBN 0201782634).

- ▶ *Inside the Publishing Revolution: The Adobe Story*, by Pamela Pfiffner. Adobe Press (ISBN 0321115643).

- ▶ *Pocket Pal,* by International Paper. (http://www.internationalpaper.com/paper/paper%20products/Pocket%20Pal%20Home.html). This is an incredible quick-reference handbook for anyone in a for-press workflow.

- ▶ *Real World: Color Management*, by Fraser, Murphy, and Bunting. Peachpit Press (ISBN 0321267222).

- ▶ *Real World: Scanning & Halftones*, by Blatner, Fleishman, Roth, and Chavez. Peachpit Press (ISBN 0321241320).

- ▶ And, of course, *Adobe Illustrator CS2 @work: Projects You Can Use On the Job* is only one book in the @work series. Look for *Adobe InDesign CS2 @work*, *Adobe Photoshop CS2 @work*, and others from Sams Publishing.

Other Resources

The following lists give a few general resources as well as several that are specific to the types of projects you may complete with the help of this book.

- ▶ Have a wish list for the next version of Illustrator? Tell Adobe! They *really* listen—I know; I helped compile the feature request lists every month for the years I worked there. Your feature requests go to the product manager for each Adobe product, as well as the development team and everyone else who has an interest in that product. Customers really do build Adobe's software.

  http://www.adobe.com/support/feature.html

- ▶ Display your amazing Illustrator vector artwork on Illustrator World.

  http://www.IllustratorWorld.com

- ▶ Everything you've ever wanted to know about OpenType fonts.

  http://store.adobe.com/type/opentype/main.html

- ▶ Pantone, the worldwide leader in color systems from the desktop to production.

  http://www.Pantone.com

- ▶ List of stock photography agencies (updated twice yearly).

  http://www.RevDrink.com/lists/stockagencies.html

- ▶ SVG—Scalable Vector Graphics—the newest technology in online and mobile content publishing.

  http://www.adobe.com/svg/

- United States Food & Drug Administration (FDA) labeling requirements for product packaging. Labeling requirements vary by product type, so search for yours using the following link.

  http://www.fda.gov/search.html

- United States Registrar of Copyrights for downloadable copyright registration forms and information, and frequently asked questions about copyright.

  http://www.copyright.gov

- When researching the viability of a logo for trademark protection, one of your best resources will be Thomson & Thomson, the leading trademark-reporting agency. Doing your own research via Thomson & Thomson's SAEGIS database and other tools is not a substitute for the assistance of a qualified intellectual property attorney, but it can save on the attorney's billable hours.

  http://www.thomson-thomson.com

- Barcode fonts for everything from books to product packaging, postal addressing to inventory control.

  http://www.RevDrink.com/lists/barcodes.html

- Lorem Ipsum generator and the history of the world's favorite nonsense text, Lorem Ipsum.

  http://www.lipsum.com/

- What are you worth? The AIGA and Aquent "Survey of Design Salaries," which queries creative professionals throughout the United States annually, compiling a comprehensive list of the median income for all levels of design career in various regions and metropolitan areas, is available online for benchmarking *your* pay rate.

  http://www.designsalaries.com

- **CreativePro.com**, an excellent news and information site for just about anything related to design, illustration, and press workflows.

  http://www.CreativePro.com

- A delicious recipe for fettucini alfredo.

  http://www.cooks.com/rec/view/0,1935,158182-247196,00.html

Notable Add-Ons and Plug-Ins

Illustrator CS2 has amazing features for any creative workflow, but it doesn't always have *every* feature needed. When you need something else, turn to these resources.

- The single largest and most focused resource available for plug-ins, scripts, swatches, symbols, brushes, tutorials, and all kinds of (mostly free) goodies for Illustrator (and other Adobe applications) is the Adobe Studio. Though many of the resources there are created by Adobe, most come from Illustrator users and enthusiasts.

  http://studio.adobe.com

- Boasting one of the best collections of plug-ins for Illustrator (as well as Photoshop, InDesign, and others) is PluginsWorld.

  http://illustrator.pluginsworld.com

- John Wundes maintains several neat Illustrator scripts on his website.

  http://www.wundes.com/js4ai/js4ai.html

- Drawing in Illustrator with a mouse just cannot compare to the freedom of drawing with a pressure-sensitive stylus and tablet. Here are the top stylus and tablet manufacturers.

  http://www.wacom.com (pronounced WAH-kum)

  http://www.aiptek.com

- Font management is critical not only to a reliable workflow but also to keeping Illustrator happy. If you don't use a font management program, you really do need to begin. Included with Mac OS X 10.3 (Panther) and higher is Apple's FontBook. If you are on Windows or just looking for more control, Suitcase and Font Reserve, both from Extensis, are the professionals' choices.

  http://www.Extensis.com

Professional Organizations and Associations

We all need to belong somewhere. The following are just a few groups among whom you may admit without shame to your newfound passion for Illustrator.

- AIGA (more than 90 years old)

  http://www.aiga.org

- Association of Medical Illustrators

  http://www.medical-illustrators.org

- Association of Professional Design Firms

  http://www.apdf.org

- Graphic Artists Guild

  http://www.gag.org

- The Society of Illustrators (more than 100 years old)

  http://www.societyillustrators.org

- Society for News Design

  http://www.snd.org

- Corporate Design Foundation

  http://www.cdf.org

About the Project

In this project, you'll learn a tried-and-true technique for identifying fonts in pre-existing artwork. Instead of creating a logo from scratch, you'll learn how to work it backward to *re*-create a logo.

Prerequisites

It would be helpful if you were familiar with placing external graphics and using the Type tool to create point type objects.

@work resources

Please visit the publisher's website to access the following Chapter 2 project files:

▸ Appendix C\Assets (Logo-From-Website.gif)
▸ Appendix C\Finished Project (where you place your finished projects)

Planning the Project

The task of identifying fonts in a pre-existing design is faced every day on the job in a kaleidoscope of different projects. The only way to plan for it is to get the clearest, highest-resolution sample of the original artwork possible, and to know you have help in this book; don't stress when you have to identify and re-create type.

In three easy steps we'll learn how to identify fonts used in a logo, re-create it with Illustrator's tools, and convert the type to modifiable paths:

1. **Identifying fonts in logos**
2. **Inserting glyphs**
3. **Converting type to outlines and massaging its paths**

Identifying Fonts in Logos and Re-creating Logo Type

Clients often just don't get the idea of resolution. In one breath they express anxiety over a designer's ability to create "high-resolution graphics," and in the next they tell you to "just grab the high-resolution logo off [their] home page," blowing whatever credibility they might have earned with their initial use of the phrase "high-resolution." I know many a designer who draws logos all day long in Illustrator but doesn't design logos per se (it is a specialized field not every creative pro gets into). These creatives are illustrators, graphic designers, web designers, pre-press people, and anyone else who may put someone's logo into a design. They redraw because they need a resolution-independent logo the client can't provide.

In a perfect world, every client would walk through the door with a vector logo already in hand—well, perfect for everyone but logo designers. Then creatives hired to work with, but not redesign, the logo could simply insert it into their designs like any other asset. Many times that's exactly how it goes; equally as many other times, the client has nothing but a fixed-resolution raster version of the logo. More and more of late, these kinds of clients have only the 72 dpi resolution logo from their website. If that's all your client has, and she wants you to use the logo in a printed piece, guess what you'll be doing.

Oh, *yeah*. You're redrawing the logo.

And you might find yourself doing it for free—as many creatives are forced to do. It will pay (or, at least cost less) to know several techniques for quickly redrawing logos. In Chapter 2, "Designing a Logo (From Scratch or From a Scan)," you learned how to re-create a logo by drawing—by picking up the Pen tool and going to town, or by identifying and more quickly re-creating shapes in the form. Now it's time to learn a third and, in the right situation, more accurate and efficient method of re-creating logos.

STEP 1 ▼
Identifying Fonts in Logos

When the client has an existing logo that needs to be redrawn, often the most effective method is to begin by identifying the typeface used and work from there. The more you work with type, the more typefaces you will recognize on sight. With hundreds of thousands of typefaces from dozens of foundries, however, you'll never recognize them all. Fortunately, there are tools that can help.

1. Start a new **8.5 × 11-in** RGB document and name it **Logo-Type Modify**.

2. Place the resource file **Logo-From-Website.gif** from the `Appendix C/Assets` folder (see Figure C.1). This is a 72 dpi, 128-color GIF image—in other words, totally useless for printing.

FIGURE C.1   **This logo may seem vaguely familiar to you. This time, however, we need to work backward to re-create it.**

3. Rename **Layer 1** in the Layers palette to **GIF**, and set it as a template—whether you dim the image is up to you.

4. Now look at the logo. Does it look like a particular typeface/font to you? (If you guess, play along for the audience at home.) What can you tell about it?

   The letters are from the Roman alphabet; that's a start. So we don't have to worry about Japanese, Sanskrit, Cyrillic, and other non-Roman alphabets. What else? Good! It's a sans serif typeface. That rules out serif, script, blackletter, and several other type classes, each representing thousands of fonts.

   The E looks like it might have been customized to accommodate the speedometer dial metaphor, so don't look too hard at it. The R and V are probably going to be closer to a real typeface than the E—which doesn't give us a great deal to go on.

5. Font management software can be a big help. In Figure C.2 are two font managers among a handful that are available for either Windows or Mac. With most font managers, the individual

letters of installed or available fonts can be examined closely for individual type characteristics—like the fact that the diagonal foot of the R extends past its bowl or the slight curvature at the inner apex of the V's arms.

Whether or not you have a font manager to turn to, Illustrator has a built-in feature that can be very useful in this situation—though that is not its primary purpose.

> **TIP**
>
> Another excellent resource is the *Identifont* website (http://www.identifont.com) which, working from a sample such as ours, asks a series of questions about present characters and serves up potential typefaces. For the record, *Identifont* found 30 potentials for this one, including the correct font and three almost identical variations of the same name from different foundries; the remaining potentials were also extremely close.

6. From the Window menu choose Type > Glyphs. Up pops the Glyphs palette. Resize the palette itself until you can see five or six rows.

> **TIP**
>
> The Glyphs palette is highly useful for inserting special characters like Copyright (©) and Trademark (™, ®) symbols, bullets (•), and other special characters such as the Euro ( ).

7. ◁△▷ At the bottom of the palette is a type family selection drop-down, a type style selection drop-down, then buttons to decrease or increase the size of the characters or *glyphs* displayed. Click on the larger mountains until the size of the display maxes out. Now scroll down until both the uppercase R and uppercase V are visible at once (see Figure C.3).

FIGURE C.2 At the top is veteran font manager Extensis Suitcase running on Windows (versions are also available for Mac OS X and Mac Classic), and, below, Apple's FontBook, a free font manager included with the Mac OS X operating system since version 10.2 (aka "Panther").

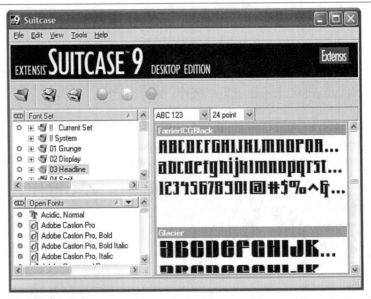

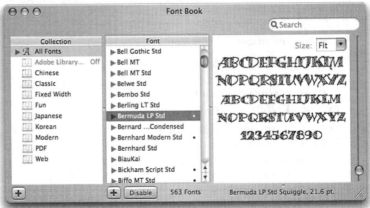

Figure C.3 The Glyphs palette showing our desired glyphs.

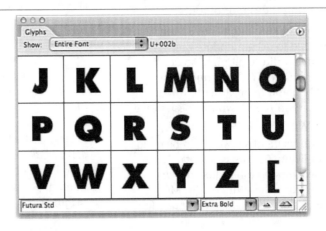

8. Position and/or resize the palette so that both R and V are visible, but also so you can see the GIF image on the artboard. At the bottom of the palette, change the type family to something you think might be the font in the REV logo.

Any luck? No? Try another type family. The letters in the REV logo look pretty thick, so, if you find something close, try changing its style to bold, semibold, extra bold, heavy, or black, if any such styles are available. The Glyphs palette only shows fonts that are installed and active; it will not show inactive fonts that may reside on your system (font managers will, however).

9. If you happen to have installed Bitstream type foundry's Futura Extra Black BT, you have (hopefully) already identified the typeface. If you don't have that particular flavor, you should have *some* foundry's Futura available (Futura is a classic that never runs out of steam). Pick the closest typeface you have.

 TIP

Included with your purchase of Illustrator CS2 or Creative Suite 2 is Myriad Pro, whose Black style would be a suitable substitute if you don't happen to have a Futura.

STEP 2 ▼
Inserting Glyphs

Now that we've identified the typeface via the Glyphs palette, how do we get the right glyphs into the document?

1. Make a new layer in the Layers palette (resize the Glyphs palette if necessary to see your document).

2. Click once with the Type tool on the artboard, approximately in the middle of the *baseline* of the REV logo. The Control palette should reflect the typeface you chose in the Glyphs palette.

3. At this point, you could just type ReV, but, because only a small fraction of the glyphs in newer fonts can actually be accessed from the keyboard, you should know how to do it from the Glyphs palette. So, return to the Glyphs palette and double-click the R. Now the e. And, finally, the V. Notice how they are inserted into your text line? This is how you get to special characters that can't be typed (for example, the Euro symbol   ).

4. Switching to the Selection tool, hold the Shift key and resize the type with the bounding box control handles until it's roughly the same size and position as the GIF template.

STEP 3 ▼
Converting Type to Outlines and Massaging Its Paths

Even if you happen to have the correct fonts installed, you will still need to massage their paths because the letters of the REV logo are not exactly as they appear in the typeface.

1. Keeping the text frame selected, go to Type > Create Outlines. From real, editable, font-driven type now come humble paths, no longer seen by Illustrator as symbols of language.

2. Still, the paths-that-once-were-letters behave as one unit. They will still move and resize together, which we don't want at this juncture. So, from the

Object menu, choose Ungroup to break up this happy family like a vindictive social worker on a rampage. Now the letter-shaped paths are completely independent.

3. One at a time, align them atop their rasterized counterparts (resize as necessary). They don't match exactly, do they?

4. Now, break out your path editing and massaging tools—the Pen, Direct Selection, Add Anchor Point, Delete Anchor Point, and Convert Anchor Point tools—and do your thing.

When you have letter-shaped paths that precisely mirror the letters of the REV GIF logo—or your own logo—you're done with this section. Save your file as **Logo-Type Modify.ai**.

Final Thoughts

This technique is applicable to almost any logo with type in it. If you need to re-create such a logo, examine the glyph(s) closely to determine which parts are features of the original typeface.

Even in cases where it would be faster to simply redraw with the Pen tool, there are distinct advantages to using real type. The fact that type can be made into outlines is of course one big advantage. But, outlines cannot be made into type. If you might need real, honest-to-goodness letters and numbers—say, for spell checking—stick with real text.

Of course, this same technique will enable you to identify and re-create type in any situation, including those cases where there is just too much text to feasibly draw with the Pen tool.

Another important reason for knowing this technique is that it comes in very handy for logo *creation* as well as *re*-creation. In fact, many logo designers often begin new designs with a glyph directly out of a font, convert the type to outlines, and then rework the path to make it unique. If your design needs a stylized A, look for a typeface that has some of the features you want, and then convert that A to outlines and finish the job by massaging its path. Better yet, load up the Glyphs palette and select any symbol font like Marlett or Wingdings on Windows or Zapf Dingbats on the Mac. See all those symbols? Just imagine how they could be used! How about taking that symbol of a telephone, converting it to outlines, and using it as a clipping mask to create a phone-shaped photograph? If you have the free Webdings font, it contains about a dozen comic-style dialog balloons that would be right at home in a pop art-style ad, poster, or invitation. There's even a pushpin icon you could convert to outlines and paint with a gradient or blend to create a realistic, 3D pushpin for incorporation into a larger drawing (and I have).

Get to know your fonts. Don't use the same typefaces over and over—how boring! Use different ones—*experiment*. Examine your installed typefaces in a font manager or the Glyphs palette. Print out type specimen sheets, which show at least the alphanumeric glyphs of a given typeface in different point sizes. In your fonts you have hundreds of thousands of pieces of clip art and new design inspiration, just waiting to be discovered and put to use in your next creative project.

Index

Numbers

design

shaped grids, 54-55

website project, 216-217

guides

angled guides, 181-182

envelopes, 78-80

locking, 181

tri-fold brochure template, 161-162

Guides menu commands

Lock Guides, 181

Make Guides, 141

guts (content) of websites, 220-222

gutters, 170

H

hair, drawing with Live Trace

converting to editable paths, 121-123

preparing for tracing, 116-117

Tracing Options dialog, 117-120

hard-proofing, 187-189

headers (website project), 219-220

Help menu commands, Welcome Screen, 17

Hide Artboard command (View menu, 100

hiding Welcome Screen, 17

highlights, 155-156

histograms, 8-9

I

I Am Pariah.com, 293

ICC profiles, 86

Identifont website, 299

identifying fonts, 297-301

Illustrator

Adobe UI, 12

advantages of, 9-10

combining with other applications, 10-11

compared to Photoshop, 7-9

future of, 11-12

Illustrator newsgroup, 293

Illustrator World, 294

images. *See* **artwork**

importing

datasets from Excel, 253

swatches, 57-58

in port (text areas), 169

InDesign, 10

saving graphs for, 249-250

inserts (DVDs)

design, 205-206

layer comps, 210-211

spine titles, 207, 210

templates, 206-207

inset spacing (tri-fold brochure), 170

intensity of highlights, 155

J-K

jars, mapping vector logos to, 51-53

decal application, 53

decal transparency, 53-54

surface images, placing and locking, 52

target surface area, defining, 52-53

jitter effects, 40-41

joining

palettes, 13

paths, 36-37

Keyboard Increment setting, 28

keyboard shortcuts, 291

Keyboard Shortcuts.pdf file, 291

Keynote, saving graphs for, 251

knitted texture, simulating, 58

knockouts

colors, 75

DVD labels, 196-197

Known Issues.pdf file, 292

L

labels. *See* **product packaging**

lanyards, mapping text to, 57-62

gradient meshes, 60-61

knitted texture effect, 58

mesh distortion, 59

projects

W-Z